Fat Man on a Bicycle

Tom Vernon is commonly regarded as a sort of partially hairy teddy-bear living in Muswell Hill. He was once a professional Elizabethan minstrel, teacher, publicity dogsbody for the Royal Shakespeare Company and all sorts of other things including being a guide in Wookey Hole Caves. Now he seems to have settled down to making radio programmes – such as the highly successful and popular *Fat Man on a Bicycle*, *Fat Man in Italy* and *Fat Man Out* – and television ones sometimes. And feeling fairly chuffed at the success of this, his first book, he is planning more.

He believes in always being adventurous except when he doesn't feel like it; always kicking people who say they know what is good for him and attempt to make him do it; and always eating a good breakfast.

His creaky Edwardian house is big enough to be fat in, but will never be properly converted because he never has time to finish it; he lives in a gentle chaos of books, music and culinary ingredients with Sally his wife, Jos and Hal his two sons, and a lazy cat.

With illustrations by
Peter Freeth

FAT MAN ON A BICYCLE

A Discovery of France
by Tom Vernon

who pedalled his nineteen stone
from Muswell Hill in London to
the Mediterranean the summer of
1979, the journey described in
BBC Radio 4's series of the
same name

Fontana/Collins

First published in Great Britain
by Michael Joseph Ltd 1981
First issued in Fontana Paperbacks 1982

Copyright © Tom Vernon 1981

Set in 10 on 11 Lasercomp Plantin
Made and printed in Great Britain by
William Collins Sons & Co. Ltd, Glasgow

For Sally

'In the heat of the handlebars he grasps the summer'
Louis MacNeice: *The Cyclist*

Contents

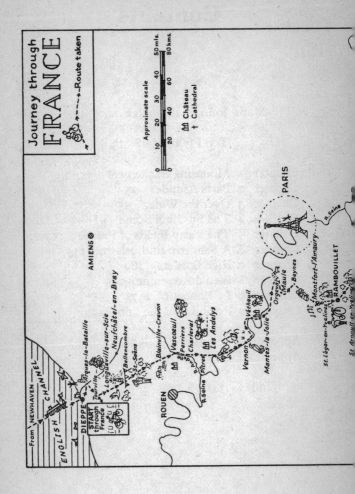

Journey through
FRANCE

🏍 ---➤ Route taken

Approximate scale

0   10   20   30   40   50 mls.

0   20   40   60   80 kms.

🏰 Château
✝ Cathedral

From NEWHAVEN

ENGLISH CHANNEL

DIEPPE

START through France

Tourville

Arques-la-Bataille

Longueville-sur-Scie

Neufchâtel-en-Bray

Bellencombre

St-Saëns

AMIENS ⊕

Bosc-le-Hard

R. Seine

ROUEN

Blainville-Crevon

Vascœuil

Perriers

Charleval

Pîtres

Les Andelys

Vernon

Vétheuil

Mantes-la-Jolie

Orgeval

Maule

Beynes

Montfort-l'Amaury

St-Léger-en-Yvelines

St-Arnoult-en-Yvelines

RAMBOUILLET

PARIS

R. Seine

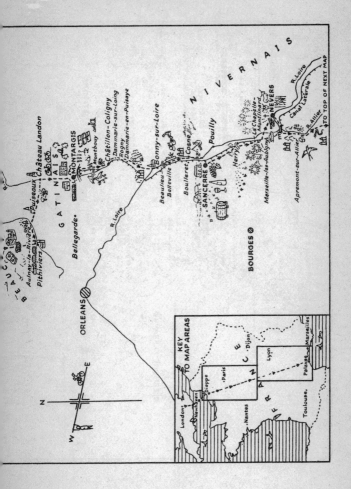

N I V E R N A I S

R. Loire

La Chapelle

NEVERS

Canal Lateralé

Pouilly

Herry

R. Allier

Cosne

Marseille-les-Aubigny

Apremont-sur-Allier

TO TOP OF NEXT MAP

Boulleret

Beaulieu

Bonny-sur-Loire

SANCERRE

Belleville

Dammarie-sur-Loing

Rogny

Dammarie-en-Puisaye

Châtillon-Coligny

Montbouy

MONTARGIS

BOURGES

Château Landon

G A T I N A I S

Puiseaux

Bellegarde

R. Loire

Pithiviers

Aurer Riva

B E A U C

ORLEANS

N

W   E

S

KEY TO MAP AREAS

London

Dieppe

Paris

Dijon

F R A N C E

Nantes

Lyon

Palavas

Marseilles

Toulouse

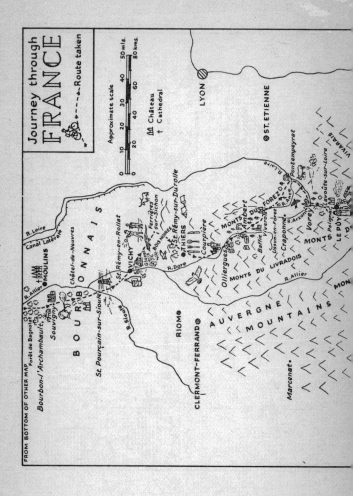

Journey through FRANCE

- - - - - Route taken

Approximate scale

Château
Cathedral

FROM BOTTOM OF OTHER MAP

Forêt de Bagnolet
R. Allier
Bourbon-l'Archambault
MOULINS
Souvigny
Châtel-de-Neuvres
BOURBONNAIS
St. Rémy-en-Rollat
St. Pourçain-sur-Sioule
R. Sioule
VICHY
St. Rémy-sur-Durolle
Ferrières-
sur-Sichon
Bon homme
THIERS
Courpiare
R. Dore
RIOM
Ollierguess
MONTS DU
Ambert
MONTS DU LIVRADOIS
R. Allier
CLERMONT-FERRAND
AUVERGNE
MOUNTAINS
Marcenat
MON
FOREZ
R. Loire
Usson-en-Forez
Baffie
Viverols
Craponne
R. Arzon
Vorey
Polignac
MONTS
LE PUY
Pontempeyrat
Rozite-sur-Loire
VIVARAIS
R. Loire
ST. ETIENNE
LYON

R. Loire
Canal Latérale

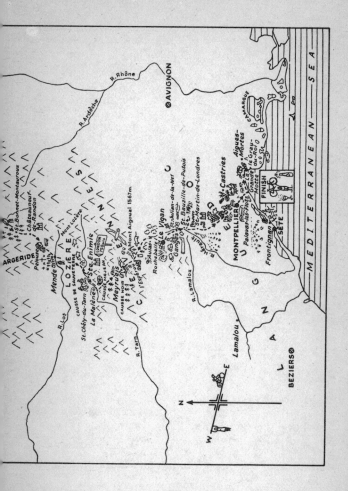

Too Fly by Half

*An author's note containing a needlessly
lepidopterous metaphor*

Some people claim to be able to distinguish fact from fiction, though personally I have given up trying. I can still tell the truth, but only as it comes – which is in little bits and nuances, particularities and half-truths, all as vague as a cloud of midges. Here are some of those flies in summer amber: perhaps they will make a pattern.

Of course it is impossible to generalize about anything, let alone two whole nations – and you cannot do with fewer, because every new traveller judges another country by his own. Some of my impressions must be unfair to France, some to England, but I have tried hard not to be partial to either, in spite of our mutual national tendencies towards chauvinism. In the conversations – which have of course been edited from my notes of the original tape-recordings – I have not corrected the Franglais of the French to perfect English, nor the Anglench of the English to good Français. I have told the journey according to how I felt about it, and how it was – though I have not gone very much into the mechanics of making the radio programmes which were the purpose of the trip. This means that one very important person figures much less in the book than she did in reality. Joy Hatwood, the Radio 4 producer who organized everything and was my doppelgänger on the road with a car full of tapes and extra recording equipment, with which I almost always managed to rendezvous when necessary. She is the first of those who have my special thanks, and among the others are: Sholto Cross, Jane Warren, Catherine Mahoney, Chris Harper and Denis Elphick; those whose names appear in the text, particularly Jean-Claude and Michèle Baudoin; many people at BBC

Radio 4, including those who accepted my idea and those who helped to make, organize or announce the programmes; very many extremely kind and helpful people working in Syndicats d'Initiative and elsewhere in France and in London; Pauline Hallam and Martine Williams of the French Tourist Office; people of good counsel in the matter of bicycles, notably the staff of F. W. Evans and the Cyclists' Touring Club; and Sally the Indispensable.

CHAPTER I

Mounting Excitement

I began as I meant to go on: sitting in the sun before the Café des Tribunaux in Dieppe in company with a litre of Provençal Rosé, a crisp loaf, a slice of oozing cheese and strawberries. It was the fifth of July. At my back – give or take a few streets and the *plage* – was the Channel: ahead – the plains, mountains and forests of pastoral France, 800 miles of grassy, leafy, rivery ways to another sea.

I had no apprehensions about the countryside, and few about the people; but the means of transportation was an unknown quantity, my own known quantity being some nineteen imperial stone, which I had agreed to carry on a bicycle from Muswell Hill to the Mediterranean, so that I could make six programmes for BBC Radio 4 about my experiences along the way.

My bicycle (which was then merely a new bike rather than a companion) shone ingenuously with zero on its mileometer, fitted that morning in the shop of M. Volet. There was not a great deal more than zero registered on my own cycling experience. I am not, and never have been, the sporty type.

Cubic when young, spherical when older, I have never believed in physical exercise, which has always been a source of discomfort and humiliation to me. At school, I was the boy who hid in the changing-room while everyone else ran compulsorily cross-country, and also the boy who froze in the mud in the penalty area, only stirring to allow yet another goal to be scored against my side. For me, the chief benefit of organized games, that Victorian glory of our educational system, has been to teach the splendour of isolation and a distrust of the motives and abilities (or both) of those who praise team spirit – which I regard as a confidence trick worked by society upon individuals.

Today, as round as ever, if not rounder, I am the man you laugh at as he runs for the bus – except that I have given up buses. Nowadays I have the bicycle, an instrument of human independence and cheerful anarchy.

One of the things that I have always held against any team-sport is that it involves so much sound and fury running round in ever-decreasing circles. Though I cannot join the village team, it is modest enough for me to feel some affection for it. But team-sports refuse to stay on the pitch nowadays: they kick goals into my living-room out of the television. The ballyhoo of commercial sport I find only one whit less objectionable than the ballyhoo of show-biz, and two whits less than politics, and it all gets us even less far than jogging, which must run second to pole-squatting as a monument to futility. The fact that life is as inconsequential as it is for most of us seems no argument for making it more so. Other ways of passing the time – music, art, literature, hobbies – tend to deepen the mind, expand it, make it more lively: organized sport contracts, trivializes, makes us more conformist. The arts encourage us to understand other human beings: sport, to compete with them. While ready to accept that you can only find out how good you are at some things through comparing performances, I have never been able to understand the pleasure in overcoming other people that seems to mean so much to sportsmen, businessmen and politicians alike. As far as I can see, the outstanding and interesting people are those who compete primarily with themselves. Sport is part of the conspiracy organized by the many to delude themselves into thinking that they are activists. Most of us are not. We are observers.

The best possible present for a non-competitive, independent observer who dislikes wasted effort and wishes to expand his mind is a bicycle. Do not be put off by unfortunate experiences of bicycles in youth. Most youthful experiences are unfortunate.

My relationships with bicycles have always been strainful. Even now that I have one of the best machines that money can buy, I look nothing like the Tour de France, except in aggregate mass. The lithe racing cyclist whirrs down the straight, sleek and sinuous as a mechanical weasel. I progress rather more like a sack of dirty laundry under instructions to make its own way to the bagwash – a danger to no one but less than elegant.

The first sophisticated machine I ever encountered was a maroon tricycle which came into the yard at home in Shropshire with some small child of five or six. That child I have forgotten, but not the sensation of mounting the machine, standing on the pedals and getting nowhere at all in the pile of sand I had decided to make my racecourse. Later on, amid the semis of South-East London, my new black Raleigh introduced me to the communal function of the bicycle, when it was used mainly for leaning upon, with a group of other small boys, in the park – a prop to boredom occasionally set in motion between one end of the rec. and the other.

To begin with, even that motion was uncertain, the bicycle having been purchased over-size for reasons of economy. My toes did not touch the ground, and it took two lessons from my father (an optimist where I was concerned and a believer in the 'push-hard-and-see-what-will-happen' method of instruction) before I could grasp the concept of the brake. I ended the first lesson in a lime tree, following a tooth-shattering jolt as I mounted the kerb. The second left me in somebody's front garden, enjoying an intimate connection with a rose bush. (My father stayed an optimist, however: some twelve years later there were similar, but rather more dramatic incidents when he taught me to drive a motorbike and sidecar. But on that occasion he was riding pillion, and that cured him.)

Living in the suburbs, the bicycle brought me a limited sense of freedom, with so many miles of humdrum uniformity between me and anywhere countrified and interesting – though Dartford Heath, where large and competent people flew large and expensive model aeroplanes before intensely envious groups of small boys, provided a superb switchback run over the gravel pits, starting from a steep hill at one end. Starting from the other, of course, it provided only a long and tedious journey back – but so much of childhood is a matter of infinite preparation for a moment of excitement that it seemed acceptable at the time.

It was at any rate more interesting that the utilitarian alternative which I was forced to adopt when I attained grammar school in Dorset, going like the snail unwillingly along the same old lanes, every hill making the most of itself thanks to the substantial frame, my inexpert maintenance, and the 3-speed gear. (I considered racing bicycles and the naked cogs that droop from derailleur gears dangerously avant-garde and rakishly improper.) Miles seemed longer then, particularly on winter nights when the only company was the temperamental flickering of the dynohub and the occasional green gleam of a slow-worm in the grass. After university and my brief relationship with the motorbike and sidecar, I gratefully turned my thoughts to the day when I would be able to afford a car, and lent my push-bike to a friend, who promptly had it stolen. It seemed most sensible on his part, and I did not grieve.

There followed a gap of some years, during which I never thought to encounter the saddle again. I did so, in the end, as the result of simple cupidity. I have almost no capitalist instincts, but those I have are unanimously directed towards the pursuit of bargains and the cast-offs of the rich, whom I have always considered to have been created for the purpose of spending extravagant sums of money to buy luxury goods which they immediately tire of, and sell to me at a considerable reduction.

It is doubtful however that any rich or titled person had ever owned the Black Pudding whom I came upon disconsolate in the local Oxfam shop. Her tyres were flat, her saddle was torn and suffering from middle-aged spread. She was dirty as a gipsy harlot, and many a leg had obviously been thrown over her in her time, but there was no

evidence that either she or anybody else had ever found the experience particularly interesting. Rather, her demeanour was that of a sturdy matron, frowzy and frazzled not by sin, but by the simple harassment of keeping up with the boredom of a limited existence. (Afterwards I came to name her the Black Pudding on account of the fact that she was extremely heavy, and acted as the vehicle for a good deal of fat.)

She had, however, one charm. She was a cheap bit of goods. The price of my seduction was £5 which is good value in any circumstances. I wheeled her home as an object that might possibly come in useful at some future date, and put her in the hall. But the future date did not occur for some two or three years during which time she cluttered up the place as only a humiliated bicycle can, reaching out her handlebars to tear passing garments, and offering her left-hand pedal to be tripped over.

Then, one day, I was without the car, and had to go to shops off the bus route. I borrowed a pump from the children, inflated the Black Pudding, straightened out the rods of her brakes, and set off. It may be that you never forget how to ride a bicycle, but after eighteen years out of the saddle, there was certainly something missing somewhere. That was apparent to the youth of the neighbourhood who passed opprobrious comments on my progress, something they only occasionally do now. Not only was there a certain unsteadiness and a feeling as of one who has only recently been released from the Cell of Little-Ease, but a considerable lack of wind – on my part. Mother Nature was OK, with a howling gale blowing head-on. The innocuous hill up to the shops defeated me. Coming down, I realized with an interesting apprehension of horror, that the kinks in the brake rods had been put there for a purpose. Holding the brakes full on, I was still gathering speed. With great presence of mind I headed for the nearest kerb, stopped by means of scraping the front wheel along it, and walked the Pudding back home to a new – and even more inconvenient – position in the hall.

But the experience rankled. I was approaching forty – a sensitive age – and to have to face up to the comparison between my faltering progress to the shops and my erstwhile flitting over the bumps of Dartford Heath was not one I cared to contemplate at the time. Out came the Pudding again with her kinks back and new brake blocks, and I began to cycle her to work, Muswell Hill to Oxford Circus. It proved to be amazingly efficient in comparison with the rush hour on public transport, and extremely unpleasant.

Overworked and very much out of condition (having taken no exercise for the past two decades other than the occasional game of tennis) I suffered no heart attack, to the surprise of my friends, but instead contracted asthma for the first time in my life. Our doctor, whom I had met twice during the previous twenty years (once for the birth of each son), was extremely unsympathetic, and spoke eloquently but peremptorily of the consequences of cigars, eating, drinking and most other things that make life worth living. Hinting darkly that in my case there was unlikely to be very much more of it left, he pooh-poohed the suggestion that cycling was in any way responsible: but I knew the asthma for what it was – the Black Pudding's Revenge. My agonies were not eased by my practice of carrying heavy ex-army panniers containing tools for the maintenance of the Pudding, and also stuffed to the brim with fruit, vegetables and cheese from Soho for the maintenance of myself.

It was about this time that a friend in a taxi happened to pass me as I laboured on the long hill up the Archway Road. Spontaneously, the taxi driver pointed me out.

'Look at that,' said the taxi driver. 'Ever seen anything more miserable?'

It was also raining.

I began to feel that life ahead was an increasingly steep descent and that I had no better hold on it than the Black Pudding's brakes. (The most regular of the ceaseless ministrations she required was the replacement of all four brake blocks every fortnight: I took every hill at a snail's pace, going up or down.) And then I began to talk bicycles with my friend Christopher, who loves them as he loves all mechanical things, being an engineer and an enthusiast for engineering.

Christopher is my opposite. Where I bulge, he knobbles. He is a man of sleeping bags, rucksacks and fell boots, where I am for beds, carrier bags and sandals. I am lethargic, he has the habitual expression of a terrier looking over a hedge towards a distant rabbit. And he is a cyclist.

He had the measure of the Black Pudding straight away. As I can recognize a nasty, vindictive temperament in a human being, he can spot it in a machine. When I pointed to the solidity of her frame and the stoutness of her wheels, he conceded to the Pudding but a single virtue – that no thief in his right mind could ever possibly desire to steal her. His own bicycle he would hustle into the office by a back door and conceal in a locked room. He had put its parts together himself at a time when he could not afford a car: it gave him pleasure, he said, to think that even his limited finances could run to a machine which in its own terms was a Rolls-Royce.

Mark you, those terms had little in comparison with my £5 bicycle. For him £5 would buy a tyre perhaps, but not much more. A bicycle is deceptively simple: for instance, in terms of maintenance, which requires not only considerable experience, but a knack. We think of a bike as everlasting, and in terms of price indices that passed away upwards when we were very young and our parents bought us something cheap. In fact, the bicycle – though remarkable value – does represent engineering sophistication which has to be paid for, but is worth having. When Christopher bought the best, Christopher was right. I knew it even as I argued the virtues of solidity and economy – even more as I turned up at work with grease and road-grit stuffed under my fingernails in the course of running repairs to the Pudding's eccentric mechanics.

So, what with my blistering doctor and Christopher's

war of attrition over the lunch table, I moved towards becoming a Proper Cyclist. But the thing that really decided me to ride to the Mediterranean (never having ridden more than twenty-five miles at a stretch at any time, and not more that half a dozen in recent years) was the feeling that I had given up being in touch with the world outside. I travelled from one centrally heated roomscape to another: sometimes I looked at fields through car windows. My relationship with the natural world my forebears battled with was like that of an armchair with a television screen – both of them forever static, no matter how much the picture changes.

All this would seem comic to an outdoor man, a farmer or a forester. But in our time there are relatively few of either, and a great many people in offices and on production lines. And a radio broadcaster is among the most detached of all. He lives under fluorescent tubes in a windowless studio, and handles words and ideas on little pieces of magnetic tape. The temptation is strong to become more and more a processor of substitute reality, not very different from a transistor in his tape machine. I wondered: 'Is there still a world out there you can touch?' and turned up the central heating another notch.

But later I went to see an old friend, Joy Hatwood, a producer for BBC Radio 4, and suggested to her that together we might roll up our trouser legs and plan a series of programmes to put the toe on the reality of provincial France, the country of the bicycle. Whereupon Joy instantly agreed to my rolling up my trouser legs, adjusted her own *haute couture*, lit yet another menthol cigarette, and set about planning – with one eye on the atlas and the other on my waistband. I am quite sure that she also had misgivings about my ability to survive a cycle trip of getting on for a thousand miles, but Joy is too nice a person to mention such things.

I was confident – or, at least, unconscious – having formulated Vernon's First Geographical Principle, viz: 'It's all downhill to the South, or they wouldn't put the North on the top of the map, would they?' It was also in my mind that, should too much exercise prove unpleasant, France is a country likely to offer compensations.

BEAUTIES OF FRANCE, AND THE MINOR DIFFICULTY OF THE FRENCH – a Note for the Chauvinist Reader by Bulwer Wellington-Ffoulkes

Every Briton loves france, but it is sometimes difficult to come to terms with the fact that it is occupied by the french. Many a pleasant holiday in the sun has been impaired by the fact that the locals do not speak The Language (English), and insist on following their own parochial way of life instead of adopting customs more acceptable in a world context (British).

Do not take them at their own value. It is well-known that the British have a monopoly in history and pastoral beauty; and that there is an Anglo-Saxon copyright in what some British statesman (Burke? Gladstone? John Peel?) has called 'liberty, equality and fraternity'.

Do not continue this book, either, for fear of contracting the nasty disease called 'francophilia' which, medical men tell us, causes decay of the British Lobe of the brain. As the poet says, 'East is east and West is west' – which means that our Nation and the french lot are poles apart: and no Channel Tunnel shall ever connect them.

B.W.-Ff.

CHAPTER 2

Parts Asunder

There is no law about taking off for the Mediterranean on a penny-farthing or a unicycle, if you choose: but the best authorities advise against it, likewise consorting with such as the Black Pudding over long distances.

Indeed, even over short ones my intimacy with the star-crossed Pudding was already on the wane. Her habit of casting off her substance as she went along, bestrewing the ground with bolts, nuts and other significant mechanical parts was difficult enough to learn to live with. Then she took to falling down drunkenly in the road when she was supposed to be leaning against parking meters; and in one of these disreputable collapses in Marylebone High Street her hind parts were run over by some myopic motorist, her back wheel irreparably buckled. She took me home waggling her bottom forlornly from side to side, and imparting a most peculiar feeling of instability to mine. It was as if she was a rejected lover making a last, vain sexual advance.

The morning after, I went round the bicycle shops for a replacement wheel-rim. I learned, at about the fourth or fifth establishment, that there are back wheels and back wheels, and the Pudding's was the other kind. When I eventually tracked one down in a hippy bike shop which did not mind dealing in antiquities, I was unwise enough to undertake rebuilding the thing myself.

Anyone who has only consciously observed wheels as wheels can have no idea of the sensation of Nature's germens tumbling about his ears which is conveyed by the spectacle of a hub and a rim without any visible means of connection except for a random bundle of little bits of wire to go somewhere between them. Any spoke may go to this side of the rim, that side of the rim, over this other spoke, under that one. It is like knitting a suspension bridge, and at the end of it all the middle is not in the middle, the outside goes round like an ouija-board under the influence of Nostradamus, and the spokes twang like a piano dropped down fourteen flights of stairs, heard somewhere around the thirteenth. True, there was nothing that could not be disentangled by the interested gentleman in the bicycle shop with the aid of a good pair of wire-cutters, but the experience was unforgettable, and the prospect of repeating it in French insupportable. I decided that the Pudding would have to go as soon as I could find a replacement.

As there are back wheels and back wheels, so there are bicycles and bicycles, and bicycle shops and bicycle shops to sell them. In some of the shops you may also buy prams, squeaky dolls and plastic ducks that swim upside-down in the bath; assuming that you wish to purchase a bicycle in combination with any or all of these, such shops have obvious advantages.

My engineering friend Christopher would have none of them, foreseeing the delightful prospect of buying something expensive by proxy. At the lunch-table, conversation was of nothing but cranks and cog-wheels, and his rhubarb crumble grew cold in the spoon as he discoursed upon the desirability of double-butting. (I have made some observations upon this interesting subject myself, which will be found at the end of this book, in Appendix I: On Bicycles.) Like an incantation, the names of Reynolds, Claud Butler, Holdsworth (Christopher was a Holdsworth man himself), Condor, Peugeot, Campagnolo, Shimano, Dawes, Motobecane, Brooks and Mercian rolled off his tongue and splashed into the custard for, as in the Iliad and certain Shakespeare plays, the more you repeat lists of impressive-sounding names, the more impressive everybody else thinks they are.

So it came about that one day I took myself down to the

Cut at Waterloo – through the scrawny, yelling street-market and past the lost-looking Old Vic to the double-fronted shop of W. H. Evans. Evans the firm – for Evans the man has long since pedalled off on the greatest ride of all – will sell you more or less whatever you fancy off-the-peg, but they are renowned for their Very Own Touring Bicycle, which they will tailor to your requirements like a bespoke suit and tell you patiently what your requirements are if you are new to the subject. (Nor are they by any means unique in this, for one of the beautiful simplicities of the bicycle is that it needs little more than the bits, a few jigs, a brazing torch and a small number of other basic tools to build the individual model, and there are cottage industries doing so up and down the length of the country.) But for the newcomer to cycling, the Evans bicycle has the advantage that – though its bits may be varied if you know how to vary them – there is a basic specification for you to start off from, and nice people to tell you not to do silly things with it. In some shops, where no complete bicycle is to be seen, and boxes of identical-looking equipment at far from identical prices await the arrival of The Racer and Real Expert, the novice feels like a man who has gone to buy a suit, and has been told by the tailor that there are many kinds of individual sleeves, hems, gussets, button-holes, skirts, lapels, trouser-legs, zip-flies, ticket-pockets and the like in the shop, and what would sir suggest flinging together to make some sort of garment?

During the early lunch-hour Evans is besieged by West-Enders via the Bakerloo Line, South Londoners from round about and City folk off that little maggot of an underground shuttle that leaves from the Monument. There are queues of enthusiasts anxious to have long earnest conversations with the men behind the counter, and queues of other enthusiasts equally anxious that they should not. (All bicycle shops are among those most apt to generate queues, though in this respect they are far out-classed by builders' merchants. Bicycle shops are also the most trippable-over shops there are, with the possible exception of warehouses specializing in hatstands, and kennels specializing in dachshunds.)

I did not feel totally comfortable among the enthusiasts, most of whom had the knobbly, outdoor look of Christopher, and none at all the gently-contoured indoor look of me. But we were one in admiration of the thin, many-coloured lines of bicycles. They had about them a touch of medieval pageantry, as if they were about to ride into the lists with glittering rims, a gleam of mudguard and a flash of bright enamels – clear blue, red, green, gold, with blazonings of heraldry.

I thought that the shop was all there was to see at Evans, apart from occasional glimpses into the little back workshop where they did the assembly, until I was shown a secret door concealed behind an arras of cards of spares and accessories as if it were just any old bit of wall. Beyond the door a dark wooden staircase thumped hollowly down to a basement into which daylight filtered obliquely, though there was red fire from the brazing torch and sparks spitting off the grinding wheel. Apart from a small kennel of secondhand bicycles in a dusty corner, that cellar was the domain of Harry Healey, frame-maker: veteran mechanic of many a great cycle race in his younger days, working out the tail end of his career at the stained black bench. Grey-haired, peering a shade more intently through his glasses than he used to, he padded round in his cycling shoes after riding to work despite a heart attack and doctor's orders.

On the old white matchboard of the walls were carefully inscribed graffiti – the jottings of an anchorite, Harry Healey's personal philosophy.

'They're just little things that occur to me now and then when I'm working, you know – and I chalk them up. A little personal wisdom for posterity, you might call them.'

There are cold cynics and warm cynics: those who never loved life, and those who did and got their fingers burned. I thought that Harry Healey was probably one of the latter:

down-to-earth, with a sense of humour as practical as an
Austin Seven changing gear – a quick rev-up, followed by
a crunch.

'Here's one just right for you, Tom: "Blessed are the
sleek, that they do not inherit the girth."'

Stuck in the shadows of his small, low-ceilinged cellar –
brazing, filing and grinding frames day after day – he retained a great enthusiasm:

'Man isn't a slave to the bicycle,' said Harry. 'It's not
like the motor car. It doesn't pollute, it's not a status
symbol, it's cheaper than walking. I once worked for old
Harry Whitlock who used to win the London to Brighton
Walk every year before the war – and he used to go through
a pair of shoes on that fifty-two miles: I can go there and
back, and you won't notice any wear on the tyres at all.
Walking through the countryside's a bit slow and in the
car it's too fast. But the bike is just the right speed. It
doesn't play your feet up like walking does over long distances and you're up higher than the average car, so you
can see over hedges.'

'Perhaps I ought to get a penny-farthing,' I said.

Harry took me seriously. 'Bit dodgy downhill; a bit of
a job to get off. They don't make things the way they used
to: they make them a damn sight better now. The basic
bike hasn't changed much in seventy or eighty years, but
we've got new materials. To get their bikes light, they had
to make them weak, whereas we can now make them very
strong. Fine-drawn tubing came into existence because of
the advent of the bicycle; the bike really developed the
roller chain – and the differential on a car was developed
for the tricycle. We were the first large-scale bike manu-
facturers, which is why most of the bikes in the world are
modelled on British ones. There's no earthly reason why
the chain wheel should be on the right-hand side, but they
all are – even in China.'

Engineering has its miracles, its towers, its superhuman
complexities that make you feel small, but talking to Harry
Healey I found myself in the presence of an engineering

achievement that makes people feel big. The bicycle is a small miracle, but more than that: it is one that has evolved in harmony with human beings, a marriage of metal and muscle.

'When I get to France,' I asked him, 'will they be able to recognize me as an English milord by my bicycle?'

'They'll recognize you by your frame: the fact that it's a bit poshed up and finished better. The French make good bike frames, but they don't tend to bull them up the way we do. Otherwise, you're going to have a right mélange – you'll probably finish up with French or Italian rims, German spokes, Jap gears, Swiss brakes. You need good brakes – some of the chaps touch fifty or sixty miles an hour, coming down the mountains in the Tour.'

'I wasn't going to go at fifty or sixty miles an hour,' I said.

'They don't pedal down at that speed. You've got to remember some of those drops go on for twenty miles at a time – they're old pack-horse tracks that have been made into roads. With your weight,' said Harry, introducing an unnecessarily personal note into the conversation, 'you just sit back and let your avoirdupois take you.'

So it would, I thought, but not at that speed if I and my Swiss brakes had anything to do with it.

'You'll get fed up rushing down a mountain at that speed,' Harry persisted. 'After a while it'll pay you to stop and let the rims cool off – have a blow, or a brew-up. But one great advantage of a bike – however unfit you are, or if you're getting old like I am – it's much harder going up the hills, but coming down is just as good as it ever was.'

'You'll slim down,' added Harry, as I left. 'You don't see many fat cyclists, do you? Strangely enough, you don't see many bald cyclists either. I think cycling's good for the hair: all the bald cyclists I know lost their hair in their twenties – but that was hereditary. I've got a feeling that wind through the hair stimulates the roots. Better than chicken-dung, I think.

'You don't see many people riding bicycles looking

bored: you see plenty of people in cars looking bored – and frustrated. In fact, the majority.'

Upstairs in the shop I sat on a machine to see what size I was: in bicycles, as in trousers, the length of the inside leg is a key measurement. Gary, the manager, wrote out the specification and said I could have any colour I liked, so long as it was black, because it is the only colour you can touch up satisfactorily. I paraded my little knowl-edge and asked was it true what I'd been reading, that on the Continent they stick a broomstick up their front forks as an additional precaution against the rigours of the cobblestones? It appeared that I did not have to bother about that, or about the other great problem that I had had with the Black Pudding in the place where the pedals go through.

'I've had a lot of trouble with my bottom bracket.'

'Trouble with your bracket?'

'Yes.'

'Loosening up?'

'Yes.'

'You need your bottom bracket very tight.'

With which valuable counsel, I left the shop.

It was not really necessary, I thought, for me to go and see a doctor but Joy insisted, having discovered one she thought was particularly appropriate for me since he was both a cyclist and a dietician. To Harley Street I went there-fore, to the consulting room of Dr Nigel Oakley. He had slightly more flesh on him than my own discouragingly spare practitioner, which was a considerable comfort; but, all the same, he was carrying an awful lot less than I was.

'If you'll just step on the scales here ...' said Dr Oakley in a tone of interested anticipation. 'Oh my goodness, we're going up rather a long way, aren't we?' (reverting to the medical plural under the stress of enquiry, and clattering his weights like a long-standing inmate of the Bastille). 'Perhaps the damage isn't that bad.'

'It can't be that bad,' I said.

'It's somewhere ... oh my goodness, it's over ... er ... over eighteen stone, isn't it?' He gave up being tactful. 'I think you're almost exactly nineteen stone.'

'Oh dear,' I said, partly because I understood some expression of penitence was expected of me, and partly because it was several pounds more than I was used to.

Dr Oakley was still seeking a way of palliating the horrid truth. 'If we switch over to kilograms ... that makes you ...' (he gave up again) '... amazingly heavy ...' (politely) '... you don't look as heavy as this, actually ... somewhere about 121 kilograms.'

It is always a pleasure to surprise a medical person, especially when they are so courteous as to start searching for extenuating circumstances before you even have a chance to mention your large bones.

'Now I'm going to take your height: stand up and make

every centimetre you can.' So I did, but it was not enough. 'You can easily work out what your ideal body weight is by taking 100 off your height in centimetres.' (It sounded a suspiciously symmetrical formula to apply to human beings, but one thing the fat man learns early is that you cannot argue with a doctor on the question of ideal body weights, which are not so much ideal, as many times hallowed and sanctified.) 'You're almost exactly 6 foot ... 183 centimetres ... minus 100 ... comes down to 83 kilograms ... which puts you a good solid 40 kilograms overweight.'

'Big bones,' I began, 'run in ...'

'I don't think the alibi of the bones (which has been used many times before in this consulting room) really washes when you've got a discrepancy of six stone.'

I am sure that there are many other alibis I could have presented, had I thought of them at the time; for instance, that my childhood had been imbued with a profound moral concern for eating so that a deep anxiety for the starving Chinese soon burgeoned in my infant conscience: at which I ate my rice pudding to the final grain, and dutifully asked for more (though I could not see clearly the precise method according to which the Chinese might thereby be relieved). 'Doctor,' I might have said, 'I listened carefully to my elders when they told me what was good for me. I learned that bread was good for me because it was cheap, butter because it was delicious; further, it was said that milk made strong bones, that people who did not eat jam offended those who made it, that sugar gave energy, that a good fried breakfast policed the body against an underworld of prowling germs, that a good lunch kept you going, that a proper observance of afternoon tea was a prop of the British Empire, that a substantial dinner was necessary because the lunch at school could not be as wholesome as the lunch you would have got at home, and that a late snack and a glass of hot milk helped you to sleep. Later, I discovered that English ale had overcome the dietary deficiencies of generations of English labourers and was therefore especially suitable for lunchtime consumption by an office-worker. There were other forms of food that had no particular virtue in themselves, but were necessary ritual accompaniments to the forms that had. Any important occasion was distinguished by ritual eating and drinking. In short, all the dietary folklore of a poor society was produced to prepare me for living in an opulent one . . . also, I happen to like eating.'

There is never time to say such things – nor are they relevant. What is, is: as we plonk a gargantuan gob of butter on our baked potato, who spares a thought for the formative years of the cow?

But as it turned out, Dr Oakley was a most agreeable man: for a start, he agreed with me about jogging.

'Just jogging to go round the block and end up where you started is futile: some people can do it, but then some people can row miles on a stationary rowing machine. Cycling to work, or a country trip at weekends – if you're competitive, something like squash which can be socially congenial as well – those are the sort of things you won't give up after a week because you're so unconscionably bored by them.'

In a brave attempt to throw off his medical conditioning, he even began to agree with me about breakfast.

'Almost all the obese patients who come to me say they don't eat breakfast. That means they have an enormous lunch, put their feet up afterwards, get soporific and go to sleep: it's the worst possible combination.'

So we discussed breakfast: Dr Oakley favoured wholemeal bread and chunky marmalade. I said that was all right, but I liked a couple of eggs, half-a-dozen grilled rashers and some fried tomatoes or creamed mushrooms to go with it. If he could find a good sausage, I said, one or two of those were not to be despised, and wasn't it a pity that kidneys had lost favour? In the matter of frying eggs and tomatoes, I said, I had my own special methods, if he was interested, and strong opinions on the cutting of bacon – very thin and lightly grilled so that it curls up like

34

a worm in cement. You get a nice clean egg if you film the frying-pan with olive oil or butter, set the bottom of the egg and finish off by adding a splash of boiling water, then covering so that the top poaches, which it does quickly (and warms your plate as well). Tomatoes also need covering and cooking briskly in lots of butter until the juice runs and you boil it all down to a savoury emulsion with plenty of salt and black pepper. Lemon juice is one flavouring for thinly sliced mushrooms briefly sautéed in butter, but for a cream sauce either fresh basil or a delicate combination of rosemary and cinnamon are better.

But it was precious little good talking about that sort of breakfast if I was going to France and, furthermore, the lunches were liable to be excessive: did we not foresee a difficulty there? And, by the way, were French dogs dangerous to English cyclists on account of France having rabies? Was any adverse effect likely to result from the continual flexing of the knee joints on the bicycle, and would the maintenance of a crouching position over long periods lead to any permanent deformation of the vertebrae? Would I get bicycle-lag, or culture shock as a result of prolonged impact of the French psychology? Since I had been advised to 'toughen myself up' in preparation for my days in the saddle, what would he recommend rubbing in for the purpose ... liniment? turps? dubbin? (I did not ask all these questions for myself, but as a broadcaster you are expected to behave like a friendly idiot in case there may be a friendly idiot somewhere in your audience who would like to identify with you.)

And I asked, optimistically: 'How much weight will I lose?'

'Let me ask you something: how long did it take you to put it on?' This was plainly one of those questions like a roulette wheel with a croupier in the habit of parking his chewing gum under the same number. I kept silent. 'I always tell my patients: however much exercise you take, however sensibly you eat, you won't lose much more than a pound a week.'

But, obligingly, he did a rough sort of sum based on the assumption that, in the best of all possible worlds, cycling might burn up 4 calories a minute and – given that fat yields 9 calories per gram, that there are 28·35 grams to the ounce and that the trip might be about 750 miles of cycling at 10 miles an hour:

$$\frac{\text{`}4 \times 60 \times (750 \div 10)}{9 \times 28 \cdot 35 \times 16} = 4 \cdot 4091707 \text{ lbs,}\text{'}$$

said Dr Oakley, or words to that effect.

'What? Five pounds? All that way?'

'Yes.'

'But at that rate how far would I have to cycle to get off six stones?'

$$\frac{\text{`}6 \times 14 \times 16 \times 9 \times 10 \times 28 \cdot 35}{4 \times 60} = 14288 \cdot 41\text{'}$$

said Dr Oakley: 'By rough arithmetic, comes to almost fifteen thousand miles.'

It confirmed everything I have always thought about taking exercise.

'Be careful about your diet – nothing worse than cycling along with colic and other intestinal problems, and having to rush behind a hedge every twenty yards.'

I left.

Then, one day, I sealed the fate of the Black Pudding with a small-ad in the local paper, and I took the tube down to the little shop at Waterloo to collect my brand new bicycle, also black but shiny and beautiful. Its pedals spun like bees trapped in a Mobius loop, it bowed its drop handlebars like a charger pawing the ground, it stuck its saddle in the air like an over-endowed dowager. It was a proud beast, an aristocrat among bicycles.

I found that, whatever the doctor might say, I felt as if a miraculous diet had taken stones off overnight. Suddenly I was converted to a real cyclist – no longer an unwieldy accessory on top, detachable for the purpose of pushing up hills. I entered a state of delightful symbiosis with an end-product of a long line of engineering evolution. It was one of those once-in-a-lifetime sensations that only those who have experienced a long relationship with a Black Pudding can appreciate. A definite swooping sensation would occur on the down, and a feeling that a well-oiled bicycle genie was helping me to push on the up. The brakes stopped me without fuss, and farewell to the juddering, squealing inefficiency I was used to in the dry and the total helplessness in the wet. A feeling of soft clicking and gentle lubrication pervaded me.

The left-hand toe-clip had its difficulties at the start. The right-hand one is fine: you slip your foot into that one before you move off. You get one push and then you teeter along playing a wobbly-game with the left-hand clip and the law of gravity. Gravity dictates that the toe-clip hangs underneath the pedal, whereas you want to get your foot into it on the top. The theory of accomplishing this is that you flick the pedal nonchalantly, so that it swings round, bringing the clip up with it to encapsulate your foot at the instant of apogee. In practice, you flick it with your toe, whereupon it spins like a dynamo: then, while you are waiting for it to stop, the left-hand kerb moves rapidly into the middle of the road and hits you in the front wheel.

My bicycle had only the one serious disadvantage common to all good bicycles. Owning such a thing is like carrying a fillet steak through a game reserve, or a naked girl through a regiment. You can't put it down for a moment. A bicycle ties you up unless you tie it up – to something good and solid, with something good and solid. I grapple mine to a parking meter with hoops of steel whenever possible, and the fact that the hoops probably weigh as much as anything I've saved by buying an expensive light-weight frame is one of life's little ironies. But that is not all. When you have grappled your frame (and, cunningly, passed your hoops round the back wheel at the same time) you have to consider the front wheel (which,

on an expensive bicycle, may be worth up to £50 in itself).
So you have to take that off, at which your proud steed
bows to the ground like a camel with the colic. If you have
enough space left in your hoops, you can grapple the front
wheel to them as well, so that you don't have to carry it
with you inside wherever you are going, along with the
panniers, the handlebar bag, the saddle-bag, the drinking
bottle and the lights. And the pump. Of course, none of
this will prevent the infant vandal from stealing the quick-
release mechanisms from the wheels, but you just have to
put up with that, as you have to put up with the scratches
on your shiny new frame from all the grappling.

The bicycle is an instrument of freedom, and – as with
other freedoms – it is necessary to make compromises (in,
for example, appearance). It is undeniable that the elegance
of the bicycle belongs entirely and exclusively to the bicycle; just as it is no use a lad going out with a beautiful
girlfriend in the hope that he will look any less of a hob-
bledehoy. He will, of course, look worse. Elegance has to
come from somewhere: it leeches on its surroundings and
sucks them dry, leaving the knobbly bits and awkward
corners. If you are not careful, not only will you appear
before whoever you have come to see loaded down with
panniers, front bag, back bag, drinking bottle, lights and
pump, but you may also be wearing the sort of costume a
North Sea trawlerman would be likely to adopt for a hard
day's work gutting herrings on the high seas in a force 10
gale – i.e. a cycling cape, a cycling bonnet with a horrid
little pom-pom on top and cycle clips.

Cycle clips may well be valuable to North Sea trawler-
men in that they prevent the entrails slipping down inside
the socks, but in the world at large, they have become a
folk-symbol of failure. To make a geographical comparison: if *haute couture* is Paris, cycle clips are somewhere
around Wolverhampton. The effect on the observer must
be something to do with the way the trouser legs bulge
out and flop around above the ankles, or it may be that
there are implications of subservience in the resemblance

to harem trousers, or the likeness of the clips themselves to fetters.

Given the low class status of cycle clips, their aesthetic disadvantages, and the way in which they nip the calves of those of us who are ample, I am not surprised that more original thought has not been devoted to cycling costume for workaday and town wear. Leisure garments are no problem for most people who can obtain cycling shorts with chamois leather seats 'eccentrically stitched' for greater comfort, or touring shorts 'double seat, reversed seams, heavy-quality fly, vent bottoms & etc.' (I quote from the magazine of that friendly and helpful organization, the Cyclists' Touring Club, and cannot say who needs a heavy-quality fly or why, or what is a vent bottom). For the country, the knickerbocker in whipcord, tweed or moleskin is not only still available, but is still worn (which, considering that it came in a century ago, gives it well-nigh the status of a national costume, especially if worn with diamond-pattern stockings). There are also 'knee-length spats – fit under toe' and a cut-down variety of plus-fours known, logically enough, as 'plus-twos'.

But for the fashion-conscious cyclist in town, cycling wear is deficient. The more aesthetic of my friends are given to recommending me to wear flowing robes, but such are impractical on a bicycle and would probably require the purchase of a lady's model. For those in tune with muesli, wood-burning stoves and wholemeal bread, an ecologically evocative alternative to cycle clips would be a simple wrapping of old rags for the feet and legs, in the manner of an Anglo-Saxon legging. For the man in the City, brightly-polished riding boots and jodhpurs provide that extra touch of formality. Bishops' gaiters are delightful to those with an enthusiasm for bishops. Mosquito boots may be worn for the summer parties and Wimbledon, and among members of the Young Conservatives a brightly-coloured Wellington may be expected to strike a colloquial note of bonhomie.

For the Scot, the dress-kilt is a natural garb, though the

sporran should not be so long as to dangle in the pedals. (Indeed, the introduction of a bicycle sporran with attachments to the handlebars is long overdue for the Northern patriot.) But for the everyday town wear, the obvious garments are Elizabethan doublet and hose. The hose are easily washable, or may be patterned in horizontal stripes to minimize the effects of contact with the chain; their weight may be varied to suit summer or winter; and tools and sandwiches find a ready home within the capacious folds of the doublet (in the case of the former, producing an attractive jingling sound as you walk, and with the latter no risk of squashing the more mollient fillings (tomato, sardine, egg mayonnaise etc.). Yet other alternatives to cycle clips are to wear waders (though in this case the tops should be tightly stuffed with old newspapers in wet weather to avoid trickling and condensation), or tucking the trousers into the socks.

I wear bare feet and sandals almost all the time, thus being unfortunately debarred from becoming a leader of high fashion in this respect. I had met with a severe sartorial rebuttal in the form of a series of polite, but dismissive conversations with thin young gentlemen in bicycle shops about the availability of eccentric stitching and reversed seams to people who take my size in shorts. Indeed, the only shorts I could find to fit me in the whole of the West End and North London were from a firm which provided tropical kit for darkest Africa. They were a sedate garment, and I rejected them in favour of my ancient, grubby tennis shorts. I had a narrow escape with the T-shirt too, on account of the fact that the programme's producer had been reading up on the Tour de France.

'I want you to have a *maillot jaune*,' said Joy.

'I thought that was a swimsuit.'

'It's a yellow shirt, and they wear it when they're leading. The Tour will be on when we're there, you know. Don't you think it would be fun if you put on your *maillot jaune* and cycled across their route?'

'I think it might get me lynched.'

'Good. Well, I've ordered a yellow one anyway.'

It was only the fact that the day I was due to cross its route the Tour de France was on a train (why, I cannot to this day imagine) and that the T-shirt factory could only supply white that preserved me from committing what is probably in French law an offence equivalent to spitting on the tricolour. Instead, I had a T-shirt with a picture of me and the legend *Le gros type à vélo*; this meant that whenever I went into a shop in France, I had to keep my arms folded across my chest for fear the proprietor should conclude that I had developed a convoluted English way of insulting him, which he would revenge as soon as he worked out quite how I was doing it.

I would have been glad to follow the good doctor's recommendations that I do a bit of training before I went, but I had no time because I was working hard. I would have been glad to cut down on the drinking and the eating, but because I was working hard, I needed comfort. But I did find time to check that I was actually capable of cycling fifty miles before I set tyre to French soil (after which it would have been rather late to find out).

It was a Sunday morning before even religious people had got up; it was going to be a fine day, but began as cool as a church. I loaded a pannier with cape and a bright yellow banana, in case rain should fall or breakfast should be elusive, bumped down the steps and took to the Cambridge road (fifty miles was quite far enough for a start, without choosing to go somewhere hilly as well). Muswell Hill was mute; I was the only sprightly thing in Bounds Green; the North Circular Road was yawning, and I was far out on the A10 before London had woken up. I had the doubly virtuous feeling of one who had both got up early and is self-propelled.

The Cambridge road is an unpretentious dual carriageway; and it is on such unloved roads, where no one ever stops, that the motor car is revealed in its true selfishness and messiness. It howls past leaving its debris on the way in showers of sweet wrappers and crumpled crisp packets exploding from little, sticky hands, gently falling apart in scraps of rubber, twists of metal and little globules of glass, as if a lovely chandelier had come out to the country for the day only to be set upon by cruel bandits who stripped it of its internal connections. If something falls off a bicycle, the whole thing probably stops working and you have to get off and screw whatever it was back. Therefore the cyclist notices the prodigality of the car, bits of whose substance lie every few yards along the oily verge. It is as if we human beings ran throwing off parts of our body as we went: here a finger, there a toe, an ear, an arm, first knee joint, second elbow, until all that was left was a high-speed torso rolling rapidly into the distance. More pathetic, and very close to you on a bicycle, is the unwilling debris of the motor-car: a cat with flame-coloured fur, a hedgehog, a rat, little bags of guts with the zips broken.

And so I came to Cambridge in four hours including a fifteen-minute stop for breakfast. I was astonished, delighted, hardly stiff. I parked, went into a shop and emerged to find a gentleman in a tattered overcoat in the act of wheeling the bike off.

'You must be joking, mate,' I said, in a state of some incredulity.

'You can't park that bicycle here,' he said, relinquishing it loftily. 'This is the University of Cambridge.'

With which he picked up his worldly possessions in his four carrier bags and departed before I could think of a suitable reply.

Examining my pannier, everything appeared to be there, but the banana had turned quite black.

'Is this rapid ripening the product of vibration?' I thought. 'A change of air? Or is it a side-effect of the theory of relativity: if mass approaches infinity towards the speed of light, do bananas approach excessive ripeness at bicycle speed?' (I am fascinated by Einstein, who holds with me the same sort of status that the Book of Revelations does with Christians – never to be read, incomprehensible but exceedingly impressive.)

I made a mental note to experiment with plums, pears, pineapples, melons at a later date, possibly even Beaujolais Nouveau, but have never got round to it.

THE FIRST DAY

I have heard it said that there are people who leave for a journey in a state of great tranquillity with everything prepared the night before. On Tuesday 3 July, I rose with only a medium hangover at 5.30 and sat down amid the rubbish of the farewell dinner to complete the booklet on forms I was writing for the National Consumer Council, all other flat surfaces in the house being occupied by small heaps of packing and strategically placed vital notes to self. At nine o'clock I penned the last line, pushed aside the bowl of sometime salad that had been quietly rotting under my nose for the previous three hours, and began to rush up and down the house, from heap to heap and note to note, trying to work out what I had forgotten. At half-past ten, just as I had got the state of packing into my head, a troop of journalists arrived for the photocall, and put it out again.

I spent the next one and a half hours riding up and down the road in a solar topee – this being thought expressive of the spirit of the enterprise – while the photographers crouched, climbed walls and rolled on the ground, shouting 'Good, good' and 'Again, again' to the interest of the neighbours and passing traffic. I simulated exhaustion and fanned myself with the solar topee. I flourished a loaf of French bread (whereupon it broke in half), I raised a wine bottle to my lips in a festive manner: in short, I did everything a man setting off for a cycling tour of France might be expected to do. The photographers left.

Then another one arrived, so I did it again, contorting

my features in the strained and over-excited expressions appropriate to a figure of fun, as if someone below the level of the picture were busy trying to put a minnow into my navel.

I detached myself from my ordinary life by small stages – the packing of a pannier, the loading of equipment into Joy's car, the search for a way to tie the handlebar bag on securely since it had £2000 worth of BBC tape-recorder in it. Then, suddenly, there was Sally, my wife, and Jos and Hal, my two sons, waving in the doorway; and I was waving back from further and further and further down the road (my practice with the photographers having stood me in good stead): the preliminaries were over and something separate was happening.

Down Highgate Hill there was a noise like high wind in grass in my ears, and I knew that my voyage was imminent. I delivered my two carrier bags of 'Gobbledegook' manuscript and official forms to the man at the National Consumer Council who gave me a glass of wine on the doorstep; he said he had planned a party to see me off, but I was two hours late, and everybody had gone. Here I felt a weight off my mind and my back wheel, and as I set my watch to 2 o'clock by Big Ben and moved off over Westminster Bridge, I felt at last that I had actually begun: that I was a freewheeling vagrant with no fixed abode but a bicycle, and no moveables other than a pair of legs.

I began as a conservatively rolling stone, for I have an inveterate tendency to travel via places I know, even if they are rather off the route. Or perhaps it was a homing instinct on the part of the bicycle, but it came about that I found myself riding down the street market in the Cut, towards the bicycle shop. A police car was edging towards me through the crowds. As it squeezed past, the driver leaned out, a Northerner by his accent:

'I hope you don't scratch my paintwork going the wrong way down a one-way street.'

Even as a respectable member of the middle classes, I

know better than to talk back to policemen with wheels;
they are not at all the same thing as policemen with feet.
But I felt even more detached from society: not only a
vagabond but a law-breaker, a desperado in my own small
way. I rode down the rest of the one-way street on the
assumption that the policemen in their car would be unlikely to ease themselves off their cushions for anything
less than a bank-robber.

It is very difficult to know how to behave on London
roads with a bicycle. A few cyclists are quite po-faced about
the Highway Code: most are like me, and take a certain
amount of licence; others ride like the Battle of Britain.

LONDON HIGHWAY CODE FOR THE ADVENTUROUS CYCLIST

How to behave at traffic lights

Green: Go straight through.
Amber: Go straight through, rather faster.
Red: Go straight through, looking to right and left.

One-way streets

There are no one-way streets.

Lighting your bicycle

Try to ride under street lamps wherever possible.

No parking, no right turn and other signs

These are for cars, and do not apply to bicycles. Ignore them – except for signs saying 'Hospital', which you should note down for future reference.

London bade me farewell in the person of a chemist-lady in Brixton. The morning's rush had left me with a number of things undone and the most vital of these was a strong recommendation from a cycling journalist who had rung up before I left.

'Get some Vaseline for your bum.'

'Sorry?'

'Some people put on talcum powder but it just cakes up in the sweat. Vaseline, every day. And get some racing mitts for your hands.'

The chemist-lady had spectacles and a tendency to purse the lips: she was one of those chemist-ladies who like to hide themselves away behind a mask of make-up, like an ancient Chinese concubine. She was the sort of polite, efficient lady to make the male feel inadequate when he goes to buy perfume as a present, and to take the bright young female down a peg or two by pontificating clinically about the colours of lipsticks. I took the small Vaseline: the large one would not do, I said, because I was on a bike.

'Have you come far?'

'Just starting actually.'

'Where are you going?'

'The Mediterranean.'

Then the extraordinary happened: the primness vanished, the mask cracked into a landscape of wrinkles so that the great grin underneath could get out.

'Oh how lovely: go where you like, stop where you like. Good luck.'

She saw me to the door, all smiles.

'Have a safe journey!'

And that was the first lesson of my trip: on a bicycle you are nobody's enemy.

I was all set for the second lesson to occur because I knew what it would be – how you see the countryside and smell the countryside in a way you never do from a car. But South London *will* go on and on: from Brixton and Streatham with their patina of humanity acquired over generations, to Norwood and Thornton Heath and Croydon, which do not feel like places where people live and die so much as places from which people commute. Every greengrocer's shop had a red wave of strawberries overflowing its counters that July afternoon: and the handlebar bag looked as if it would be excellently adapted for eating on the move – a sort of bicycle nosebag in fact. But I saved that pleasure for the country: no one can eat strawberries in the streets of Croydon and enjoy them. I turned off the Brighton road at Purley into a deceptive patch of green and bought my lunch there, from a grocer who stared most suspiciously at the legend on my chest as if *Le gros type à vélo* was French for 'Stolen from H.M. Prisons' – but the houses started again; suburbia was a line stretching from anywhere to infinity.

And then, suddenly, it was country: dual-carriageway country winding uphill, but it was country all the same and I felt another of the tendons binding me to working life pull softly out of my brain. The pace was no longer the same: half-way up the hill, something rural scuttled in the undergrowth covering a bank – a red-combed, wallflower-brown, proverbial chicken afraid to cross the dual-carriageway. On the other side of the hill I lunched on the verge with tiny-leaved vetches flowering inconspicuously among the grass. I could not yet quite shake off the feeling that I ought to be rushing somewhere, but the standard pork pie was like pork pies used to taste before you realized they were standard, and the tomatoes had a tropical flavour. (Was this the same accelerated ripening at bicycle speed I had observed with the banana?) I raised my can of lager to the outdoor life. There were doubtless beaded bubbles winking at the brim but, being in a tin, I could not see them at it.

The miles to East Grinstead went down slowly and Ashdown Forest proved to have almost as many hills as trees. As I trailed up one, I passed a cottage with an old woman – shrunk by age until she was too small for the furry boots which she wore in spite of the sun – sweeping her lawn with a besom. Flick, flick – peering carefully, glasses not being what they used to be – flick with the twigs, and a scrap of paper made a slow progress across the grass. Flick, flick, flick, and the old lady trip, trip after it in her fur boots.

By Wych Cross, 600 feet up in the middle of the forest, the strains of cycling were screwing a fine crick into my neck, pulling the toes adrift from the ankles to make room for an ache somewhere in between, and thumping the palms of the hands into great red blotches.

'If these are English hills,' I thought, 'what are French mountains going to be like?'

I laboured through Nutley where there is a signpost to Cackle Street, through Uckfield, and after seven hours in the (increasingly hard) saddle I came to a couple of long cottages on the corner of the lane to Isfield, and established there that the pub I was seeking for the night did indeed lie off to the right – for I had no energy left for random exploration.

After a couple of miles I came to a tangle of elderflowers and old buildings just like Miss Haversham's house out of *Great Expectations*, and next to it the white gables of The Laughing Fish, with a flight of Victorian steps leading to a friendly bar and behind it a bespectacled landlord beaming interestedly through the gothic doorway at the road and me. Stiffly, I walked my machine up through the vegetable garden to a sagging barn, and chained it up to the beams, feeling guilty for bringing a Londoner's distrust into such a rural spot.

For Isfield has grown more peaceful, not less, over the years. On closer examination, Miss Haversham's house turned out to be the old railway station which has gone the same way as the local navigation went a century before. The narrow-boats once followed the Ouse over twenty miles upstream of Lewes, but flour mill, paper mill, barges and everything are all long gone, and The Laughing Fish has moderated its expression to a philosophical smile.

There are two great luxuries after seventy-six miles of cycling: one is a pint or two of beer (Beard's in Lewes brew a fine natural ale with a tang to it) and the other is a hot bath. After the latter I bethought myself of the advice of the cycling journalist and lay on the bed with legs in the air rubbing Vaseline into my main point of contact with the bicycle. It was probably not strictly necessary to adopt such a flamboyant posture, but it convinced me that my limbs were still capable of motion, which was at that moment a welcome reassurance. However, I was not completely happy about the application of Vaseline, for my considerate advisor had neglected to specify whether it

49

should be rubbed before cycling, or after. To this day, I have no idea, nor do I know if it is really necessary, for I rubbed it in at every possible opportunity, just to be on the safe side.

As I sat in the bar with a rump steak and a cat that came in with the dishes and went out when they left, I thought that if I were leaving England forever, I could not imagine a better place to spend my last evening than The Laughing Fish. Good beer, plain food, no pretensions and a vase of stocks on the table. There was the sound of true English tranquillity – the random thudding of darts mingled with unhurried conversation. Next to me a frail old lady was dreadfully disturbed by the extravagance of her friends.

'Brandy! It's very dear. You shouldn't buy it. I don't like it. I might take a sip at it, but that's all.'

She sipped. The landlord told me an opera singer was coming to stay the next day: '... an important part at Glyndebourne, quite famous, have you heard of her?'

It was all very peaceful.

THE SECOND DAY

I woke gingerly next morning to the gentle rumbling of barrels from below, the muted cooing of distant wood pigeons and the nearby twitterings of the infant James, son of the house. I lay flat for some time, wondering whether it might be dangerous to move my extremities in case they should be inclined to drop off – limbs because of cycling, head on account of Beard's bitter. It was seven o'clock. Having tested my concentration by staring closely at the ceiling, I concluded that the head was all right. Likewise, getting out of the covers and sitting up produced no sensation of the limbs detaching themselves; instead, a tendency for everything to be far too stiffly held on.

Over breakfast I had the company of the infant James, a young person of enquiring mind and a strong interest in beards.

'What for? How do you work them?'

Had I got boys, who was looking after them and what time did I go to work? We went off to the old shed at the bottom of the garden to put the bags back on the bicycle.

'What *is* a pump?'

It was time to leave. I mounted before a group of interested school-children waiting for the bus. As I rode off, there were loud scraping noises from behind: I dismounted rapidly.

The landlord, who had obviously been on the watch for some instant calamity, hurried out. The school-children became even more interested. Examination revealed that, in the cut-and-thrust of debate with the enquiring infant, I had put the bags on the wrong way round. The landlord helped me put them right. More farewells: I left, again with scraping noises since it seemed to be too early in the morning to get the feet into the toe-clips. As I turned the corner of the lane I could see the landlord gazing after me, looking doubtful.

There is a great feeling of virtue about riding a bicycle through the start of a fine day, and a great deal of pleasure. There was a hazy sky with the sun just showing through, and a lark: I passed meadows like green lawns afflicted with grassy boils; a hayfield, and an old brown horse with a sagging back and belly standing solemn but useless guard over a group of expectant Jersey cows. Birds, birds, birds in the hedgerows. As I rounded the bend above the Barcombe 'Cock', I saw the Downs ahead, the last sunlit barrier to the sea. In fact, they are not what they seem: the more you ride towards them, the more they retreat, and at last they open a passage for the river Ouse and you have only to climb quite a brief hill to look down upon Meeching, as the town was known until the beginning of the eighteenth century, when they tore down what remained of the old wooden piers, and built Newhaven.

THE CHANNEL CROSSING – a Guide for the Consumer by Bulwer Wellington-Ffoulkes

We British are a seafaring race, and think nothing of voyaging to foreign parts, even though it may be pretty unpleasant when we get there. The Ocean, however, has a very bad reputation with consumers (being given to typhoons, tidal waves, hammer-headed sharks, sea-serpents and the like) and you should ensure that you have a qualified captain (or, if possible, an admiral).

Having ensured that your car is safely stowed (*well* away from the walls and other vehicles because there is always a certain amount of movement on board ship, particularly during storms), insist on being taken to the captain. Tell him to show you his credentials, and obtain answers to the following questions:

1. Are your bilges tight and in good order?
2. Are you willing to go down with your ship?
3. Will you marry me? (For use only in the event of shipboard romance taking place.)

On request, the purser (pronounced 'boatswain') is required to furnish you with a full passenger list and a seating plan of the lifeboats. Do not hesitate to use foul language: it is considered polite among sailors.

Ladies should remember to give the First Officer their cup size, both in inches and centimetres, for their *brassière de sauvetage*.

B.W.-Ff.

My bicycle looked lonely stabled in the thundering, thumping hold of the *Valençay* with none but cars to keep it company. It is remarkable how little like a ship a ferry appears from the inside: a mixture of indifferent hotel, railway train and underground car park. Usually we look at ships from the outside, and then they seem to have a rhyme and reason all their own, going their own way on their own voyages, everything about them adapted to their relationship with sea, not at all a floating shanty town, a hotch-potch of accommodation for human beings centred on the duty-free shop, a small wooden dungeon with iron bars that fold up in international waters – that is, just beyond the end of Newhaven jetty. Cell upon cell of boxes of indulgence were waiting to be let out by the jaileress, a comfortable blonde lady of great patience in two languages, and a fine head for figures that added up in pounds, francs or any combination of the two, as befitting one who is always inter, never national. It was her easy trip across the Channel – no queues at the counter, no intense huddle around the list of customs allowances uncongenially posted above a skull and the legend 'Rabies is a killer'. There was only a solitary nun with a lapel badge saying 'Lourdes' who stopped to read the tariff of tobacco and alcohol, but went off without buying anything to take along as a little present for whichever holy sisters she might have been planning to stay with along the way.

'I've brought you a small gift, sister: a litre of single malt.'

'How kind, but the Mother Superior only allows Calvados and cigars.'

After about half an hour the nun returned, read the tariff again, and moved on. Then I noticed that processions of people were doing it – all bored, all on a circuit of the ship, strolling past the sleepers on the benches, the sunbathers on the boat-deck, the rattling grrummmphing funnel. But the most bored person on the ship was the small boy standing in an agony of poverty before a giant electronic game sending phantom shapes aimlessly back and forth across its screen, back and forth like the ferry across the Channel – a great iron hotel going through the water with tremendous expenditure of energy yet totally without impact on its environment apart from the odd box of rubbish for the sea birds to fight over; and the wake like a broad road behind.

CHAPTER 3

Over the Water

The hold of the ferry is one of the few places a bicycle cannot wriggle out of ahead of the cars. I stood wreathed in exhaust fumes as the engines revved, like something nasty coming up from the underworld. Nor was my exit elegant, encumbered with a heavy tape machine slipping and sliding from backbone to stomach so that I could gather the stereo sound of the musical clank that is the fanfare to France as you roll up the ramp into the certified French sunlight. On a bike, however, you don't roll up, you pedal up – and if you are in too high a gear to start with, you do so wheezily. And at the bottom of the place where the clank is there are great chasms in the plates where a bicycle wheel will go through. So I had to get off for them. Then at the top of the ramp, there were chasms in the form of tram tracks – I had forgotten all about such things, how they object to a bicycle travelling in the same direction and seize it and shake it fiercely to get rid of the rider. Fortunately there was a flat stretch at the top before I rounded the corner towards my reception committee from the tourist office and the cycling club of Dieppe.

There was a small but creditable quantity of Gallic cheering, accompanied by hoots from my horn as the bulb got in the way of my lower stomach as I dismounted, as it thereafter continued to do throughout the trip and, indeed, does to this day – the full stop on the end of a ride.

'What a trip, what a trip, ha-ha,' said the man from the tourist office waving his arms in huge delight.

'*Quelles vitesses!*' said the short rather fierce-looking ancient who was the president of the cycling club, staring at my gears. 'With these you can go up that.' He raised his

hand vertically; there was a tone of disapproval in his voice
that anyone could contemplate getting up a hill so easily.
Later, I discovered that he was almost seventy himself, and
had recently taken a trip to Harrogate, where he had cycled
a hundred miles a day for a week.

'It was beautiful,' said his fellow cyclist, M. Jean
Poirson, over an aperitif at the hotel. 'Unfortunately it
rained all the week.'

M. Poirson was a tall, spare gentleman – always behind
one pair of handlebars by reason of his languid Edwardian
moustache, but scarcely less frequently on a bicycle as well.

'This year is the big year for me. I'm training hard: my
last trip was 600 km in two days. You can't believe that,
can you? It sounds crazy, but there's a big cycling trip in
September – Paris-Brest-Paris, 1200 km in four days; and I
said to myself, "I would like to do that, just once in my
life." It's a sort of challenge.'

My aperitif was Suz: a golden liquor tasting over-sweet
at the start and over-medicinal at the end.

'It's not challenging me,' I said.

'When you get used to cycling, you go further and further: one day you want to do something exceptional in your life. I started cycling as the best way to see a bit more round Normandy. People are taking cycling very seriously in France.'

'Is it something in the national character?'

'There is a difference with the English spirit. We are more professional in France: the English are amateur – they like sport for fun. Here everybody is going a bit further every day and working very hard: it's the same with jogging. It's our inferiority complex – trying to compensate.'

He surprised me. 'Inferiority? In a beautiful country with the best wine and the best food in the world?'

'Yes, we are eating too much: as you say, we have good wine and good foods, so we try to sweat it off. You will lose weight I'm sure.' (M. Poirson cast an estimating eye around my navel.) 'Ten kilos at least, and you will enjoy food better.'

'I enjoy it rather too well now,' I said.

'No, no, you will lose weight. You like garlic? That's surprising because so many English hate it. On a cycle, you eat in restaurants you never discover in a car. You talk to wonderful people – you have time to talk to them: you take the side roads. Cycling becomes a sort of drug. Do you understand that? You will understand later.'

The sun was going down on the horizon, its light trickling down the lanes of France into the sea. I thought of empty miles and golden days trickling ahead. I was not, after all, in Harrogate.

THE THIRD DAY

Like Caesar's Gaul, Dieppe is divided into three parts – coming, going, and staying put. The British are comers and goers nowadays, but for over a century the town supported a sizeable colony of genteel exiles eking out their pensions and remittances with their eyes fixed longingly on where Brighton would be, if it were not for the horizon. An old inhabitant, M. Georges Guibon – ninety-three years old and lamenting that the memory is apt to be less than it was when one gets past ninety – nevertheless remembered the days when French living was cheap, and the British community was 600 strong, with a high and a low church of its own, British chemists, British grocers, and even Indian servants, imported by the colonels on half-pay to remind them of the Raj. British artists, more and less respectable, lived here too, among them Beardsley, Ruskin, Sickert and Wilde.

'An Englishman,' said M. Guibon, chuckling into his carpet-slippers, 'an Englishman was not a foreigner, but a friend. To this day, the English and the French have more in common than they think.' He added, with a touch of chauvinism: 'When I am in England, I do not say I am French. I say I am a Norman – and of course a Norman is more than an Englishman. I was not at the Battle of Hastings, of course, but I went to Hastings to see it.'

Since the days of William the Conqueror, the mailed glove has been on the other fist. Most of the original Dieppe was burnt to ashes during a bombardment by the British and Dutch in 1694, and in 1942 there was more destruction in the disastrous allied raid in which 1000 soldiers, mostly Canadians, died for little more purpose than to teach the Higher Command a few lessons about how to conduct the future Normandy invasion.

The old part of the town that survives is mainly eighteenth-century, but on a cliff at one end stands the turreted castle which is now a museum, containing among other things a fine collection of ivory carvings. Jehan Ango, a sixteenth-century merchant prince of questionable morality, was the man who established the trade links that made the town a centre of that art. Shipbuilder, privateer and known as 'the Medici of Dieppe', he was rich enough to lend money to one king (Francis I of France) and powerful enough to conduct a private war with another (the King of

Portugal) and come off better. Apart from a tomb, his individual monument is an elaborate Florentine dovecote which he intended to be the best in Normandy. This five-star residence for birds is at his country manor along the coast at Varengeville: his Dieppe palace (which was of wood) burned down in 1694.

Trade links remain but, I was told, ivory carvers (like elephants) had become fewer: there was one left in Dieppe. White tusks have given place to yellow bananas as a principal import – so that dishes made with them have almost an honorary status *du pays*, along with *sole dieppoise*, soused herrings, apple tart, shellfish of all kinds (the town guide proudly claims two out of every five shellfish consumed in France are fished from Dieppe), and the local equivalent of *bouillabaisse* – *marmite dieppoise*. Every year a school of posh cookery attracts about 2000 Francophiles who can't bear to get away from the kitchen stove.

There is still an English connection to be made with the front door of the Hotel Windsor, which says '*Tirez*' at the top and 'Pull' beneath. The cafés in the scrubby dockside street bear names like le Brighton and le Newhaven as they wait for the passing trade to stop passing, which it mainly does during the wait for the ferry, bad-tempered after its long drive and fulminating against the incomprehensible organization of ferry bookings on busy weekends, and the lack of proper queuing spirit; the warm clothes are at the bottom of the boot, and the office looms on Monday morning. The children nod in their chairs, and though the food and service are still French, they are rather too close to the British for comfort. I feel sorry for those little restaurants ruled by the sailings of the ferry – for no one eats there on the outward trip from England, but rushes off towards the great gastronomic vision of the French interior.

I had broken the rule on my first night in France, and dined several cuts above the ordinary dockside establishments at L'Armorique – though it still had cranes, like steel giraffes, peering in at the window. For 70 francs, it produced a creditable fish soup – tomatoey, peppery, with croûtons and garlic mayonnaise – fillet of sole poached with a creamy tarragon sauce, and profiteroles in hot, bitter chocolate. At the next table, they were eating clams that wriggled as they felt the lemon juice, giving me a momentary feeling of what it must be like to be flayed. Then, to lay the Muscadet to rest, I strolled beneath a half moon in a deep blue sky to the Café des Tribunaux in the centre of town for a *café-cognac*, and back to the hotel past a genuine *pissoir*, legless at that time of night but still hissing to itself under the flying buttresses of the church of St Jacques.

It took me ages to get to sleep – I always forget the reverberating quality of French streets, and the exuberance of the native car engines. When they slumbered, a large husky church clock took over, and from 6.30 a foghorn belled distantly through the light morning mist. French birds took to fighting busily under the window, the cars woke up again and motorbikes began practising for the races; a siren wound itself up, someone tipped a load of bottles on to the pavement for a remarkable length of time considering the existence of the laws of gravity, and I had to get up and open the shutters.

A fine sunny morning came in, with a smell of roasting coffee, and just the right atmosphere of difference for a first morning in a new country. Opposite was a messy elegance of balconies and shutters with that typical air of refined dowdiness with which French buildings suggest that they have seen a good deal of life and have now settled down to domesticity with many an interesting memory to bloom the routine. They are like the middle age of a pretty woman, with elegance still among the discreet lines at the corners of the eyes, and the serenity that comes from having been much admired.

Lawns stretched from the hotel to the pebbly beach and the sea. A large woolly dog promenaded gravely among them. After him a fat lady, waddling. After her an even fatter lap-dog advanced at double-waddle on four short

legs. I too found Dieppe a fine place for promenades —
along the harbour wall where old men took the sun and
small boys with all the time in the world threw pebbles at
other pebbles until a boat went past; or down the main
shopping street (which they have banned to cars nowadays) with a practising oboe sending music of spasmodic
plangency over the stylish shops and the flocks of dumpy
ladies buying the stokings for lunch. And so did I, joyfully,
for French food shops feel so much crisper than English,

as if the contents mattered more (which of course they do).
I bought soft cheese, strawberries and wine – and wheeled
my bicycle back to the Café des Tribunaux (which is in-
escapable in Dieppe and always recognizable on account of
its Bavarian half-timbering, which looks totally out of place
in this otherwise stone town) balancing that glorious thing,
the first *baguette* of the holiday, on my handlebars. There
are flowerbeds in front of the café and a little well, the
Puits-Salé, which lives in a wrought-iron cage with a tin
galleon on top: there I sat in the sun and lunched. And
that is where we came in.

★

Whether it was anything to do with the power of Provençal Rosé I don't know, but it turned out to be trickier than I thought getting out of Dieppe without going back to the front and following the tourist signs, which I scorned to do. There was a tendency among the gears for them to get muddled, and the chain came off, and there was no sign of the hill which I remembered as leading up to the main road, the N15. I finally decided to follow a large yellow van marked 'Guildford' – which, if it had come all the way from Guildford, was doubtless going somewhere important, and rolled out through the suburbs and down the social scale of architecture.

First came villas rather like some of the Edwardian houses in Muswell Hill, apart from their quality of French up-and-down-ness, which is to do with the vertical lines of the shutters making the windows look rather thinner than one expects; then workmen's terraces, and wooden chalets in the Alpine style with a gentleman in blue dungarees scratching himself reflectively in one porch. The road was up here and the yellow van took a diversion: on my bicycle I went straight on, bumpily, seeking rurality as if I were already 500 miles on my way.

Not five minutes from Dieppe, I encountered my first goat in the very midst of subtopia – a white creature manifesting all the traditional goatish independence, scowling at the grass beyond its chain and sticking up its tail at a rude angle. Soon I came to a church that had failed to make up its mind whether to have a spire or a tower, and had compromised on something that looked as if it were intended to be a device for spearing angels on the wing, but had caught a specially large one which snapped off the point. I was at Arques-la-Bataille, which really should be called Arques-les-Batailles, for not only was there a famous battle here in 1589 when Henry IV defeated a force over four times as strong as his own 7000 men, but German flying bombs flew into Britain from the woods nearby during the last war, and William the Conqueror defeated

the local Count of Arques only six years before he moved
on to England.

There I made up my mind that I was definitely on the
wrong road, so turned off cross-country uphill by the
ruined castle with grey walls stretching right across the
hill-top, and trees standing sentry within. I came out on
the plain above Dieppe, with sun and marguerites everywhere: and I was hit by an amazing sense of space – of
the whole country before me. Above, there were larks with
the whole sky before them. We seemed to have a certain
amount in common, except that it was bumpier on the
ground, for I took a farm track to Tourville, with nettles
getting at my legs.

The hamlet began with a crop of new, white bungalows,
set up on a mound as is common in France, presumably
to accommodate the all-important wine-cellar. In one, a
housewife stood before a patch of fresh earth apparently
willing something to grow. It didn't. The rest of Tourville
had done much better and had managed roses; and in the
town square I met Alice in Wonderland, a nymphette
riding round in the dust on a cycle rather too small for
her, whiling away the time between childhood and growing
up enough to be off after the boys; she wore a pink check
Alice in Wonderland dress, and had long Alice in Wonderland hair, golden down the back. She led me astray, for
while I was watching her I missed the sign to Manéhou-
ville, and careered off down the road to Miromesnil, where
Maupassant lived in the pointy-turreted château, and I had
to turn round and come back to the square, where Alice
was still tracing circles in the dust with a face of beautiful
boredom.

It was a fragrant afternoon. There was the scent of cut
grass, and the heat that broke off the road in waves made
the green wheat smell as if it were already full-grown, gar-
nered and ground at the mill. Over the uplands there were
just the wheat and me: then the road turned down through
a grove of beeches and there was company ahead. A slate-

grey spire; an already familiar mixture of neat white new houses and straggly old ones; an orchard with a fluffy company of ducklings asleep with their mother beneath a tree; and an extraordinarily crowded graveyard with the local dead riding to the last trump in double-decker tombs.

Across the river in Anneville-sur-Scie is one of the larger cider factories in Normandy: a lot of the production, however, still goes on in a small way in farms, for family use and private sale.

'Even if it is not pasteurized, people prefer farm cider. It is the fashion in France: all the products coming from the country, even if they are dirty, must be good: they drink *everything*,' said M. Philippe Baron of the *cidrerie* Duché de Longueville, which is named after a celebrated medieval duchess from the next town downstream. From a brave laugh in his voice, it was plain that he felt slightly wounded at the trendies with a country craze rejecting his cherished professional product for the amateur at almost double the price.

The *cidrerie* looked as much like an enlarged farm as a factory. True, there was a tall brick chimney, but sheep bleated in the field next door, there were bright beds of marigolds and puce roses, a half-timbered cottage on the far hillside – and trout in the stream running below the office windows. M. Baron and I crossed the bridge to a kind of concrete car park 300 yards across with channels in the bottom where the truckloads of apples come in late September and early October, to be tipped out in rolling hillocks of green and yellow – for there are no red varieties.

When the *cidrerie* was founded in the 1920s, apples would come from farmers, but no longer. 'They would rather have cows,' said M. Baron. 'That is why, ten years ago, we planted our own orchards, which is very unusual in France. The best varieties are Muscadet and Antoinette – and from each of them we make a special *cidre de qualité superieure*, dry or soft. *Cidre de table* is made of mixed varieties, but all the apples are – what is the word? – without sugar?'

'Tart.'

'Yes, tart.'

A lactic sort of smell hung over the *cidrerie* – or perhaps it came from the jam factory next door. There was not an apple in sight. M. Baron told me how they wash the fruit down the channels and over the stream, bobbing above the unsuspecting trout, to three sprawling presses looking like something out of a power station.

'How many kilos do you press a year?' I asked.

M. Baron was imperial. 'Five hundred thousand tons. A lot of juice: ten million litres. Apple juice – nothing else. We are allowed to add gas, but we don't like.'

We went to see the juice. It was imprisoned in stainless steel tanks forty or fifty feet high, its progress towards cider arrested at different stages of fermentation.

'In some tanks, it is juice,' explained M. Baron. 'Others already with alcohols. We have to stop the cider working, and we do this by refrigeration. From January 1st to 31st December the temperature is 3°C, always the same.'

'Is the cider any different after a year?'

'No. It is a short process. In one month or six weeks, cider is made.'

'Why keep it then?'

'Because we cannot bottle it in one day,' said M. Baron, with kindness.

In the bottling shed, there was a hissing of steam and a clattering like the world xylophone championships. Metal pathways curled in and out of each other. Nudging each other along them, as straight up as the Brigade of Guards doing the softshoe shuffle, went the bottles.

'Other people are making a lot of disposable bottles,' said M. Baron. 'Of course we would prefer, but we don't want to waste such glass: it is not *normal*. As far as ethic is concerned, we don't want.'

The French system of returnable bottles, *consignés*, seems to work much better than ours. Standard litre wine bottles are universally returnable, and it is pretty nearly as easy to get your deposit back on fizzy drink bottles. Small shops take them back readily at the till, big supermarkets usually have a kind of bottle purgatory somewhere at the back where a bored recording angel gives you 50-80 centimes for each of the glassy elect he passes through to life eternal, and damns the rest in a dustbin. The system is not infallible, but is much better than anything in Britain, probably being helped by the fact that most small foodshops are linked to chain supermarkets and by the vast consumption of table wine in standard bottles, to destroy which would be waste of a particularly conspicuous kind.

The French are a conserving people, perhaps partly because so many of them have recent links with the peasantry: you see it in butchery and *charcuterie*, where everything finds a use, instead of the less attractive bits having to be sold off cheaply, as in England.

M. Baron and I left the bottling plant: outside were glass mountains. One of them, it turned out, was of a bottle which was eminently disposable, even more than other champagne-type bottles, which have never got into the returnable system.

'We made a very, very bad experience,' said M. Baron, scowling at the offending container. 'Last year we said we will do something very special. We let make a special bottle for us. We let make also special label – gold and black, very nice. We have not sold one bottle. Not one.'

He decided it was no good going on scowling at such a ridiculous situation and took to chuckling instead. 'Nobody has bought *one* bottle of this.'

'Why not?'

'I don't know. It was unusual. Incredible.'

'To be honest, I always wonder that you can carry on selling cider in a country where wine is so cheap. In fact cider must be pretty nearly as expensive.'

'No. Cider is a bit *more* expensive than ordinary wine. They drink it with meals in Normandy, the north of France and the west coast. In the rest of France, they drink cider only occasionally when they are thirsty, like a glass of beer, a glass of cocoa or what else.'

'Do you export any to England?'

'No. We tried, but the taste is not the same.'

I knew that certain wines do not travel well, but this was the first time I had ever heard of such a thing with cider.

'Just by going across the Channel?' I asked.

'Yes. No. The taste of the English people.'

'Are you sure you didn't put it in the wrong bottle?'

'No. The taste of the English cider is really different from the French cider. We went to England and have visited *cidrerie* and it is really different.' M. Baron's voice took on a tone of puzzlement. 'They put what they want in a bottle of cider – marmalade, chocolate, what they want.' He flung out his hands in a gesture which included me, the entire factory, and a nearby herd of very fat cows. 'In France we are obliged to use only apples, and of course at the end the taste cannot be the same. I do not say French cider is better: I say it is different. Everybody will judge.'

It was plain that there was no doubt in his mind as to what the verdict ought to be.

'Ah,' I said, 'you're just being polite.'

'Drop in for a drink next time you're round here,' said M. Baron, even more politely, and I made off up the valley of the Scie with my mind on the cider I had not got round to tasting.

If, as M. Guibon had said, an Englishman is not a stranger in Dieppe, he is still less of a stranger in the Norman countryside. There is a difference in that element of town architecture that has gone rural (where we have our standard Victorian red-brick invader, Normandy has the straight-up-and-down would-be château style) but the gardens feel like English gardens, with roses and very un-French runner beans, and the cottages are like English cottages as they ought to be – a trifle tumbledown and workaday, rather than pink-washed and pretentious. They are long and low with all their construction undressed for the architectural voyeur: maize-coloured plaster with milk-chocolate half-timbering and a ridiculous number of doors;

the original long-houses with the animals at one end, the family at the other and a storeroom above. The trees in the orchard are generally of that lichened antiquity that gladdens the heart and gives small apples, if any. Sometimes you see a family pig rooting for windfalls in the grass as if sties had never been invented, much less pig farms.

I crossed the river at Longueville-sur-Scie and passed an old white water-wheel, to climb gently up through the woods. Even going uphill it struck me that cycling is the nearest you can get to gliding without going up in the air: the faintest rumbling from the road, a discreet clicking of cogs, and little plunks of stones flying out under the tyres – these were all the sounds of my passage. There were smells of woodsmoke and fungus, piquant elderflower, coy honeysuckle, creosote from fence posts. The woods were ash, nut, beech and pine. A bicycle ride is a great tuner of the senses: a large pigeon flapped heavily out of a treetop to dive-bomb the road before me and sounded like a jet fighter, a passing tractor like World War 3.

Crossing the wheatfields on the ridge, I came down into the neighbouring valley of Muchedent, where the rambling rivulets of the Varenne briefly come together in a single bright stream with long green weed floating with the current, fine as Ophelia's hair. As I came over the bridge, they were remaking the road with a bed of crushed chalk. My wheels sank: I got off and walked past the tiny old church without spire or tower, and felt like a medieval pilgrim.

Some way along the main road up the valley was a solitary roadside café with a sign. I was a few yards past when the legend registered on the nutritional lobe of my brain. I wheeled round and approached it again to make sure: *Cidre de ferme 7.50 F* it said. I dismounted. The café had a tiny round bar, tiny round tables and a large round *patronne* chatting to the single customer, who appeared to have come in from the fields primarily to natter rather than buy anything. They looked at me with that expression of indifferent scepticism with which small cafés frequently greet the stranger. On being asked for cider, the *patronne*'s worst fears were realized: here was a mad Englishman not come in to sit down and drink in the shade like a normal civilized person (i.e. a Frenchman) but proposing to take a bottle of her precious brew and bump it up and down on a bicycle in the sun.

Out of the refrigerator came a green champagne bottle, with a suspiciously overdone tangle of wire round the stopper keeping the vital spirits in. The *patronne* waddled back to the counter (for her own vital forces had burst their bounds long ago and hung about her in rolls). She had on her face the expression of one who carries a small but uncertain time-bomb.

'It must be cold,' she said – as one might remark, 'Do not on any account remove the firing-pin.'

About a mile up the road it came to me that the bottle in the bag would already be getting warm and, if my own temperature was anything to go by, would be likely to reach critical mass well before the end of the afternoon. There was only one solution. Waiting until I was decently past the only other occupant of the landscape – an old woman gathering nettle-tops – I stopped and sat myself on the

verge, peering through the thick green glass of the bottle
at the murky fluid within, which looked indeed like something most authentically out of a farm. Gingerly, I set to
work on the wire tangle and was just getting to the last
knot when it vanished from my hand, borne by the stopper
towards the outer reaches of the atmosphere, and followed
by an alcoholic geyser from the bottle. It is very difficult
to win in single combat against a fountain of fizz: either
you stick your thumb over it, in which case it spurts all
over you, or you catch it in a glass, which is as much as
to say that you don't. Having no glass, I improvised a
third method on the spur of the moment, which was to
stick the end of the bottle rapidly in my mouth. I cannot
recommend this method: for weddings it is socially in-
elegant; for practical purposes, it makes you understand
what it is like to be a petrol tank (and after the initial flood
of enthusiasm it spurts all over you anyway). The remains
of the contents of this erratic bottle, now even murkier
than before, were rustic and delicious – though I have
bought quite sophisticated sparkling wines in the South
of France for two-thirds of the price. It is a mistake in
France (especially for the tourist) to think that by buying
direct from the producer you will necessarily save money.
But, apart from the pleasure of buying fresh vegetables
(for example) directly from the land, there is a snob appeal
in things rural and, perhaps, a continuing affection for the
peasant way of life that keeps up prices.

I set off again at a fine pace. In the pretty village of Bellencombre, they were ringing the church bell and had
hung out the flags for me – bunting, green, yellow, white
and red across the road. I did not stop to make a speech
just in case they might press me to stay an unreasonable
length of time, but pedalled to St-Saëns with the cider
bubbling in my legs, past a château with a flight of white
doves over it, down a long avenue of ash trees.

What struck me at St-Saëns was not the forest of Eawy
with its famous 6 km ride through beechwoods, the Allée

des Limousins, nor any reminiscence of the composer
whose family home was here, or the oversized Romanesque
church that stands looking like a white elephant in the
square by the cross-roads, but the two coach-loads of
policemen who passed me as I was following a short stretch
of Route Nationale towards a more congenial minor road.
Perhaps they had had a hard day, but they looked as if they
were uncommonly unsympathetic to the world, and as if
they expected the world to be uncommonly unsympathetic
to them. There were wire screens to let down over the coach
windows in case they were stoned, which struck me as the
sort of precaution it would be better not to take unless you
absolutely had to: and that, if you absolutely had to, the
relations between police and public might be in rather a
bad way. The British love to pat themselves on the back
because the 'bobbee', as the French call him, does not
carry a gun, though our self-complacent euphoria on this
count has been driven to moderate itself in recent years.
The French police system is complex, with blue sorts and
brown sorts, and village sorts and town sorts and secret
sorts, but the thing we have to congratulate our nation on
is that British policemen tend to smile just a bit more
frequently than French ones.

After being taken a trifle aback by the double coach-load
of scowls, I made it my business to watch out for policemen
and note down how they looked. The village *gendarme* was
most human-looking and was observed on several oc-
casions to smile and often to chat, though usually in a
slightly superior manner. With this exception, the habitual
expression of the French *policier* is of one who has, unawares, trodden barefoot on a toad. It is not endearing.
And there seem to be rather a lot of them: a French girl I
met said she did a count on journeys through Paris (about
as far as Marble Arch to Hampstead) and London (South
London to Hampstead): in Paris she saw twelve policemen,
in London one: that summed up the difference for her, she
said.

As I came up the hill and turned left off the main road,

the cider seemed to have gone flat in the limbs and head: it had been a temporary defence against the heat of the afternoon. The journey had only been forty-one miles, but to the end there was a wearing succession of undulations over the hill-tops to St-André-sur-Cailly and the N28 from Neufchâtel-en-Bray where, at the cross-roads, was a long inn with virginia creeper growing on its chest and rustic insouciance at its back. This was the Auberge Henri IV, named after the Protestant king who had won the victory against the Catholics at Arques, and had travelled round during the Wars of Religion having other battles all over the place in the most kingly and religious manner possible.

Cycling does get up a good thirst and good appetite. While I was waiting for the trickliest bath tap in the world, I spied from my window the sign of a Routier restaurant, which is to the Francophile English middle class as a fine fat truffle is to a fine fat sow: something to be instantly seized upon and never mind the earth round its roots. I drooled in anticipation.

So, later, I slunk out of the side door of the hotel, where the menu was upwards of 50 francs, and pattered a hundred yards to the lorry-driver's caf, where it was upwards of 30. French lorry-drivers seem to have the same sort of public relations going for them as do London taxi-drivers: 'We are all jolly good fellows, kind to animals, love children, work for charity and never charge anybody double fare.' Certainly, with the size of the lorries that blow gasoline farts like thunderclaps in the dead of night in echoey French towns, some kind of public relations pitch cannot but be necessary even among a nation of fairly abject internal-combustion fanciers. That summer, the monsters had little stickers on their backs saying: *Les routiers sont sympa.* So they might well be, but the certainty is that anyone can be pretty sympathetic with the sort of meal under his belt that I got in that caf. It may be, I thought, that there is no difference between the English lorry-driver and the French, but in that case the people who serve him are a different dish entirely.

As it happened, I had a recent experience to compare it
with: the palace of sliced bread at which I had breakfasted
on my training ride to Cambridge had charged me 70p for
a cup of strong tea, two slices of the ritual commodity
buttered, two more slices fried, a rasher, a re-heated
sausage with its end cut off, baked beans and a giant-
jumbo-grand-economy-size mini fried egg. It was self-
service with plastic tables and the stuffing coming out of
the seats.

There were bright red tablecloths in the French lorry-
driver's caf, and sparkling spoons, and little lamps. There
was German beer and English beer on tap and a plump,
pretty country waitress offering a whole crab sulking redly
on a plate of mayonnaise to start with; veal chops cooked
in cider and cream; a cheese board with Bleu de Bresse,
Emmenthal, Camembert and Pont l'Evêque: there was
apple tart to finish, all for just over £3, with service.
The house wine, a good Côtes de Roussillon, was a cheap
extra. I thought: if I was a lorry-driver, I would not drive
in Britain. In fact, as I discovered later from experience, I
had stumbled upon a *relais routier* of a refinement which
was *extra*, as the French say. I have never found another
as good, though *relais routier* food is usually plentiful and
seldom bad value.

That was the end of the third day, with some 117 bicycle
miles on the clock, not counting the Channel.

OBSERVATIONS ON THE GASTRONOMIC
DIGNITY OF FRENCH LORRY-DRIVERS

Oh royal is the *routier*
Who quits the road to dine
On *confit d'oie* and caviar,
On cockerel cooked in wine.
Whose e'er-expanding stomach

Is the pride and honoured guest
Of half-a-hundred roadside chefs
From Abbeville to Brest;
Th'egregious waitress wafts her steaks
All savoury 'neath his nose,
'Not cooked too far?' she asks. 'Ça va?'
He cries, 'It goes, it goes.'

His manners are exceptional,
Bright white his hankerchee;
Never a spot, be't cold or hot
Falls on his dungaree;
His bread is brisk with crust so crisp
It crackles like the fire:
His veal with cream a mollient dream
Of satisfied desire:
Oh happy is the *routier*
Born to the silver spoon,
Whose well-stuffed tum may sigh 'yum-yum!'
Where'er he stops at noon.

THE FOURTH DAY

I was surprised to find, on Friday, that sleep seemed to
have knotted up my ravelled edges with Gordian knots.
Perhaps I was getting used to cycling – or perhaps it was
that the morning was fine, with just a trace of high cloud
in the sky, and the minor road to Vascoeuil gentle through
wheatfields and old orchards of leaning trees. At the hamlet
of la Pommeraye an extraordinarily dilapidated barn made
me wonder what sort of animals they could be keeping
there. As I came round to its other side, I saw the answer:
people. I was looking through a hole into the past: this
was peasant life of a century ago – or two, or three for it
makes no difference – an existence of tumbledown bore-

dom with an old iron well and a nettley duckpond. We conceal rural poverty better in England.

The road crossed a stretch of plain and bowled downhill into Blainville-Crevon, which was getting ready to go to sleep in the sun for the day. There is a fifteenth-century church here with carved figures, but the buildings which caught my eye were a vast clap-boarded barn of a garage, straight out of the early days of motoring when you took your car to the blacksmith to get it fixed, and a four-square town hall standing to attention behind its flower-beds on the green.

The Mairie is the indispensable seat of civic life in France, even in the smallest village: it must be the seat, because you never see anybody walking in or out. The desirable features are generally a portico (so that if anyone were to walk in or out, they could do it in style); a balcony to fit on top of the portico (to make speeches from, if anybody will listen); a minimum of one, and preferably three flagpoles (for hanging out tricolours); then something in the way of windows to go either side to make the whole thing look properly dignified and symmetrical. Such French town halls are formal and pompous, but in a parochial way that somehow lends a charm to their self-importance – to the traveller, as to the novelist. This part of the country is the place in which Flaubert's romantic Madame Bovary got so bored – just down the road through a stream valley of wild watercress and butter-cups, is the village of Ry, which he named 'Yonville L'Abbaye'.

I prefer Ry: it seems a pity to lengthen one of the few short place-names in a country over-much inclined to saints, châteaux and prolixity. It must be partly because French is not my native tongue, but in France I miss the hobbit-like quality of British names like Piddletrenthide and Cold Christmas – quaint, domestic and earthy. Never-theless, in Normandy I delight in the exclamatory town of Eu, and near Houdan is the hamlet of Moque-Souris, which has to be a literal translation of 'Micky Mouse'.

There is a Brains-sur-le-March in East Brittany. Best of all, however, I like the name of a little place in the area of Bellegarde which lies to the south of the road from Pithiviers to Montargis – Chien Cul, 'Dog's Bottom'. It is a name not to be found even in the excellent series *Carte Touristique* 1.100000 issued by the Institut Géographique Nationale: but, nevertheless, you will come upon it by the side of the road on one of the little blue signs with which the French announce their very smallest housing clusters. Such names, in England or France, are pieces of escaped language, fragments of fantasy popping up for no reason at all in the middle of a workaday world and in such a world any strange intruder is welcome.

Ry now has a Bovary museum including one of the strangest and most inappropriate monuments any novelist could have – 300 mechanical dolls woodenly acting out scenes from the novels. (There is a more formal Flaubert museum at his home in Croisset on the Seine west of Rouen.) Tourists stop at Ry before going on the few miles to the Château de Vascoeuil, now conscientiously restored as a museum for the nineteenth-century historian Michelet and a centre for modern art. It being lunchtime, which is as sacred in Normandy as anywhere in France, I saw the château by pressing my nose to a vertical bar of the ornamented gates, so that my eyes might have an uninterrupted view either side. There were pretty-pretty gardens and a creamy stone up-and-down house and round tower with the sort of roofs that make buildings look as if they are wearing medieval hats.

I rode off with a dent in my nose: though Vascoeuil formed part of the defensive belt with which in the twelfth century Richard Coeur de Lion sought to guard the chastity of his Normandy against the invasive French, I was *en route* for the great padlock itself, the Château Gaillard. I was travelling down the valley of the Andelle, with the Forest of Lyons across the river to my left, where Henry I died after eating his celebrated surfeit of lampreys at the Abbaye de Mortemer. There were no lampreys at the village grocer at Perriers-sur-Andelle, but perfect Brie, château-bottled Minervois, sexy tomatoes (indecently ripe and full of juice) and fine plums, all of which I stowed carefully in my pannier, with a tart from the baker opposite and a couple of those thumb-thick crusty loaves the French call *ficelles* which are airy crust when you buy them, and stale two hours later.

With some regret I turned off the valley road at Charleval – partly because my only route up over the plateau to Les Andelys began with my longest hill yet and a main road, and partly because the Andelle flows down to the Seine at Pîtres, where the road runs beneath the Hill of the Two Lovers, whose story was written by the twelfth-century Marie de France, who has a certain claim to be the first French lady popular novelist, though she spent most of her life in England.

The lovers were Raoul and Caliste, daughter of the King of Pîtres (so the story goes, though from the size of the town today the kingdom must have been on the modest side). The king, acting in the arbitrary and needlessly competitive manner beloved of legendary monarchs, stipulated that he who should win his daughter's hand and any other portions of her anatomy that took his fancy must first run to the top of the hill opposite, bearing the lady in his arms. History does not record the proportions of Caliste, or whether she dieted before the event, but Raoul achieved the impossible, only to drop dead of exhaustion at the top, whereupon his briefly affianced followed him to the grave with romantic haste. Their hill-top tombs are not to be found today, if they ever were, but the area is still the *Côte des Deux Amants* as irrevocably as *côtes de porc* are *côtes de porc*.

My appointment at the Château Gaillard was not till half-past three. I chose a conveniently-angled bank by the side of the road in the green country on the top of the hill and conveniently angled myself on it for lunch. As the level of the Minervois went down, I dropped with it to end up snoozing akimbo in the ditch. (There is an interesting

77

tendency for the legs to fly apart when food and alcohol lean on the hidden spring.) I was at peace with the world, and it was all downhill to Les Andelys.

Coming from the east there is no question of asking directions to the Château Gaillard which sprawls out over a promontory of hill-top, a great gap-toothed ruin, with one fat white tower, shaped like a cooling tower, still intact. From the other direction it is not quite so obvious, and so it was that I discovered that when they say Les Andelys, they mean the 'Les'. In Le Grand Andely, which is where you might expect a castle to be, little has survived the last war apart from the church of Notre Dame. Le Petit Andely – which was luckier – is spread out along the Seine with two high points – one a slender spire, replacing a predecessor which lasted from the fifteenth century until a gale in 1975, the other, the château.

'It's up there,' said the lady trimming her flowers, pointing to a lane which came down the hillside with the uncompromising directness of a falling stone. I would gladly have contented myself by looking over the château with a pair of binoculars from ground level, but the arrangement was that I should meet the deputy mayor, Dr

LeMercier, at a gateway there: the Porte de Plaisance. It was a funny name for a gate, but perhaps chimed in with the château being Gaillard.

I engaged bottom gear and started to work off lunch. The road had obviously been designed as a defensive tactic by Richard Coeur de Lion, who built the place in 1196 with all the experience and high technology learned from the crusades. Plainly, its purpose was to keep an enemy down, not let visitors up. I got two-thirds of the way: then, puffing, I saw an additional climb up a dusty path to the château itself. I turned up it and got off inelegantly – my foot slipped on the gravel, the bicycle went one way and I the other. There is no problem about this distribution of component parts except when you keep holding on to the handlebars. If you do this, the bicycle's sideways movement *away* is converted instantly to downward motion *to*, and the chain wheel digs its teeth ferociously into your leg, leaving punctures like the trademark of an oily vampire.

I sat sweating into the dust and a small French dog came and sat by me. Together, we watched my knee swelling to twice its normal size.

'Ah,' I thought, extrapolating from long-past biology lessons, 'that will be the knee-cap fractured, and the synovial fluid leaking out: will it need draining off, I wonder, before it festers?'

I limped up to the castle in the sun, pushing the bicycle – for even in rural France, I did not dare to leave it in a place where there was nothing to lock it to. I saw at once that there would be no difficulty in locating the Porte de Plaisance, since as far as I could see only one *porte* remained. I settled myself on a rock and waited for 3.30. Below were the red-tiled roofs of Le Petit Andely, green river banks, an island in the curve of the broad blue river.

Three-thirty came and went with no sign of a mayor. A stentorian guide with a French moustache arrived and bellowed at a group of tourists from a plank bridge over the moat. Richard Lionheart built the castle only three years before his death: within three more years, Philippe-Auguste of France had laid siege to it; another year and the Château Gaillard had fallen – it is said, thanks to a soldier who very courageously climbed up through the lavatories, an exploit for which one can only hope he was well rewarded. With the castle, fell the rest of Normandy. Later, the story went on, was the adulterous Margaret of Burgundy strangled here with her own hair? Nobody seemed to know for sure, but the possibility was a good talking point.

Adequately lectured, the tourists went away.

'Perhaps,' I thought, 'there's another gate on the other side.'

I hobbled over to the guide.

'Could you tell me,' I asked in idiomatic French, 'where-finds itself the Porte de Plaisance?'

'No, no, no,' said the guide, with the intuitive response of one used to dealing with the French of foreigners. 'The Port de Plaisance, the marina; it is down by the river, naturally: where else would it be? One will not find it up a mountain, will one? Ha, ha!'

'Ha, ha,' I said. He was a friendly man, and chatty.

He led me to the edge of the hill: there was the marina, with a small group of people standing on the bank, gazing intently down-river.

'Everyone is down there,' said the guide: 'M. Ravensdale, he who was once a British ambassador; Mme Ravensdale; M. Raymond from the French television; and Dr Le-Mercier, the Deputy Mayor.'

'Truly?' I said, uncertainly.

'But yes. They are waiting for a journalist from the British radio, who is pedalling on a water bicycle up the Seine.'

'Ah yes,' I said: 'thank you' – and flew down the hill with gratitude for good brakes and a sensation of what it would be like coming up again if – as now seemed unlikely – I was to have a tour of the castle.

The little group of watchers on the water's edge had not

been expecting an English cyclist to turn up behind them from the direction of dry land, even one who was able to take charge of the situation in fluent French as soon as he had been introduced.

'*La perdrix –*' I began – I can't say why, but it is on my tape-recording of the event – which continues: '*Mais, mais mais mais j'ai – er – on m'a dit qu'on – que – quelqu'un a – er – a dit qui – er – c'est à pédalo.*'

'*Oui,*' said the man from French television, understandingly.

'*Mais, c'est – ce n'est pas à pédalo.*'

'Aaah,' said the man from French television, in a very knowing way.

Explanations continued in English, which everybody seemed to speak except the TV man. It appeared that during the course of international communications the phrase 'coming along the Seine' had been changed to 'coming on the Seine'.

'Some people say you are coming with the bicycle – floating on the Seine,' said Mrs Ravensdale, a breezy lady, in whom French birth and marriage to a British diplomat had produced an accent set somewhere between the Champs-Elysées and the royal enclosure at Ascot.

'Pedalling,' added her husband, interrupting with the motive power.

'We thought you were pedalling from Newhaven more or less, or somewhere in front of Calais in a funny amphibian bicycle. We were a bit confused: we saw this Californian man on the TV in the air, so we thought you were more or less doing the same thing.'

'I don't think I shall ever do that,' I said.

'Well we hadn't seen anything in the *Daily Telegraph* about it, so we wondered if it was true or not. *Il est venu par le ferry-boat de Newhaven à Dieppe,*' she added, for the benefit of the man from French television.

'It's not at all *sportif,*' said the man, in French, and a great deal more besides, which Mrs Ravensdale translated.

'He telephoned to the head of the service-navigation in

Rouen to know if this man pedalling on the water had come by.'

'*Il était très étonné*,' said the TV man.

'He said no; he thought it was a humbug – what do you call it in English? He said he thought it was an oaks.'

There was a brief discussion as to whether, if I had come on a *pédalo*, it would have been feasible to do so, and whether it would have been more difficult to pedal up the Seine than cross the Channel, on account of the currents.

'We wondered if you would have a favourable wind,' said Mrs Ravensdale.

'*Voilà, c'est tout*,' said the man from French television, plainly of the opinion that it was far from enough.

'But it's very funny all the same,' she said.

The Deputy Mayor broke in: 'Excuse me, will you ride your bicycle for the photographers: then after we go to the Mary.'

'The . . . ?'

'The Town Hall.'

'Thank you: that will be delightful.'

It was a relief not to be going up to the château again. My knee was throbbing and I felt about the place rather as Margaret of Burgundy must have done.

At the town hall, they broke out the champagne, even though the guest of honour had not lived up to his almost biblical reputation, and Dr LeMercier made a speech about the many things we have in common and the great numbers of English tourists he hoped to see in the town. But there was already a great Englishness about the place, what with the Norman gardens and thatched cottages I had passed on my way here.

'*Fermettes*, they are called,' said Mrs Ravensdale. 'It is very chic to convert them.' (I thought that in England that process had been at its height thirty and more years ago. The Ravensdales' own house was bought from Conan Doyle, who had two sisters at the famous finishing school of Mlle Pomponne de la Boulet (unless it was Poulet) 'a very old French family'.) Tom Ravensdale, a man with all the modest charm of the diplomat, spoke winningly of the joys of retiring to the *cuisine* and countryside of France.

'There are very many historical associations with England, and the countryside's very much like the south of England: we only have a little patch of ground ourselves, but we try and keep it as much like an English cottage garden as possible.'

Thus was our national presence preserved in Normandy, without the necessity for Richard Lionheart and his castle. I cycled off below its cliff, with the one remaining tower sticking up like a fat stone thumb in a futile gesture of derision to its conquerors, the French. I have been back once since: by chance I hit the day of the Fair, which was the most stunningly miscellaneous and teeming hotch-potch I have ever seen – a straggly, crowded shanty-city of stalls with surrealist congeries of rubbish and would-be curious or useful *objets trouvés*.

LACK OF A PROPER ENGLISH SPIRIT AMONG THE FRENCH – a Note for the Chauvinist Reader by Bulwer Wellington-Ffoulkes

It may be useful to the English traveller in france to know that it is wise to avoid Lays-on-the-Leas on early Saturdays in September, on at least one of which a heavy concentration of the french may be expected. On a recent visit to our former Norman dominions, I found Lays-on-the-Leas Parva all right, but Lays-on-the-Leas Magna was badly clogged up with what the french call a *jour de foie*, which I penetrated despite futile attempts of one of those imitation policemen with the wrong sort of hat to divert me from driving among the stalls.

My progress, which was accompanied by shouts of welcome from the populace, was eventually arrested by a road-block of roundabouts and vegetable sellers who refused to move, despite my continually blowing the foghorn I always carry beneath the bonnet on trips abroad to let the natives know I'm coming.

Luckily, I was able to make clear my determination to proceed by driving fast through a gap between two stalls and made good my escape with only minor damage to the front suspension.

B.W.-Ff.

There are various traditional prejudices of the English against the French, viz: that they eat frogs' legs, are naughty, talk too fast and smell of garlic. But one of the most profound differences between the societies operates secretly, though it can hardly fail to be fundamental. It is the obvious point that the French do not have the English class system, which is the bubonic plague of our social life, our politics and our industry, and the lack of which must be an inestimable advantage to all other countries. (Think how different life would be if you thought other people were equal to you.) This is not to say that the French do not have their own discriminations, élites and elects, but class is not instititionalized as it is in England – tending rather towards meritocracy where we turn to fossilized snobbery. It can be no accident that the French have taken the word 'snob' from English, though they have altered the meaning to suit better with relatively trivial bourgeois pretensions: with us, snobbery is part of a world-order defining the structure and stability of our society. I cannot speak for Celts, but the Englishman at least can never escape the consequences of his class. He may climb, he may descend, he may embrace, combat or studiously ignore, but he always acts in relation to it, in the same way that the lapse of the lapsed Catholic is always defined by his former religion. As the French took 'snob' from us, we have borrowed from them the word 'déclassé' (though we never use it, because you cannot lose class in England, though classlessness is theoretically possible).

I was off for a quick scamper up a family tree, to discover whether I might have a right to sit and scratch myself in its branches. I was going to Vernon: partly out of simple curiosity; partly because that was where Joy had booked the rooms; and partly because of childhood brainwashing. My seedling sense of class had put out its roots in the social equivalent of John Innes No 1: a rich compost of pretension mixed with a grit of poverty.

To my parents' small and shabby house would periodically descend a cohort from a regiment of monstrous paternal aunts, who came from a place where people dressed up to drink sherry with each other in the evenings. (As I grew up, I too was given some of this beverage, which usually turned out to be indifferent South African mixed with something nameless for reasons of economy.) I thought of them as 'the silver teapot brigade' for not only did the people own silver teapots (as we did) but they made tea in them (which we didn't) and had tea-services they used *all the time* to serve cucumber sandwiches with limp component parts, and old ends of fruit cake. The only fresh things around were usually flowers, for the goddess Economia ruled over their households, that they might afford a woman who was a 'woman' and not a cleaning lady, and was prone to a sinful indulgence in television sets and large families. For occasional short but glorious periods there might even be a cook (who was indeed extremely necessary, in spite of the fulsome compliments with which the teapot brigade garnished each other's dishes on a principle of self-preservation).

When one of the teapot brigade entered our house, an offensive would be mounted on several grounds, viz: that our family was failing to engage in regular manoeuvres with other members of the teapot brigade; that church parade was being inadequately observed; and that a proper respect

85

for family tradition was not being inculcated in the young but future Head Of The Family (me). The latter offensive being the only one capable of sustained bombardment, that would then become the main prong of the attack, with fragments of doubtful genealogy hurtling over the teacups and silver teapot (which we had of course produced for the occasion). Thus it was that I learned how one beautiful Vernon starred in a novel by Walter Scott (which had to be respectable, even if boring), how another ran away with her coachman (which had to be interesting even if hardly respectable), and of my God-given right to a selection of stately homes and estates, which for some unaccountable reason appeared to be being occupied by somebody else, though in at least one of them it would still be an obligation upon the local verger to ring the church bells if I entered the parish. (I thought to myself that for this I would need a harbinger – of whose existence I had recently learnt at school during a lesson on *Macbeth* – to tell the verger that I was coming, unless he had prepared for the eventuality by living on the boundary.) There would be a short discussion on the family vault, the family tree and an invocation of William the Conqueror. The brigade would then retire in good order, often leaving behind alms in the form of some worn-out household object which we would have to throw away. (Among the teapot brigade this form of delegated rubbish disposal was known as being 'very kind'.)

It was this sort of education that led Vernon to turn his tyres through the Forest of Vernon in quest of a family seat which, in view of the throbbing condition of his knee-cap, he hoped would prove comfortable. On the way was a menhir marked in the forest, but he missed it. Fancy that: missing a menhir.

'The English proliferated enormously,' said M. Laurence, glancing absentmindedly at my midriff. '*Vous êtes certainement, cher monsieur, le descendant.*'

We sat in the corner café of the Hotel Roussel, drinking

beer and Pernod below a formula 3 espresso machine and
watched over by the *patronne*, a woman of fine proportions,
most of which were distributed rearwards. M. Laurence,
waggling his *legion d'honneur* beard with Gallic emphasis,
was a local historian; Sabine, a pretty student, the daughter
of another, and M. Fiche was the third in the party of those
prepared to discuss my ancestry. Titles, escutcheons, fiefs
and the like hung in the air in a cloud of glorious vagueness.
It was strange, but flattering, to be mentioned in the same
breath as the long-dead earls of Vernon who so proliferated
in England under William the Conqueror or 'the Bastard'
as everyone would persist in calling him.

'The British sprout is better than the French one,' said
M. Laurence referring not to a desirable accompaniment to
roast lamb, but to the fact that the French Vernons died
out over six centuries ago.

'It is an enduring race, certainly. I must know whether
your family crest bears bunches of watercress.'

I said that it did, for I had it on the authority of the
Chief of Staff, Silver Teapots.

'Does watercress grow here?' I asked.

'It did when the Seine was clean,' said Sabine.

M. Fiche interrupted. 'It still does in the neighbourhood. But there was a legend which spoke of a certain
gardener in 1198 who opened the gates of Vernon to the
French king Philippe-Auguste when he was fighting
against the English, and that gardener entered the town
with a big bundle of watercress on his back.'

Marvellous, I thought, to be possibly related to such a
hero, or at least to an earl who might employ such a
hero as his gardener. Better was to come:

'About seven or eight years ago,' said M. Fiche, 'I went
to England for the benediction of a statue of Saint Ajuta.'

'Makes a change from Butlins,' I thought.

'St Ajuta was one of the sons of the earls of Vernon
here.'

I was related (possibly) to a saint: in an instant access
of moral virtue, I modestly refrained from comment,

reflecting merely that my many desirable character traits had to come from somewhere.

'A lot of researches were done in Partsmouth in the celebrated driving school there, HMS *Vernon*,' M. Fiche went on. 'They found that the admiral and Saint Ajuta had the same roots. The tradition in your family, does it go up to the Admiral Vernon?'

'*L'Admiral Vernon est bien connu par ce boisson de rhum,*' put in M. Laurence.

'Everyone knows in France that he invented grog – some sort of punch,' translated M. Fiche.

'Of all the things I've heard, that rings truest to family characteristics,' I said. 'Watering the rum of those in no position to object. But what does it mean, my name?'

'Many places along the Seine are called "gwern" or "vern" – like "Verneuil" – and the origin is the same. The word gwern or Gwernon means swamp.'

'A swamp? I'm named after a bog?' It was a terrible anti-climax for a close relative of a saint and an earl who employed heroic gardeners (as was practically certain, with only a little matter of nine and a bit centuries of ancestry in England to account for). I changed the subject: I did not like the turn of the conversation into swamps. Any moment now, and I would discover myself to be descended from a frog.

Menhirs are extremely dangerous.
Many people are thought to have been bored to death by them — T.V.

I was briefly comforted at dinner that night by dis-
covering that there was a local Vernon liqueur, made out of
nuts. But I found it nondescript. That was the end of the
fourth day, 165 miles gone.

CHAPTER 4

The Swelling Scene

THE FIFTH DAY

I hit my first long stretch of Route Nationale on the way out from Vernon along the Seine. The river curves up in a great hoop near here, like a boa-constrictor with indigestion, so the main road was a short cut: otherwise, I would have wound my way over the north bank, for its associations with Monet: the village of Vétheuil with its church; Giverny with its waterlily gardens where the painter spent the last forty years of his life in that magnificently futile business of trying to flash over to someone else the momentary glories inside his head.

But that Saturday I was not heading for Impressionist country, but skirting Paris where the cilia of the great city and the marks of the Second War were unobtrusively everywhere (not scars, but blanknesses in the traditional appearance of the country). There is a characteristic style to a Route Nationale near a centre of population: a subtopia of garages, boorish fences, straggling houses, workaday factories and dusty, unloved countryside; and my journey lacked for none of these. Even the people had changed: there was no '*bonjour*' or '*salut*' among cyclists that Saturday morning, as I discovered after several suspicious glares in my direction. The preferred thing seemed to be to take your bicycle and ride it somewhere else, or so I guessed from the cars that passed with bicycles lying lack on the roofs, slowly rolling their front wheels in ecstasy as the wind tickled their bottom brackets. Taking the locals up on their spirit of rivalry, I was astonished to overtake three other cyclists myself on the road through Rosny-sur-Seine,

where the great prime minister Sully left two wings of the château unfinished as a memorial to his king, Henri IV.

Mantes-la-Jolie was anything but *jolie* on the outskirts, and not particularly in the centre: out of town, my road kept company with a motorway, a festoon of electricity pylons and a factory landscape with chimneys everlastingly erect like forlorn giraffes trying to see something nice somewhere. I felt as if I had been cast in a movie by Antonioni without being given an opportunity to object.

It was not until the road turned away from the Seine that the land stopped being flat and rolled over into a rather over-organized countryside of field, market garden and orchard. I came to the village of Orgeval in good time for lunch, turning off through a fringe of commuter villas up a lane to a long, old house on the corner.

There was a vociferous dog at the fence, and a small boy on the lawn. There is a profound scepticism about small boys addressed stumblingly in French: when I do it, I always feel I am destroying their faith in the adult world. However, we agreed that I was *chez* the Cottave family, that he was a young Cottave, that other Cottaves were variously out or asleep but that, since I was the man who was coming to lunch, he would go and fetch his grandfather. I was just congratulating myself on my command of language when the small boy advanced to a deck-chair under the apple tree on the lawn and spoke to it in perfect

English. The other side of the deck-chair grew arms and a head, and ultimately separated itself into two parts, one of which – an old gentleman in shorts – came towards me, on his lips the accent of the home counties. Indeed, they were, he said, his home: he was on holiday visiting his daughter, Judith, who had married a Frenchman. It made the world feel slightly smaller. And did I know his other daughter who lived in Muswell Hill?

'By name only,' I said defensively in an effort to stop the world from shrinking almost to nothing.

One by one the Cottave family assembled in the cool of the stone-floored living-room. Robert Cottave came down from upstairs with the look of a man who has sat too late into too many nights on too many committees: he is a leader of *Force Ouvrière*, the socialist trade union (for in France there are only five unions divided according to ideology rather than trade). His green-eyed daughter Gigi returned from work, and her mother Judith made her entrance with a bag of steaks exclaiming vigorously that she didn't cook, couldn't cook, wouldn't cook, and that there was nothing special for lunch. It didn't sound like France.

But it was: the steaks were delicious. We ate a piquant salad, cheeses and drank wine from the far south, Costières du Gard, in honour of my eventual destination.

'In thirty-two years in France,' I said to Judith, 'have you become formidable? That's what strikes me about the difference between French and British housewives; the French will argue like hell to get the best.'

'I try to do it discreetly. Fruit and vegetables of course I always pick out for myself in the village: when I go to London I do the same – my sister frowns and has to pull me away. I'm still "the Englishwoman" in France and now I'm "the Frenchwoman" in England. But argue – yes, I can, I do.'

'The French love fighting with each other,' said Gigi, 'it's one of the games they play. When you shout at somebody it doesn't mean you hate them; it means you want something off them.'

'In France people are prepared to argue and dispute in social life,' said Robert, 'but at work we had a very disciplinary situation: the boss was the boss, period. An old tradition. Though it's changing since 1968. Everyone has a feeling he will find a special way to cope with the boss and get some personal benefit out of it. The peasant mentality remains the dominating one in this country. For example, a peasant won't take credit, he will wait till he has the money to buy the thing himself: this is still a general attitude. Most French people stay very close to the land – their father or grandfather was a farmer, and they usually keep contact with the family. My grandfather was the one to quit the farm to become a teacher; but I can still see in myself some reactions very near to the *paysan*.'

It was shortly after I left the Cottaves that my shame took place. I had gone down a twisty bend and up a little hill when the producer's car drew alongside.

'It's three o'clock,' said Joy, 'and we've got to be at St-Léger-en-Yvelines by four: you'll have to put the bike on the car.'

'I can't do that,' I said. 'It wouldn't be right. I'm not supposed to be going by car to the Mediterranean.'

'You've gone miles out of your way to Orgeval: it doesn't make any difference to the length of the trip. You've done more miles, if anything. Anyway, there are going to be television cameras waiting.'

I thought of the man from French television waiting patiently at Les Andelys for the water cyclist; I could not disappoint another fellow-professional. It was only twenty or thirty miles and what Joy said about having covered an equivalent distance was true. But I didn't like it.

'It's going to be the big "ooh la la" if I turn up in a car, isn't it?'

'I'll let you off in the forest a couple of miles before.'

'Someone will see.'

'No they won't.'

'They'll want to interview me in French.'

'Very possibly; get off and get in.'

So I got in, carrying my mileometer which had fallen off as I took the front wheel out, with 200 miles registered on its disapproving clock. The bike shop at Dieppe had hung it on without a nut. Over lunch I had been praising my French car and the service I'd always had in the past from French garages: everybody round the table had looked a bit dubious at that. Perhaps they were right. The Frenchman is anxious to preserve his status as a professional. Hence the excellent service at good establishments combined with make-do and bodge at other ones, which in England would be more inclined to say, 'We can't' or more likely, 'We can, come back on Monday/Wednesday/next week/next month/can you manage without it till autumn?'

There was a disgruntled, frantic drive across farming country to the Forest of Rambouillet, through Maule, Beynes and Montfort-L'Amaury – pretty, paved and hilly. There had been no sign of subtopia since I left Orgeval: I was heading for country that stands in relation to Paris more or less as the Thames Valley stands to London, though it is much more like real country, with far less development, nor is the prettifying usually as obtrusive.

The Montfort in Montfort-L'Amaury is the same as in Simon de Montfort, the tough and turbulent thirteenth-century Earl of Leicester, who took his iron hand both to those who did not share his own particular brand of religious bigotry and to his king, Henry III, from whom he succeeded in transferring a great deal of power to the first English parliament. Simon was born in France, and came back to live there more than once; but Montfort-L'Amaury is now more associated with Ravel, since his house La Belvédère has been turned into a museum to the composer.

Just after the town, the Forest of Rambouillet begins, elegant and stately, and I was let out into it a few minutes before four o'clock, with the car streaking off ahead like the wrong end of a telescope to keep the appointment.

It was a simple matter to refix the front wheel and the dangling mileometer. All I had to do was to hold the bicycle frame up with one hand while with the second I held the mileometer in position: then I eased the right-hand side of the wheel into that side of the fork with a third hand, the left side with a fourth and slipped the tyre past the brake-blocks with a fifth.

But I was full of guilt: there was no way that I could explain to a TV audience that I had been in a car, but not for long, and that if you added up the miles they would be even more than the number you first thought of – especially in French. I should have to brazen it out.

But did I look like somebody who had been cycling all day? I could ruffle my hair, but where were the sweat stains on my T-shirt on that hot afternoon? Any that were there had long dried off during lunch: I would have to ride hard and get some more. I set off furiously.

But the trees were tall, the forest cool, and the faster I rode the nearer I got to the TV cameras looking fresh as a daffodil, and trumpeting deceit. There was only one solution. Grimly, I held the brakes almost full on and pedalled hard in low gear. Another cyclist passed me on the other side with a wave. He looked puzzled: he was obviously finding it difficult to understand how it was that a fat man on an expensive bicycle should be whirling his legs at an incredible rate and yet be travelling like a snail along a perfectly straight, perfectly flat road. A French couple had parked their car in the woods and were sitting by the verge ahead. They observed my approach with interest. They continued to observe it. They kept looking. My approach continued. Their attention did not wander: they had decided that since there were no other moving objects around, even one moving towards them like that movie cliché of someone running into telephoto lens was better than nothing. It struck me that when I came abreast of them in a few minutes' time, they might say

'*Bonjour*', in which case I would either have to delay my reply (with the risk of them thinking that I was anti-social or deaf and dumb) or answer straightaway and do the rest of the crawl past them in endless silence. As I came close to them I decided I had had enough, took off the brakes, changed gear, and shot past like a rabbit suddenly aware of a weasel. They did not say '*Bonjour*': perhaps they were too surprised.

There was a drop or two of dishonest perspiration on my brow as I came out of the forest, but it was probably due to embarrassment. However, it would have to do. Fortunately it was downhill into the village – I would be able to make an entrance at speed. I swooped down, whirring upon the bend at the bottom where I could see Joy standing with two chic people: a neat blonde and a man with an executive tan: the cameras had to be round the corner. I arrived, panting conscientiously but not ostentatiously.

'How are you?' said the chic man with the tan. 'Be careful here, it is dangerous.'

It seemed like a funny beginning to an interview. Nevertheless . . .

'What a beautiful place,' I began, in the cause of international relations, 'a magnificent forest – and very cool in it too,' I added as an afterthought, 'very cool.'

'You can relax,' said Joy, 'no TV cameras. Apparently it's a triple time on Saturday afternoon in French television, and they didn't think you were worth sending a crew.'

'Never mind,' I said, nobly. A car came round the bend, and I understood why it was dangerous. 'Perhaps we should go to the hotel,' I suggested, picking myself up from the kerb over which I had stumbled in my flight.

The village looked like England, with flowers and gardens and long low houses, the nearest of which had thatch settled cosily round its cottage windows, and a would-be lych-gate below the virginia creeper on the side wall. At the gate, stood a thin pale woman and a plump chef with check kitchen trousers and a Gallic moustache which looked as if it would like to grow up to have its ends waxed one day. There was a smiling garden visible under the thatch of the would-be lych-gate, and a smile under the thatch of the moustache, for M. Delfer, chef-proprietor of the Auberge de la Belle Aventure, shared with his wife a fine gift of friendly welcome. He was king of the kitchen, she queen of the hotel, but they had areas of mutual territory such as the garden, the bar and – presumably – the bed, since there were two little Delfers running around poking their noses into such aspects of the hotel business as were not too high for them.

'I think the boy will do the cooking, or perhaps the reception at the hotel,' M. Delfer told me. 'I want him to work in my house. It's a family business: my mother had a restaurant before me – near Lyons, where they grow good wine, Hermitage.' He wheeled off my tired

bicycle to join his in the garage, remarking that he liked a spin in the Forest himself when he could find the time ('Yes,' I thought, 'should be very pleasant without the brakes on') and Madame wheeled me off to my room and everybody else to a little white table in the garden.

There was a bowling alley in the garden (or to be more precise, a bouling alley); a well and a sort of rustic cowshed that was probably a summer house; some barrels sitting on the grass waiting for an explanation of what they were doing there and why someone had painted them blue; a dead tree fruiting electric light bulbs; and a ticktock of ping-pong on the lawn. The guests were a lolloping black dog (seemingly incapable of keeping his limbs and ears in orthodox relationship to his body) and a set of people who looked either chic, or as if they were taking a short vacation from being so and were likely to revert at any moment. There was a blonde with a languid face like a golden retriever, inspecting her nails; a swarthy young gentleman with a perpetual grin and a high-pitched laugh; and an imitation Great White Hunter in khaki, looking muscular and bored.

It dawned on me that I had not only changed scene rapidly that afternoon: I had also changed milieu, and had come unawares upon a social institution – *le weekend parisien*. That was the explanation for the well-kept people, the flowery village and the unassuming comfort of the *auberge*: city money, subsidizing the Forest of Rambouillet – anciently a playground and hunting-ground of Paris, and still so. I had heard at lunch that there were wild boar nearby, not fifty miles from the capital – and the decor of the auberge strongly suggested a luxurious hunting-lodge, though it might be that most game no longer ran upon four legs, but on two.

My room was approached by a gallery which ran all along one side of the top of the house: red-shaded lamps had given up the struggle to illuminate the opulent art nouveau wallpaper, and dropped a few sulky pools of yellow on the thick carpet instead.

'Ooh,' I said to Madame, 'all the rooms have names – Christine, Blanche, Astride ...'

I was in Eugénie. There was a picture of her on the wall – an Edwardian floozie, dressed in black stockings and nothing else, artistically embracing a penny-farthing. She did not look like a serious cycle-tourist. Not at all.

I came down to the garden again and joined *le weekend*, which appeared to be being conducted among citizens of some financial stability. Even at my own table, with a long glass before me, I felt not wholly in place, friendly though the two people were who had come down from Paris to welcome me on behalf of the Tourist Board. M. Disler – the executive tan – was in charge of tourism for that area, the Ile de France. He was well fleshed and relaxed, and his trousers were ironed like a white mirror. His companion, Mme Leyton, had trained her prettiness firmly into elegance. She looked as cool as if her clothes had just come out of a fashionable refrigerator.

Then there was me. The perspiration which had eluded me in the forest now came out in the sun to dribble down a brick red face to a T-shirt that had plainly been so dribbled on before. Below this veteran associate of my sweat glands were tennis shorts that looked as if they had been used to clean the car (though in fact they had only been used while I was mending the car). Bare, thick peasant legs below with old sandals curling up in despair; a bushy beard above tangling into matted hair completed the impression of a mentally deficient brigand newly emerged from the mountain after a life-time of debauchery with a pack of wolves. Not for the first time or the last time, I was struck by how impressively elegant the French can be – and not only the well-off and citified, like these, and not only in comparison with me. Whereas the English tend to shamble and roll their clothes round them, the French march and pirouette, with all their personality laced up tight so as to push their competence at living to prominence. Where we ignore other people, or do not intrude upon them, the French tend to be constantly aware of their relationship to someone else, and jockey for position. They were doing it at table tennis: quarrelling like sparrows, flamboyantly competitive.

We chatted peacefully to the twittering of birds on the poplars at the end of the lawn and the tick-tock, tick-tock of the tennis table. Suddenly there was a far-off, spasmodic trumpeting, as if a herd of mad elephants were rushing upon us over extremely rough ground which made it difficult for them to catch their breath. They came nearer and turned into a frenzy of car horns that tooted and blared in a maniac crescendo through the village and diminuendoed into the distance.

'Someone must be hurt,' I said, 'or is it a fire?'

'A wedding,' answered M. Disler. 'It is the custom; they must do noise.'

'It's for everybody to know,' Mme Leyton interjected.

FAT MAN ON A BICYCLE

'Before, people walked on the streets to be seen, now they are lazy.'

The chef-proprietor came over from the ping-pong where he had been jumping up and down and shouting in the process of battering one of his richer guests under the table.

'I was in the Bee Tea Harch,' M. Delfer informed me, proudly.

'Sorry?'

'The BTH,' said M. Delfer. 'I was in Glasgow at the British Transport Hotel: at Gleneagles too, and I know very well Leeds and Liverpool.'

'Very cold, Glasgow,' I said (in place of what I wanted to say, which was that I hoped he had not brought too many British cooking habits back with him).

'Very,' said M. Delfer, and went back to bouncing around at his table tennis, slamming the ball with such vivacity that he broke it in half, and leaving me apprehensive lest he should offer me a box labelled 'Traveller's Fare' for dinner. That evening, however, about the time we had uncorked the bottle of Bouzy (which is a still champagne) and got down to the foie gras in aspic (which the Parisians, with whom I was getting quite friendly in a brittle sort of way, said should be eaten with sultanas) I realized that any interaction that might have taken place between M. Delfer and Glasgow had been very much to the benefit of the latter.

We ate all together at a long table in the garden, Mme Delfer having announced a general menu at a general price, any objections? This kind of comfortable, if expensive informality was obviously why almost everyone there was a regular customer – and the others were not going to dare to say anything above an undertone – so we all passed the evening in a casual good fellowship quite untypical of anything else I saw in northern France; and M. Delfer dashed back and forth from the kitchen to play ping-pong between courses.

'It's a friendly place,' he told me, 'therefore people come

back time after time, manufacturers, big shopkeepers, people with money – for a sense of *bien être*.'

There was certainly a sense of togetherness. My neighbour, a lively *coupeuse* from a smart hairdresser's in Paris, confided to me that it was in London that she truly learnt about life and – aah – about love, which was a very gratifying thing for an Englishman to hear. She had vivacious dark eyes, and was built on similar lines to Eugénie as far as I could see, though it was difficult to tell without a penny-farthing.

THE SIXTH DAY

It seems that I awoke considerably before the other guests who had all finished up Saturday evening by going off to what they called a *boîte*, which by all accounts was an old hay barn full of very loud music, spot-lighting which alternated rapidly from being full on to full off, and mirror-lined walls so that everybody would have a suitable opportunity of admiring themselves. There were yellow tulips on my wallpaper with long green stems. Above the bed, Eugénie was still preparing to mount her bicycle. Hush swaddled the auberge, apart from a few Sunday birds, and an occasional burst of ferocious coffee-grinding from below; from Astride, Blanche, Christine and the rest came not even the creak of early morning bedsprings.

My bath water made a pronounced *glug* as it ran away. Investigating, as the keen amateur plumber I am, I traced the cause to the trap of a fold-away bidet hidden beneath the wash basin going *gurgle* like a large pottery animal choking in its cupboard. I folded it and unfolded it a few times to see whether such a thing would be acceptable to a British Water Board. It would not.

'If equipped with a strong spring,' I thought, 'this could give somebody a nasty shock.'

The French are always telling you that they are a logical and practical people, and quoting Descartes at you to prove it. Logical they certainly are, but when it comes to pipework, many a house looks very much as if it has indeed been plumbed by a philosopher, with a few comparatively clear runs and a great many twists and turns of argument. At least part of the reason must be the languishing of French house-building between the wars, as the result of a government-imposed rent freeze that lasted almost forty years. It is the reason why France escaped the blight of the semi-detached thirties which has ruined so many of our old towns, but it also meant that buildings fell into disrepair, that conversions were cheap-jack – and the continuity of the trades must have been broken too.

A lot of the stories about French plumbing are ancient history now: La Belle Aventure, for instance, had gold taps with sea-horses on them and a splendidly enormous bath to go with the fold-away bidet. The lavatory was positively baronial, with a tassel to pull the chain as if you were ringing for the butler or taking a modest part in Triple Bob Major.

When the British say they don't like French plumbing, what they usually mean is that they object to squatting on their haunches over a hole in the ground in a public lavatory designed by an acrobat and cleaned by a quadruple amputee. No question, public lavatories in France can be awful. In defecation, as in picnics, the French are great ones for the alfresco and when in the country it is usually wise to emulate them: France is a large, not yet over-populated land, and the results are usually not too unpleasant, except in some heavily touristed areas. In hotels, ventilation is usually poor and often appalling, and in a moderate private house may be nothing more than a minute grille communicating at length with the outside air by means of a tiny and tortuous pipe. All this, and the effluvia which hangs over some towns because of the discharge of washing water into surface drains and streams, is a function of planning regulations: it is the way things are – everybody seems to survive, and it may even add a certain romanticism of atmosphere. You cannot beat French

plumbing: you just have to be thankful for the best, try to avoid the worst, and appreciate the rest as an eccentric art-work.

I went downstairs, and found M. Delfer pottering back and forth between the bar and the kitchen to the gentle plod of a baroque trio sonata on the wireless. His kitchen was a long, low galley running the length of the restaurant, its spotless tiles and business-like stainless steel permanently on display to the customers as something to be proud of, from the vast fridge to the double charcoal grill – one side for fish, the other for meat. There we held a curiously involuted conversation about food. The trouble was that M. Delfer did not want to be rude about Britain, and I could see little in British catering to be polite about. It was the old 'Do read my poem and tell me *absolutely frankly* what you think of it' situation.

'In England, you like more broccoli,' said M. Delfer. I

think he meant cabbage. He liked English lamb; he thought French beef was better. In England, the boss used to tell him not to put so much alcohol in his dishes.

'I think alcohol is more expensive in England, maybe?' M. Delfer excused his criticism. 'It is a nice kitchen, the English kitchen, but it is very different from the French cooking. In England you like meat with something sweet – ham with pineapple. In France we do not have that.' It was plain that he could not imagine any civilized nation wanting such a thing. I told him how I had once been to a club lunch at a posh restaurant in the West End where they had served a mayonnaise salad with tinned pineapple to start with, ham and pineapple to continue and – to finish up – plain pineapple. We shuddered together.

I asked whether he liked mint sauce, because I knew he would not: the French generally regard it as the most extraordinary of barbarisms.

'Oh no – yes – I know.' M. Delfer writhed with embarrassment and took refuge in an anxious chuckle. 'You say French cooking is the best in the world: I don't know exactly, you know. In England I see the very good cook who like working very much with the French people.' M. Delfer hit on a happy way of improving international culinary relations. 'He gave me some *recettes*.'

'What recipes, exactly?' He was not expecting that.

'Er –' said M. Delfer. 'The Bread Sauce.' Somehow bread sauce hardly seemed to have the credentials for full ambassadorial rank.

'And The Big Turkey for the New Year.' That at any rate was larger.

'And The Yorkshire Pudding.'

'Yes,' I said; that was worthy of crossing a frontier. But however deep M. Delfer's loyalty to his time in Britain, he did not seem to be making practical use of a vast range of British dishes.

I administered the *coup de grâce*: 'Do your customers *like* the English recipes?'

M. Delfer crumbled. 'They said it was good, but they were not used to it.' He rested his case on a swamp of faint praise. It sank immediately. 'If I cook English food here, I think my clients say, "What happened?" but if I cook French food in England, they say, "Please do."'

M. Delfer told me that his working hours had lengthened considerably since he left England, from eight hours a day, five days a week, to fifteen hours a day, seven days a week. Of course he was now running his own house and could pop off to the garden for ping-pong between times; he might be expected to work harder as a chef-proprietor; but even so, catering jobs in France were generally much more exacting. He had an under-chef and a boy to do the washing up, he said. His wife, who worked the same sort of hours as he did, had a waitress to help her.

'The work is too much, but I think, "When I am young I must do this, for when I am old I will not want to." I was not very taken with my trade at first but after five or seven years I liked this *métier*, for the more you cook, the more you love it. Some days you are not good for the kitchen: it's like a painter – one day spectacular, another not. I am not an artist, for I think anybody can cook, with experience: but when you love your business in your heart, you are artist in every job. Imagination is very important in the kitchen: if you have just cutlet and potatoes, it is just cutlet and potatoes, but if you take some garlic, parsley, tomato sauce, then ...' He raised his eyes to heaven, and smacked his lips. 'I don't know what I shall cook tonight – perhaps a cheese soufflé, or a chocolate soufflé. I do what my client like. I don't say, "This is what we have"; I say, "What do you want for your dinners?"'

It was a peaceful lounging day in the garden, with the Parisians preening and niggling at each other over the ping-pong table.

That night we all dined together again on *salade niçoise*, raw ham cut so thin you could see through it, and the promised cheese soufflés, airy as two gigantic yellow fungi, swelling on the golden tablecloth under a lemon-coloured moon.

THE SEVENTH DAY

Monday was getting off to a slow start, with M. Delfer pottering around the beginning of his fifteen-hour day. He pottered out into the empty street with me, bade me a friendly if quizzical *au revoir* and pottered back again. I turned the corner and passed a brightly buntinged town hall at odds with the grey morning, then headed into the forest which has a cycle track to Rambouillet going right through the wood.

The land is flat here, for I was approaching the plains, the forest spacious and tall. The oak trees and the beeches were stock still down to the smallest leaf: the birches hung limply, waiting to see if the mist would turn to rain. The birds were optimistic: their songs were the only sound apart from the distant hum of a plane and the running of the tyres.

They have some picturesque names in the forest. I came over the cross-roads of the Six Feet, past Cut-throat Pond and round Hare Circus; the trees became even more stately as I rode, and the track turned to a broad path and then to a road which could hardly make up its mind whether it was a man-made object or something which had just grown there, for the forest was gently settling its debris over it, and leaf-mould was soothing the edges of the tarmac.

The Forest of Rambouillet is a remnant of the ancient Forest of Carnutes that has managed to survive as the result of having friends at court. They lived – and live still – in the sober-sided château, squatting uptight in its over-sized gardens, with their elaborate formalities, their lawns, their avenues, their vast, boring canals. 'What am I supposed to do in this Gothic toad-hole?' asked Marie Antoinette, when her husband bought it to gratify his passion for hunting, for the building was worse in her day, the principal

architectural feature being the fourteenth-century tower whose claim to fame is that François I died in it.

So Louis XVI build her the famous dairy in the form of a classical temple in which she could play at milkmaids, making cheeses in porcelain pots, while he returned to his own 376 *moutons*, imported from Spain, on the trotter, for stock breeding. Louis XVI was not to know that he was creating a line more enduring than his own, for the Rambouillet coat of arms bears a sheep to this day (and an interesting motto), and the descendants of those merinos still live on the estate at the Bergerie Nationale, which is more than you can say for the French monarchy.

I followed the bumpy road into the town past the barracks, which is the headquarters of a tank regiment and where a bored soldier was lounging on guard at the gate as if he had had an exceptionally heavy weekend. At the château, the road bends round and I bent with it, for I have a long-standing grudge against the French monarchy, in that it was responsible for taking me on an interminable school trip to Versailles when I was a child, which made me understand how easily a king who lived in that comfortless pile could sign death warrants, promulgate injustices, despatch hundreds of thousands to their deaths in a war: anything, as some sort of distraction from his ever-aching feet. Nowadays, they make the President of

France live in the Château de Rambouillet sometimes, but at least it is smaller than Versailles and, not being a hereditary monarch, the President has had his chance to avoid it and only has himself to blame.

So I passed by the château, the aviary, the sheepcote, the ice-house, the Grotte des Deux Amants (where two lovers were struck by lightning) and Shell Cottage, which is enough to make an oyster turn in its bivalve, for the decor is exclusively molluscular. What I really wanted to know was what sort of cheese Marie Antoinette made in her dairy, and what it tasted like, but I doubted that a guided tour would tell me much about that. I speculated, however, that she probably made a soft cheese like Camembert or Brie that did not require a great deal of pressing, rather than something like a Cheddar where the physique of the milkmaid is important. (As they used to say in the West Country, 'The bigger the dairy-maid, the better the cheese.') Though I suppose she could always have called a footman to put his foot on it.

Like the soldier at the barracks, Rambouillet was tired after the weekend. I have seen it seething on a Saturday, but that Monday the town had gone into a grey study, with silent, shut-up shops, and was living its life behind closed doors, one of which was, fortunately, open to me.

The door belonged to a smart middle-aged house in a neat garden in the Rue Pasteur – which was appropriate – for Dr Planté is a medical man, and important at the local hospital. Still more appropriate was the name of one of his twin daughters who greeted me in company with a husky-voiced dog: I am probably one of the few living visitors to Rambouillet who can claim that they had the door opened to them by Marie Antoinette.

'She is well named for a daughter of Rambouillet,' said her mother, pouring out a welcome aperitif of punch (pronounced 'poonsh') which she had made herself from rum, cane sugar syrup and a proprietary mix of spices.

There was something very pleasant about being within

reach of a traditional French lunchtime, with melon, a chicken that tasted like a chicken cooked with lemon slices in lemon sauce, and Madame's stunning raspberry sorbet: particularly when such domestic tranquillities are things of the past for many a city-dweller.

'That Paris life!' said Madame with a sniff and a shrug. 'Take the metro, work, metro back home, eat heaven knows what, snatch a bit of sleep, get up, take the tube ...! More sorbet? No? Then a little marc de Bourgogne made by my cousin: we call it "*la goutte*": it's very strong.' She proffered a bottle of an ominously transparent-looking liquor rather as an English housewife might offer a dish of her maiden aunt's plum jam. Marc is made from the residue of the wine vat, and I had drunk it before in a supermarket version which tasted rather like distilled stables; this was a very different thing – strong certainly, but smooth and subtly flavoured as well.

On the walls of the dining-room were pictures of England for – as he told me – Dr Planté was an enthusiastic town-twinner, and had been so since 1956. I would have expected a place like Rambouillet with the presidential country retreat in it to opt for Windsor or Chartwell, but Great Yarmouth was the choice.

'Very different towns,' I said.

'Very,' agreed Dr Planté, 'but after twenty years we have come to the conclusion that the features of the town are not as important as you would think. It's a question of people, and we have been very lucky in that.'

Hardly could I prevail upon Dr Planté to make distinctions between the two nations.

'For a man to love another country, I think he must first love his own. I am ferociously French, but when we sit down in committee with the people from Yarmouth, we forget nationality: it's a sort of family now. We have some-times different points of view. We are quicker, we are dreaming much more than they do. When we have an idea, we would like it to be realized immediately, whereas they want to wait, to be sure. But men and ladies are men and ladies in every part of the world. I am from the south, my wife is from Burgundy: when we met for the first time, she was completely unable to understand me. My way of life and accent were quite different, yet our families have been French for generations.'

But surely, I asked them, they must have noticed national differences of some sort? Yes, said the Plantés, they had been struck by the surprising quantities of choirs and tennis courts in Great Yarmouth.

'A great problem the first time was to understand why the British houses had not cellars under them: we had many discussions with people there as to whether this was because there were some problem in making concrete, or because the soil was too sandy.'

'No shutters too,' put in Madame. 'And in England you have not a wall between your houses: in Rambouillet, we have all big wall. We like very well to separate.'

'Yes, it was surprising for us to spend the evening sitting by the fire and to be able to see the lights of the cars in the street. This is completely unknown in France: we have many poetries about the shutters shut and the pleasure of being inside.'

'When I go to England, it makes me smile when you are in a bus and you can see all the bedrooms because there are no shutters,' said Madame. 'You see exactly the same dressing tables. We cannot understand that. We were invited to a party and two ladies spoke of the furniture of the other and one said: "My daughter had bed and chairs like that": and the other said: "Oh, I am very pleased: my daughter has also the same." I said nothing, because as a French lady I was horrified. It was terrible for me to think my daughter would have the same things. If there are two women with the same dress in a room, the French woman goes out and changes; the English woman says, "Ah you've bought the same dress – *formidable*!" *Ça, c'est la différence entre nous – voyez!*'

As I headed off for the country I turned briefly from my

path on a small pilgrimage to a not-very-distinguished housing development in which an old man in a beret was holding a colloquy with a housewife bearing a long loaf, beneath a sign reading *Place de Great Yarmouth*.

As I travelled through St-Arnoult-en-Yvelines (where parts of the church may date back fifteen centuries and more) and Dourdan (with the remains of its great thirteenth-century castle), the forest maintained a presence. The sky was a purple-grey: evening primroses along the road were fully out in the dark afternoon. I felt a quieter country coming, and took to stopping occasionally to begin a collection of wild flowers pressed in my dictionary (which meant that I was thereafter unable to use it for looking up anything). Cornfields encroached more and more on the woods which retreated defensively into clumps of trees. The road straightened, levelled, dipped through Etampes with its ancient churches, hiding in a last outpost of green. Round the corner out of the town there was a stretch of bone-shattering *pavé* left in the road, presumably to slow down cars coming the other way. I rumbled over it, and uphill into a different landscape: the plateau of Beauce, where the last gleam of influence from the big city goes and the fields stretch to the horizon.

Comparing my watch and the road markers set at every kilometre, I found I could make half a kilometre in a minute. Rhythmically I sped through the uniform landscape, which looked as if it would be more so when disease got hold of the occasional thin avenue of elms by the roadside, until I came to what appeared to have once been a farm, spreading its outbuildings over the plain without making a real impression on the emptiness of its surroundings. It was the Auberge de Courpain and there I tied up my bicycle just as the first few drops of sullen rain were beginning to fall.

HOW TO COOK THE ENGLISH – a Guide for Foreigners by Bulwer Wellington-Ffoulkes

So the common people have got their common market, and serve them right. A mongrel internationalism is the order of the day and I can only say, with Socrates, Cato and other honorary Englishmen, 'Pass the hemlock'. This french food stuff, however, I shall *not* pass in any sense of the word – certainly not without a considerable struggle – and have prepared the following instructions for issue to hotel-keepers when abroad:

1. You french are always mincing, chopping and mucking about. Remember, a hen needs grit to lay good eggs, and roughage is essential to the proper functioning of this milord.

2. This milord is an *homme de goo* or lover of refined flavours. Therefore, when you make a tomato soupe (since the real stuff cannot be had over here), be sure to add quantities of sugar, as this will make

it fit to drink. You may also apply this principle to any soupe, ragoo or cornflake, but not to roast meat, which milord eats with jam.

3. The milord's religion forbids any food which contains butter (where it could contain margarine), cream (where it could contain milk), stock (where it could contain water) or steak (where it could contain gristle). The use of alcohol in cooking, the garnishing of potatoes and the preparation of vinaigrette dressing are expressly prohibited.

4. The milord likes his vegetables cooked *à point*, that is to say, to the point of disintegration – and in *plenty* of water.

5. Brown and tomato sauces, pickled onions and vinegar shall be available at all times, and at afternoon tea the water (*not* Vichy water) must be *bouillante*.

B.W.-Ff.

CHAPTER 5

The Vasty Fields of France

THE EIGHTH DAY

The plains of Beauce are not featureless: they are all one feature. They have no middle distance, only the very far and the very close; but – focus as you choose – their time scale is on infinity. Even in a car, you feel the landscape unchanging for a while; on foot or on a bicycle you are like a pair of fellow-travellers I saw the morning I left the auberge – two bright, furry caterpillars crossing the road together; crawling, vulnerable splodges of colour on a plain of tarmac. I felt scarcely less close to the ground than they were as I cycled away. The sun was so high, the horizons so far off; distantly, larks were going bonkers in the blue.

The auberge was set by a wrinkle in the land, at the

top of a tiny fold which had encouraged the growth of a tentative hamlet. The inn itself was an oasis of expensive prettification, with the strong lines of ancient farm buildings, high walls and gateways embellished with bright puce flowers and agricultural *objets-trouvés*, including a gigantic wine-press. Perhaps the watch-tower at one corner of the courtyard was a sign that the whole complex had once been a fortified farm – in this part of the country people have traditionally lived in isolated farm units rather than villages – or perhaps it was a dovecote. But it was certain that the Auberge de Courpain was embattled against its surroundings, with a young, ambitious garden to keep the wheatfields away and carry the banner of artistic horticulture, a great deal of fierce pointing to keep the stones from looking rurally decrepit, and plenty of rigorous varnishing to keep the woodwork in order.

There was also a landlady (with her cardigan sticking up at the back like a ruff on a brontosaurus) to keep the clientele in order with the assistance of no fewer than eight guard-animals (four Alsatians, three poodles and a Burmese cat asleep by the till) and a bevy of white-coated waiters dancing attendance to the tune of eternal muzak (which, on one occasion, was heard to change, rather over-felicitously, directly from Handel's Water Music to Swannee River). It struck me that the wine-press in the yard, the ancient iron farm machines, were more than decoration: they were war trophies, set up in triumph to show that within this little space the crude world of commercial agriculture was tamed, subject of a no less commercial sophistication.

It must have been in subconscious acknowledgement of this that I had chosen *turbotine au beurre blanc* the night before, for seafood must be one of the most incongruous things imaginable to eat in the middle of a steppe, though it is a tribute to the far-flung excellence of French fish-mongering that it is available at all.

The country was fighting back: not fifty yards down the road was a large corrugated-iron barn with a sign *Brocante* (junk) hung out, and surrounded by its wares. In contrast to the *objets-trouvés* of the inn, which seemed to say, 'We may be junk, but we are very expensive junk and much to be admired', the *brocante* outside the barn had given up the fight of sophistication and was sunk in an inbred peasant utility. As I passed, an encrusted cement-mixer was keeping company with carts and a pot-bellied old boiler.

At first I found myself rushing over a kilometre every two minutes as I had the night before under the threat of rain, though there was no more than a trace of high cloud in the sky. Even on a bicycle, there can be the temptation not to be leisurely: but remembering my resolution to press a specimen of every roadside flower that I came across, I slowed, and was soon stopping at every other pedal. From either distant end of the long straight road came the occasional car or lorry in a long, slow buzz, with a quick snarl as it went past. When it had gone, the lark-song would come back again, perhaps with the drone of an invisible tractor somewhere across the geometric landscape – not a hedge to be seen, but divided into great oblongs by rough tracks. The wheat, too, and the maize – taller here than any I had yet seen – showed the pattern of its planting in shadowy lines converging on the horizon, as if a flock of one-track birds had followed the sower. Close to, the ripe wheat was not simply green: almost yellow at the ear, there was a band of blue just below the grains, and below that the green stems seemed to move in and out of each other as I passed, flickering like a stroboscope. There was almost nothing to interrupt the landscape except that every now and again there would be the small cluster of a farm far away from the main road whose verges would sometimes grow a half-hearted line of trees, often alive with the chatter of fledglings, so that there I rode through an avenue of abrupt flowerings of sound.

There are few moving parts to the great plain: the birds are too small to make any impression on the landscape, there are very few human figures, no animals;

there is just what travels along the road, and the waterers. Beauce (like most of the Paris basin) is among the lowest rainfall areas in France, with heavy competition from the Mediterranean coast and dry pockets on the central plateau and Alpes Maritimes; it is certainly by far the most flamboyant in its irrigation, with a whole hierarchy of sprinklers at everlasting drill. In private gardens, I heard domestic models go individually plut-plut on lawn and roses, like the panting of a Pekinese: from a small field came a complex sibilance as a dotting of lonely sandpipes interwove their pattern of spray. Further off, water-cannon spurted curving plumes in a slow circle, dragged along the furrows to the other end of their sentry-go by a giant, gently clicking reel of enormous pipe; and the patriarch of the whole lot was a wing of pipes only slightly smaller than Concorde, turning serenely as if in flight, with a trailing edge of spray making rainbows in the sun.

I came through Sermaises, with plain, low houses stretching phlegmatically along the road in an atmosphere of the stupendously humdrum (though it must have one of the longest bicycle shops in France); the tiny Intville-la-Guétard, and on the outskirts of the town of Pithiviers, with the needle spire of its church piercing the sky above the plains, I turned off towards the river which at that point is either the Essonne or its tributary the Oeuf, for it is difficult to distinguish between them until you are well past the village of Bondaroy.

There was little sign of the river at first, but the road left the wheatfields to one side and then dipped into a fold big enough to hide smaller fields and trees. As I free-wheeled down, a class of tiny school-children out for a day's cycling came up towards me in a crocodile, with a thin mistress charging along at the front and a fat one puffing at the rear. I reached the hamlet of Aulnay-la-Rivière as the church bell was ringing midday, stopping everything dead in its tracks for a proper observance of lunch.

My own lunch was waiting just out of the village, in

a creeper-covered farmhouse with white shutters and two round towers flying little metal flags in permanent perkiness. I had an introduction to the farmer's wife, Mme Claude Levassor.

There was a surprising emptiness about the big courtyard of dusty cobbles before the house. With the towers and the fine stone walls and the substantial barns, this had obviously always been an establishment of some style: the garden at the back had old apple trees, walks and lawns. Once, this would have been a traditional mixed farm, all mess and crowded animals, but in an age of things specialized and mechanized it had become possible for the Levassor family to manage their 300 acres almost singlehanded. The land is dry and stony here: their barley and maize ripen quickly in consequence. So now Le Grand Cour is quiet and clean – though the cobbles defeated me. I wheeled the bicycle across the yard to the welcome at the front door.

M. Levassor was a check-shirted man in his forties, looking as brown and spare as if he had just been harvested from his own fields. For him, specialization had meant becoming both manager and labourer, but especially labourer, though all the family would help on the land sometimes, driving the tractor, changing the pipes of the waterers – fifteen-year-old Frederick, fourteen-year-old Dorothy and the lady of the house, Mme Claude. (So I called her, as I later discovered, not quite correctly.)

Mme Claude was more style than apron: she had the easy friendliness that a farmer's wife ought to have but otherwise she had about her more of the poise of the town than the homeliness of the country.

'I am a farmer's wife, but I am not a *campagnarde*,' she told me in the cool, lofty dining-room. The floor was chequered stone and there was a great beamed hearth and heavy furniture looking not just ancient but ancestral; the room had only three corners – in the fourth bulged the curve of one of the round towers. It looked like a life-style of some distinction, and I said so. Mme Claude was pleased to accept the compliment to her furniture, but dismissed the rest.

'The farm is not ours: we borrowed a lot of money when we got married seventeen years ago, and we have a very heavy mortgage. Like farmers everywhere, we depend on the weather. It was very bad in '76; we lost a lot of money, and had to *serre*' (she clenched her fist) 'even more than usual. Some of our friends have got their own fields – they don't have these problems – but I like the summer because then I know my husband will be harvesting and soon we can pay the bills that have been waiting for months.' She added, with that half-wistfulness that has touched many a countrywoman in many a country: 'Sometimes I think I like to travel, but ... we have to count the money, and I think we must do things for the children so that they have a good remembrance of their childhood.'

In a small town like Pithiviers, part-time jobs are not easy to come by and if she had a full-time one, who would feed the chickens? The fixed points of her life were ferrying the children to school by eight and getting them back at five: Pithiviers has no transport for them, despite its transport museum where dumpy steam engines puff over the last remaining four kilometres of the narrow gauge railway that used to take locals the thirty-two kilometres to Toury on 60-cm track.

'I've got twelve hens because my husband says it's a farm and we need to have hens and a cock. I wanted to kill the cock last week – to eat, he has big legs – but my husband said, "No, it's nice in a farm."'

This was more like a *campagnarde* thought. I halted my spoonful of melon in mid-parabola, lunch being under way by this time.

'Wring its neck, do you?' I asked.

'I can't do that. I get the lady from next door. We have pigeons, too, because when Frederick was smaller he wanted to breed them. They breed a lot. A lot!' She evidently admired their abilities. 'We have to take the eggs away not to get more – and sometimes we have to kill them, but then Dorothy won't eat them because they are like the family. So we kill them while she's away.'

'It must be a problem, livestock,' I said.

'We had rabbits last year, but – thank God – they all died.'

Plainly, Mme Claude was right: she was not a *campagnarde*. In her attitude to animals, she hardly even sounded French. The French are brusque with animals, where Britons often show Victorian sentimentality fostered at an early age by our tradition of nursery animals, from Pooh and Mrs Tiggywinkle to the lachrymose Black Beauty. By contrast, French children's books have human beings as heroes: even Babar is more man than elephant, and Asterix and Tintin are little short of environmental disasters. They are hunters, while we have cultivated a comfortable mental gap between the well-established corpse that provides the Sunday joint, and the creature running round in a sunny-book farm – fluffy lamb, friendly pig, phlegmatic cow. Since to us animals are people, it is a great shock to come into a country where they are still animals, and their public treatment is the only aspect of French life that I can think of which would be likely to cause a riot if brought to England.

The difference begins by looking quaint. The first time I noticed it was one grey holiday morning in the Aveyron, north-east of Toulouse. Villefranche-de-Rouerge is a beautiful old town, if somewhat miasmatic with drains. The market square is a cobbled hill cuddled up against the buttresses and massive tower of the church of Notre Dame. Among the stalls of garlic, cheeses, vegetables, were tables with ducks and geese sitting contentedly in neat lines – as they had to, their legs being tied together. Beside the tables were crates containing what looked like a kind of furry engine – a blur of ceaseless motion from rabbits crammed together in a space much too small for them, all jockeying to be on top. In the country in Britain, I thought, it would be rather more difficult to attract customers willıng to kill their own food, even for the sake of the blood to add body and flavour to a *civet*. Where the British self-image is the observing one of a gentleman, the French self-image is of the hunter.

I saw the principle demonstrated when I walked beneath the arch of the buttresses, out of the market into a narrow but very smart shopping street. What kind of chic boutique I was staring into – I forget, chocolates perhaps, or perfume – but suddenly there was a whooping like Red Indians auditioning for a TV Western, and out of the spotless interior of the shop, through shining glass doors burst a hunting party of immaculately-cosmeticized women, led by a neatly-suited man waving a broom with all the flourish and inaccuracy of the headsman employed by Mary Queen of Scots. Before them ran a rat – round in circles, back and forth in jerks like a grey toy. It took me a moment to notice it, so bright-eyed, yelling and happy they all were. They picked up other hunters from the passers-by in the street, and a contingent from the shop next door, all screaming in and out of doorways in a brief frenzy, until the man with the broom laid the creature dead in the gutter and everybody dispersed laughing and immensely pleased with themselves. That incident, too, was slightly different from what you would expect to find in England.

More macabre was the side-show I came across at a village fête in the mountains that same holiday: a star attraction, advertised as a *lapindrome*. I went to see it with no idea of what it could be unless it were something like a hippodrome, only smaller. It turned out to consist of a crowd surrounding a circle of numbered boxes, a man with a public address microphone, and a rabbit. The way it worked was that the man shouted, the people bought numbers and then they let the rabbit loose in the middle to see which box it would hop into, whereupon the lucky winner pounced on it and took it home for the pot. Then they fetched another rabbit. Everyone enjoyed it greatly, particularly the man with the microphone who was able to make many jokes of an ironic character at the expense of the rabbit, which cowered amid the circle of genially hooting adults and children, and had to be prodded to get it going. In Britain, children would not have laughed, but cried.

It was also in the mountains that I saw a swarthy party of casual anglers from somewhere in the south take their tiny catch from the water and grill them live and squirming on the fire. That summer of the bicycle trip I went to a Provençal market where a duck was clamped to the scales by its legs, so that its weight would be demonstrated to a prospective customer. Its legs broke. The customer did not buy it. The process was repeated with the next customer.

But the incident I shall not forget was that of the little cat of Avignon. French cats are small and thin: it was difficult to tell whether this one was simply emaciated or whether its insides had been squeezed out of it by whatever it was that injured it. It might have been run over, though I could not see how in that case it could have avoided a broken back: otherwise its injuries might have been caused by being slammed in a heavy door, or by a powerful kick. Whatever the cause, there it was on the road, accompanied by a long-legged kitten with gigantic orange eyes and pointy ears, playing unconcernedly nearby. The mother cat would not touch the milk I put down in a reflex action while I thought what to do. It moved a little and slowly – sat down, dragged itself a little way, sat down again, occasionally mewed in pain, got up when I laid it on its side. It bled in spots on the asphalt, dark blood mixed with something internal. It would obviously have been kindest to cut its throat or knock it on the head, but I have no experience with the first and what I know of the second from rabbits with myxomatosis is that it takes much longer and involves much more brutality than you might expect. So I went to the neighbours. The man next door said he had two dogs and couldn't be bothered with cats. A passer-by said it was just a cat and what was the fuss about anyway.

A woman at the house opposite said that she was the maid, but there was a vet down the road.

It was difficult to carry the cat because holding it in front obviously hurt it and holding it at the back meant touching the place where its insides were coming out. But I put it on some newspaper in the car and tried to keep it still while I drove to the vet.

For a town vet – this all took place in a suburb of Avignon – this one was doing pretty nicely with a marble decor, and a queue in the waiting-room which went into committee on my arrival and passed a motion to the effect that here was a man with a cat, and it was just a cat and consequently of little interest, since they all had their own problems. The problems appeared to have been chosen on the basis of size and swank. A blotchy Great Dane was so great that it made the waiting-room feel like a broom cupboard we were sharing with a horse. A stern-looking couple had two Alsatians – large and small, their collars tightly yoked together. The large Alsatian had broken its leg and kept trying to stand up, which it could not do because it was tied so tightly to the puppy. All that was needed was to loosen its collar, but at the first sound of the claws of its one good front leg, scrabbling on the marble, its owner would thump it down and everyone else would assist in thumping it down. The other person in the room was a young man who had evidently attempted to cut the ears of his spaniel, which was covered with blood and in a dreadful state of fear, and had a pair of surgical scissors still dangling from one ear. Nor had that young man even the grace to look ashamed.

The vet agreed with me about the cat: it would have to be *sacrifiée*, and would cost 20 francs. I paid up in the hope he would kill it kindly, though as far as I could see, his waiting-room was full of animal sacrifices that had already taken place. And that was the end of the little cat of Avignon: the kitten I gave to Cécile and Bernard with whom I was staying, and Bernard gave it to his sister with whom it lived happily ever after. It was not until some months had gone by that it was discovered that it was not a stray at all, but had belonged to someone a few doors down the road, so I was guilty of trafficking in stolen cats. But by that time it was too late to do anything about it.

But in the Levassor farm at Aulnay-la-Rivière, the cockerel and his harem strutted round the barns and old stables where only tractors live nowadays, for old times' sake. However, Mme Claude told me, her husband was a traditionalist in many ways, one of which was hunting. 'He's been putting out water in the fields for the pheasants and partridges.'

She rose to fetch the main dish: it turned out to be a Provençal recipe: thick slices of beef marinaded in olive oil and herbs for two days and served raw. It was the sort of dish that is quite a surprise when you aren't expecting it.

'I don't like much cooking,' said Mme Claude. 'When I got married, my grandmother came from Pithiviers for a few weeks and organized the meals. She said, "Today you will give him that, tomorrow that". I've still got the book she wrote for me – how to make a *potage*, a *civet de lièvre*, *Pithiviers aux amandes* and *pâté d'alouettes*.'

The recipe for *Pithiviers aux amandes* may have come to the neighbourhood from Armenia, brought by the local hermit, Gregory, who was bishop of that country in the tenth century but gave up his palace for a cave in the village of Bondaroy which I had passed that morning. He is recorded as having baked 'a cake of honey and spices after the manner of his country' which sent the faithful into raptures.

A legend also attaches to the *pâté d'alouettes*, a pie of larks and forcemeat with or without a crust, which is said to have been served to Charles IX by brigands who captured him when he was hunting, and held him to ransom. So impressed was the king, that, when his own forces arrived to rescue him, he spared the lives of his captors and on his way home stopped off to visit the chef, one Margolet, known as Provenchère, who received the title of *pâtissier du roi* and established a long line of pâté-making larkhunters. I did not taste this local speciality since I prefer to hear my larks rather than eat them: the nearest I came to it was a mouthful or two of thrush pâté which was rather granular in texture with a penetrating taste tending to the gamey, and not really good enough to provide a convincing excuse for depopulating the hedgerows, that is, once you have got over the frisson which is the gastronomic equivalent of seeing a dirty picture.

'I couldn't fancy cooking larks, Mme Claude,' I said.

'I don't like much cooking: I cook today because you sound on the phone like enjoying life. I said to my husband, "Sounds like enjoying life, enjoying travelling and going all over the world!"' She passed me a slice of *clafouti*, sweet batter cooked with cherries.

'By the way, you must not call me Mme Claude, you know,' said Mme Claude, allowing herself a brief giggle. 'It was the name of –' She said something I could not quite catch, since she giggled again. But it sounded like 'a well-known prostitute in Paris'.

'Oh,' I said, 'I'm terribly sorry.' What patience on her part, I thought. Even if she eats larks.

After lunch, the great farmyard was stiller and emptier than ever in the afternoon sun; nothing moved, apart from the tail feathers of a token chicken vanishing round the corner of a barn. There was a tentative shimmer and a desultory post-prandial cooing from the poplars down by the river. There was not even a car to raise the dust on the road outside until the Levassors put-putted off to the fields in their Deux Chevaux to inspect the watering. I followed, bumping along the field track into the middle of nowhere, getting my wheels stuck in soil so fine it might have been blown there by the wind – and probably was. Down by a curly stream, a pump purred furiously at the end of a good half-mile of pipe: up in the fields by a straggly thorn hedge, turned one of the giant waterwings I had noticed that morning.

Seen close, its pipes and girders were streaked with rust, its stately progress accompanied with a crying of old metal. I stood beneath it with my stereo recorder to capture the sound of the shower going past: the machine turned over me like the disk of a radio telescope, like a main-sail catching the wind, like a gigantic bird that could not settle. As the water jets approached, their muted hiss swelled to a sharp patter, the shower fell cold and heavy, and the leaves bent as if a horde of invisible rats had run lightly over the top of the corn. I wondered whether anybody had ever made such a recording before: from the expressions on the faces of the Levassors, they had certainly not previously considered the possibility of a fat man standing under one of their waterers soaking an expensive tape-recorder. Nor did they think it was the sort of pastime that would catch on.

Though the collecting of snap-shots is a respectable and boringly universal progress, the collecting of sounds is apt to mark the collector as an early candidate for the madhouse. People make even less effort to use their ears than their eyes: most of them – even many sound broadcasters – cannot hear sounds in their proper places. Yet each sound has its position, and changes according to its distance and surroundings. You only need to concentrate to make your ears light up and fizz with it as if someone had connected them to a hi-fi system via a bottle of champagne. The great differences between collecting sounds and visual snap-shots, however, are that there is much more interference (you cannot hide a revving 1000cc motor-bike just out of the corner of the picture); sounds are less defined and people more suggestible where they are concerned than with visual images (a rose is a rose is a rose, but a swoosh is a jet plane, a wind or a river according to what you tell people beforehand: it can even be a bolt of lightning – which is interesting, since lightning, as you know, is silent). But the things that really set sound-collecting apart from photography are the awkwardness factor and the time factor. Even in the age of the silicon chip it is generally true that really good sound equipment is much bulkier than a camera. People who collect sounds seriously know what it is to stand festooned with wires like a do-it-yourself electric chair, weighed down with knob-ridden shiny machinery of infinite delight and irresistible attraction to any small boy in the area (and most large ones), to sprout headphones like a pair of latex cauliflowers, to wave in the air a micro-phone array the size of a football – and to do all this while attempting to remain inconspicuous. What generally hap-pens of course is that everyone stops what they are doing and comes to see what you are up to. That is the awkward-ness factor: the time factor is simply that whereas photo-graphs are instant, sounds go on for as long as they take so you have to remain inconspicuous for five, ten, fifteen minutes or more.

There is one reward: when you play back to people on the spot a really good recording of a sound that they have been ignoring all their lives, they are dull indeed if they do not recognize its quality. I played the waterer to the

Levassors: they went ooh-la-la with their eyes and shivered as the electronic water passed over them. Then they led me back to the road, puttering and lurching over the track in the 2CV, and I headed east for Montargis, leaving the farm with its twin round towers behind the trees, the conical turrets like a couple of witches engaged in earnest conversation.

The blue afternoon shone. Its few clouds were luminous wool: gleams of silver tobogganed down the drooping fronds of the dark green maize. I crossed the Essonne by the village wash-house, a shed at water level with its roof overhanging the stream like a peaked cap. Limpid swirls made glass bull's-eyes on the surface; there were patches of king-cup leaves, as if below the stream there was a giant water-boatman clinging upside-down on bright green suckers. The river meandered just enough to show its independence: the trees reflected ragged silhouettes in the water, in contrary wanderings.

The road turned out of the river valley up over the plain, deserted but for the occasional van or tractor, a farm labourer on a mobilette covered with useful bags to put things in, another with a rake slung across his back. I came into Puiseaux by a long avenue of grey setts and dusty sidewalks, past the church with a grey slate spire and out again (there is very little of Puiseaux). Then the long straight road once more, with the cream-green wheat stretching to the horizon with the subtlest of undulations, for I was heading off the plain into the Gâtinais, and the most regular planting could not disguise the first restlessness on the lie of the land. Officially, I had been in the Gâtinais since Pithiviers, but the description was as yet hardly appropriate, since *la gâtine* describes heavy, undrained land, little cultivated but given over to pond and copse and grass. Here at the edge of Beauce, the loess still blew from the fields when they were dry and lapped at the road, the thin black strip of civilization that was carrying me from Puiseaux to Château-Landon. I could see from the sandy pattern by the verge that when it was wet the encroachment became a stream and washed in a first fine layer of mud.

The clouds had gone, the sky got deeper and a haze began to build up on the horizon. The sun having positioned itself just behind my right ear, I travelled in company with my shadow, a silent blackness slipping over the asphalt like a curtain on casters. Impressed, I tried to photograph it as a kind of disembodied symbol of myself: unfortunately, it kept on wobbling at crucial moments and – though I managed to conceal the camera behind its head – there seemed to be no way of hiding the supporting arm, so that the finished results show a shadow riding a bicycle with its hand pressed to its brow in a dramatic attitude of Victorian dejection, or possibly a bad hangover.

The shadow was just wobbling for the third time when I saw the cyclists ahead. Cheered, I worked harder, and was about forty yards behind when it occurred to me that if I were to come up with them I would either have to continue by their side in conversation, which they might not want, or pass them, which might encourage a spirit of needless competition in which they would probably win. I had just decided to drop quietly behind when the girl looked back. Too late. She was a pretty, slim creature: the man was long and had the patina of health that is to be observed in very rich people who take tennis lessons and climb mountains. They both looked as if they had a fair turn of speed in them.

I drew alongside. After we had established that they were from Paris, out for the day and heading for the river Loing, conversation ran out. With a nonchalant pant, I bade them farewell and moved ahead, changing up with a flourish. The chain came off. They sailed past. Gratefully, I pulled into the side and spent an unnecessarily long time putting things to rights again. When I unbent myself from the chain wheel, they were still there. Stopped, about 100 yards away. Watching me. Plainly, they anticipated some disaster if this inexperienced English cyclist were abandoned with

his unreliable machine. I got on and moved off: they got on and moved off, looking back from time to time. We moved together in harmony, the three of us: when they slowed, I slowed, when they resumed their pace, so did I. Nothing it seemed would speed them up: they were going very slightly too slow. I began to wonder which was the more embarrassing: to ride in silence beside them or at a constant distance of 100 yards behind in obvious avoidance.

I was just nerving myself for another sprint and another one-sided conversation (what *was* the French for 'chain wheel'?) when I was saved by a small, rattly car that came like a bullet out of the distance, stood on its brakes at the prospect of a slow cycling race advancing towards it, and edged cautiously forward until I was within hailing distance.

'There can't be two of you,' said the small rattly car in English, putting a curly black fringe and a wide smile out of its window.

'Not as far as I know,' I said. Between the smile and the fringe there was a clear, assured expression, and dark eyes.

'You're staying with me tonight.' In any other circumstances, this would have been an interesting proposition: as it was, it was a pre-arrangement with an old friend of Joy's. Michèle Baudoin had taught Joy French at school in Rugby, so I had been expecting someone at least a generation ahead: now I saw that it must have been a friendship established between a very junior *assistante* and a very senior schoolgirl.

'Ah,' I said, 'you must be Michèle. I thought you were going to be one of those terrifying French matrons.' (Unaware, I set the tone of our future relationship.)

'I thought I'd drive out and see how you were getting on.'

'Am I almost there, then?'

'No, it's miles. I wasn't going to come so far, but I kept going a little bit more. Are you all right? Got our address?'

'Yes.'

'See you later then. You'll have some company. I passed a couple of cyclists up ahead. They're not going very fast so I expect you'll catch them up.'

'What's the French for chain wheel?' I asked.

'What's a chain wheel?'

'That thing: the big one with the teeth.'

'No idea.' She departed.

Sure enough, within minutes, there were the cyclists, taking it easy. I stopped and took a photograph (I still have it: it shows a great deal of wheat) but the disadvantage hardly lasted more than a mile. It was not until the village of Château-Landon that I saw my chance, triumphantly parking myself in a little supermarket full of fat women in one corner of the little square, examining the shelves minutely and emerging with a bottle of water. I cast a leisurely eye over the church, which has an old tower consisting of three ranks of Norman arches piled one on top of the other, making it look rather like a medieval apparatus for training firemen. Also in a leisurely manner, I mounted and trickled round the corner on to the Montargis road, only to spot, instantly, two well-known bicycles leaning against the wall. Rejecting the possibility of letting down their tyres as undesirably complicated, I went hell for leather out of town, and never saw them again.

Later I discovered from the dictionary of bicycling terms with which the Cyclists' Touring Club had provided me that the French for 'chain wheel' is *le grand pignon*

(or, as I prefer to think of it, *Le Grand Pignon*). But I never needed to refer to it again, nor the bottom bracket (*le logement du pédalier*), the pawl springs (*le ressort de cliquet*), the ball-bearing (*le roulement à billes*), the wire strippers (*les pinces à denuder*), the nipple (*la raccord de graissage*), nor even the seat stem (*la potence*).

So I came to Montargis: over the plain, through some rather half-hearted suburbs of randomly disposed blocks of flats, in and out of the railway station (by mistake) and at last up a narrow, bendy side street to a tall stone house, outside it a pair of art nouveau gates with a sagging neckline like an old green party dress that wouldn't quite do up any more.

135

USEFUL PHRASES FOR CYCLISTS NOT TO BE FOUND IN THE CYCLISTS' TOURING CLUB DICTIONARY

Attention! le pneumatique est crevé.

Stand to attention! the fat man has a headache.

Voyez donc ces raccords de graissage.

That is an interesting young lady.

Le ressort de cliquet est rouillé: donnez-moi un tourne-vis.

The seaside town of Cliquet is full of roués: send for the vigilantes.

Tiens! votre phare ne brille plus: avez-vous une pile?

Crumbs! your lighthouse is no longer illuminated: are you saddle-sore?

Cette bicyclette ne marche plus: il faut aller à pied.

This bicycle is no longer walking: I will have to hop on one foot.

Merde! votre potence est plus grand que le mien.

Good heavens! your seat stem is bigger than mine.

Le Grand Pignon ne sert à rien.

It is impossible to find a use for the term 'Grand Pignon'.

THE NINTH DAY

The house of Jean-Claude and Michèle Baudoin – who were not only old friends of Joy's but very soon felt like old friends of mine – had something fantastic in its personality, as if a fairy story had been forced to be practical, and made to live in a town. There was rather too much in the way of eaves, which looked as though they had started life with an ambition to become an alpine chalet in their own right but had never quite made it; the stonework was crazy paving that had somehow got stuck upright (there were odd little patches of red brick in it, such as a child might put in to see a pretty colour); long white stones hung over the corners of each window like a pair of witch's teeth. Inside, it rambled from room to room and devoted much energy to its hallway and staircase. The small garden contained a wooden grotto for the rattly car; a lawn (which, like all little lawns, showed not the remotest sign of having any notion what it was doing there); a home-made rock/flowerbed/fountain complex with waterworks that seemed not to; and a superb cut-leaved birch reaching and rustling right up to the windows of the little attic room where I slept in Michèle's grandmother's feather bed.

There was also a conceited wardrobe which was not, however, half as stuck-up as the immensely pompous tall clock in the living-room, with flowers on its waistcoat and a heavily loaded pendulum swinging like gilded intestines behind a glass panel. Like many French clocks, it struck twice in case you missed it the first time, which you almost always did. Of course, strictly speaking, the bell is always wrong second time round, but this does not matter to the French who are utilitarians in their way of making things, which – like their attitude to animals – has a different spirit to our own, being more about people and less about the artefact itself. French engineering, for instance, has a tendency to hang bits on the edge where the British like to integrate within. Even in these days of multi-national design, you can still see the contrast in cars and sophisticated goods, and when you come down to the world of drainpipes and wires, it is plain indeed – rambling down the walls of the houses and strung through the air in a municipal festoon. National habits of workmanship are scarcely less distinctive than national *cuisines*.

Who but the French would ever have developed the

concept of the triple-barrel mousetrap (presumably on the principle that you cannot have too much of a good thing)? Yet there they were in a supermarket, a thick block of wood bored with three parallel tunnels with some nasty apparatus within them: the theory was that the mice could come up one at a time and poke their heads in so that in the morning there would be three little corpses neatly side by side. (I did not buy one, thinking that English mice might not know what was expected of them.)

There was also an interesting contrast in gas-lighters. My old British one at home has two pieces of metal and a flint holder. It has now been joined by its French equivalent – which has eleven pieces of metal, two springs, one washer, a wooden handle and a grinding wheel.

It was very difficult to get people in Montargis or anywhere else in France to discuss this artefactual nationalism, because to them of course it was the way things naturally were and therefore unworthy of remark. Michèle and I screamed over the lunch table in an effort to shout each other down on the question of which country had the worse garages: I said England, she said France. From either side of the Channel we produced affecting parables in which clean-cut mechanics shot like arrows from their garages after closing time and – with honeyed words and old-fashioned courtesies upon their lips – succoured the distressful traveller at minimal expense.

'You find what you look for,' said Michèle. 'Go back to England, look at it the same way you are looking at France, and you will see.'

'Things must be more efficient here,' I said, 'if only because the French ladies are so much more terrifying.' (I was not being quite fair.)

'Tell us how it is when you meet those terrifying French ladies: what do you do, fall off your bike?'

It was not until I met Stuart Cunningham that I discovered an ally. He was a Scot, but only just. His profession brought him to Montargis – to be maître d'hôtel of one of France's best restaurants, the Auberge des Templiers at Les Bézards, a few miles south of the town. A big, gently spoken man, his Edinburgh lilt had taken on occasional continental inflexions. His children, he said, spoke only French (working in catering, he only really saw them at breakfast and on his one hectic day off a week). However, he had kept one link with Britain: a collection – a small one, in fact the smallest possible, but very distinguished – of Aston Martins.

'My father was very interested in cars. When I was a wee boy he always said: "If you have some money one day, buy an Aston." It always stuck in my mind so I bought one – and then I bought two.'

'You turn up at the restaurant in them?' I asked. 'In front of the customers?'

'Petrol's too expensive: but if it were the same price as in Scotland I'd drive them at least twice a week.'

He agreed with me about standards of service. When the closed sign went up in Britain, that was it: in France, there was always a way to get round things.

'They take life a little easier here, perhaps. It's more lively; there's more contact with people.' He reverted to the question of garages. 'Here they still offer to clean the windscreen: I can't think of that happening to me in Britain in the past couple of years or so.'

'See?' I said to Michèle. 'You formidable French lady, you.'

'We have a saying in this country,' said Michèle, 'if my aunt had any, she would be my uncle.'

Michèle was very much like the French gas-lighters mentioned earlier in these pages. She had a certain French elegance, a lot of interesting moving parts, and continually produced sparks. She was a lot prettier than the gas-lighter. It was not that I failed to get on with her, but by nature she was a winkler and I have a tendency to be a winkle, that is, one who is prodded rather than one who prods. Each of us, therefore, slipped into a ready-made relationship, both being used to our opposites, my wife Sally being a winkler too, and Michèle's husband Jean-Claude a quiet and gentle man, though he looks rather like a Napoleonic hussar.

'Violence – that's a typical character of the French,' said Jean-Claude with extreme mildness, over lunch, though the only visible threat of it to date had been when I displaced Michèle's chicken pâté to put my tape-recorder in the middle of the table.

'*Donnez-moi un oeuf,*' said Catherine (the smallest Baudoin, with chestnut plaits and a smile like a ripe melon), plainly apprehensive that the fat stranger would clear the board before the famished eyes of herself and her elder sister, Stephane, shooting up through adolescence under cover of great bangs of long brown hair like a gamin spaniel. Jean-Claude cut the bread, so crisp that it sounded as if it had firecrackers in the crust.

'The French driver, for instance, is terribly violent,' said Jean-Claude, still mildly. I told him I agreed with him. I'd seen a lot of signs of aggression in French: for example, the proper way to speak the language was aggressively, I was convinced.

'The British used to get on my nerves,' said Michèle, 'so calm, so quiet and relaxed – and I knew all the time that deep inside they were not. I'd call them, "you hypocrites!" at that moment. But social relations are more pleasant than with these gesticulating, excited people.'

'That's what I was saying about the French matrons,' I said. 'They always look as if they're going into a shop to have a row about the quality of the goods.'

'What's so particular about that?'

'The British never complain – or many of us don't. I find it very difficult to make a scene.'

'I don't make a scene in public when I go shopping! He's at me again, he's at women again: French ladees terrify him!' said the French ladee. So I changed the subject: a natural winkle should never argue with a natural winkler, any more than a snail should argue with an inquisitive thrush.

MICHELE'S CHICKEN TERRINE RECONSTRUCTED

Take the meat off a chicken, dice it small and leave it to marinate overnight in brandy with herbs, salt and pepper, accompanied by a rather smaller quantity of minced pork meat from the *charcutier*. Next day, hard-boil as many eggs as will stretch from one end of your terrine to the other, and concentrate a tasty stock jelly from veal bones, the chicken carcase, a large onion, carrot, bay leaf, clove of garlic, black peppercorns, white wine and any brandy not absorbed by the meat. Arrange the two meats in layers in the terrine, starting and finishing with chicken and running the hard-boiled eggs through the middle as in veal-and-ham pie. Strain the stock over; cook in a medium oven for 1½ to 2 hours. Let it cool in the oven and – preferably – leave it to stand in the refrigerator for at least two days to allow the flavour to develop.

I learned from the Baudoins that Montargis with its suburb of Châlette-sur-Loing was one of the most cosmopolitan towns in France: the half-hearted flatscape I had come through the night before was Vésine, serving the industrial part of the town with housing for many immigrants – Portuguese, Spanish, Yugoslavs, Turks, Algerians and other North Africans – giving rise to familiar stories of police discrimination, overcrowded housing, and Irish jokes – except that here they were North African jokes making particular play with the immigrants' funny French accents.

The town is an agglomeration, to use the local word, that has lodged itself at an intersection of road and water.

There are 126 bridges in Montargis, houses that tumble their backs down into the stream, and a lake in the town itself so that it is sometimes called 'The Venice of the Gâtinais' in a considerable excess of local optimism. The waterways are the river Loing and its accompanying canal that lead south from the Seine and turn into the Canal de Briare (the Canal d'Orléans, now declassified as a waterway, joining them to the north of the town); the roads are the cross-country route from Orléans, to Sens and Troyes, and the Route Nationale 7, the Parisian's traditional highway to the sun, evocative of holidays and hymned by Charles Trenet.

Even more significant to the town than its liberation from the Germans on 23 August 1944 was its repulsion of the English on 5 September 1427, after a two-month siege, for this feat secured it royal favours resulting in three centuries of prosperity. Though it hardly looks it, the history of Montargis is golden: saffron was grown here, the honey of the Gâtinais is no less famous than its well-flavoured fowls, and there was a gold chain factory in the town.

Montargis passed into royal hands towards the end of the twelfth century and the royal hunting forest still lies across the river to the north-east. In its centre are the sought-after villages of Paucourt and La Pierre du Gros Vilain – a menhir (which I missed – but which was the scene of an incident which gives Montargis something in common with Aberdeen, Edinburgh and Peking – each being famous for a dog).

This one lived in the fourteenth century and is celebrated, like all respectable hounds, for its devotion to its master, a gentleman of the court of Charles V. The Chevalier Aubri was murdered in the forest with no one to see but his dog which watched over his body for three days and nights until hunger drove it from the spot. Returning to the château at dinner-time, it pounced on a courtier called Macaire, bit him, snatched the food from his plate and made off into the forest. The next day, the same thing happened. This, and the sending-out of a search party, is a praiseworthy but fairly run-of-the-mill example of dog-gedness: the hound's moment of glory was yet to come, when some bright legal mind decided to match the hound in trial by combat with Macaire, he being provided with a stick and the dog a refuge in the shape of a barrel. It may have been that Macaire was very poor with sticks, or the dog very good with barrels, but the man lost and – this being an infallible proof of guilt – was peremptorily ex-ecuted. What happened to the dog I have not been able to discover, but most likely it lived out the remainder of its life in luxury, surrounded by the medieval equivalent of doggy chocolate drops. Certainly the worthy animal now has its statue outside the town hall; in fact, so do both participants, since it is in the form of a sort of canine Laocoon, but you are only allowed to cheer on the dog.

That night I met Stuart Cunningham again, this time at work as maître d'hôtel, when Joy, the Baudoins and I all drove south on the N7 to the tiny hamlet of Les Bézards, in which the Auberge des Templiers is by far the most significant object. Entering the rambling alcoves of the restaurant, which showed signs of having been consider-ably extended over the years, was rather like tip-toeing into an ante-room of heaven, in that it held out every pros-pect of an experience that would be better than you deserved. As in heaven, there was a great deal of very white white in the way of draperies of the attendant cherubim, and our spotless tablecloth reached – decently – to the ground. There were no harps (which was excellent, the harp being a most unsatisfactory instrument even on earth) and no other forms of muzak (which was even better); there was a prospect of lawns beyond the windows (which were, of course, French).

We sat spaciously on high-backed velvet benches and when we were settled, Stuart Cunningham – a large pink St Peter in a dinner jacket – turned the key on the best restaurant meal of my life. Earlier, he had told me how, in France, the restaurant business was not a job, but a profession: during that evening, I came to the conclusion that – on that level – it was not a profession either, but an art form, an orchestration of graceful flavours. Medieval theologians used to argue about how many angels you could get on the head of a pin: here the question was how many delicate contrasts could you cause to hop up and down on the tastebuds, like a mouse on an electric typewriter. I felt deliciously out of my class, that I had strayed into a higher gastronomic society.

As the waiters danced in and out, *mousse de foie de volaille, sole colbert* and *canard à la berrichonne* crescendoed to increasingly elaborate accompaniments and the liquid notes of Montrachet and Chinon, the wine of Rabelais; a second movement began with a champagne sorbet, there was a reprise of richness with the cheeses, and the gastronomic symphony came to an end with a pastorale of strawberries. Yet the art of the whole thing was such that – after all this – I felt a little self-indulgent perhaps, but not at all greedy.

After the coffee and Armagnac, and the other guests had gone, we sat into the night with the maître d'hôtel, drinking his champagne. He told me how an English auction house had sent a man over to look at the cellar, some of which had become too valuable to use – customers for wines at more than £100 a bottle being difficult to come by, though I was surprised to learn they were not unheard of. (One bottle had been brought reverently up from the cellar, only to slip out of the waiter's hands on to a stone floor.) But not only rich people came to the restaurant: others would save up for a special meal – it could be the local dustman, said Stuart Cunningham, though in this particular restaurant it had not been. Every so often a group would come and say, 'We have so much to spend: what can you do for us' – having put their money together in *la cagnotte*, the piggy-bank.

We drove back to Montargis in a furious thunderstorm, with rain sluicing past the wipers and steaming off the road in the lights, but against the sensation of well-being im-

parted by the Auberge des Templiers the storm was power-
less to prevail.

Eating my way across France, there had to come a point
when contrasts in national eating flashed before my eyes
and made me ask, 'What on earth is the matter with British
food?' As we drove home from the Auberge des Templiers
in the rain and lightning, the road to Montargis was my
road to Damascus in this respect.

I lay back and thought of England, and the thought was
not edifying. It was particularly of a gracious and human
university town, whose inhabitants should walk barefoot
through the streets in penance for allowing a good number
of their local restaurants to stay in business, if my fairly
frequent experience of eating there in the cheap to middle
range is anything to go by (i.e. paying as much as would
buy an excellent three- or four-course meal with wine in
provincial France).

I recalled one particular restaurant to which I took my
family to lunch. The building occupied a superb site by
the river, but the interior was like a tramp in a white tie –
inappropriate and dirty. Grime-stained magenta walls
wore the cerements of a once-trendy decor, which also
featured old plush cinema seats showing greasy patches of
wear, moth-eaten stuffed animals, and the inevitable
candle in a chianti bottle (with a horrid growth of dirty
wax upon it).

The waiter had never waited before in his life. It was no
great problem that he failed to bring things, since he could
be sent back for them, but someone should have told him
not to put our plates of food on the floor before putting
them on the table, which he did in order to economize on
the effort of climbing a short flight of steps.

The bread basket, a plate of one emaciated slice, was
the accompaniment to a first course of chicken-liver pâté
and vegetable soup. The soup was clear on top, with a
sludge of old cauliflower and worn-out carrots beneath.
The stygian-coloured pâté had a taste like no other I have

ever had, and came from an anatomically interesting chicken whose liver had bones, which were scattered in small splinters throughout.

Three dishes came up from the floor for the second course. The *entrecôte bourgignon* was a shiny, floury, dull gravy (which showed no signs of having been introduced to Moroccan plonk, let alone Burgundy) covering tasteless meat. The roast lamb was frozen slices imperfectly re-heated in Bisto gravy, accompanied by mint sauce tasting like a splodge of grass cutting mixed with vitriol. Pizza (small and frozen) came with the usual accompaniments suitable to a dish of starch: i.e. a potato which magically combined all the unfavourable qualities of boiled, fried and roast potatoes; tired tinned peas, re-heated cauliflower in extremities of nudity and carrots, brothers to the long-drowned fragments in the soup.

There was a tinned pear with a ball of inferior ice-cream that was 'Poire Melba', fermented fruit salad, and instant coffee.

The worthy citizens of that ancient university town sat there and ate it, and so did I. We were all of us either fools fit to eat at a pig-trough, or the most abject cowards. Worse, I had the horrid feeling that some of my fellow guests in that bistro (in Britain, the word may be taken to be a corruption of 'Bisto') had been there before, and returned. As a Frenchman remarked to me: 'The English will do almost anything to avoid making a fuss.' He was right, and we pay a terrible price as a result. Much of our public cuisine is a shame, a sham, an incompetence, a greediness and an exploitation: some of our private cooking is slothful to the point of paralysis, and bog-ignorant. Making a fuss would help, though the disorder is more complex: we have dry rot of the culinary tradition.

The quality of the Auberge des Templiers was understandable and obtainable by reason of a co-operation between staff and guests, both sides having agreed to care about the food, so that any interaction between them tended to raise standards rather than – as commonly in

Britain – depress them. Of course, such splendid restaurants must be irrelevant to most people most of the time, but their example, and that of the great chefs past and present, are not. In France, the aristocratic tradition of cookery, with chefs achieving remarkable refinement and luxury for a privileged class, has ensured that people have something to aspire to. In Britain, the greater importance of the squirearchy meant that cooks would have a less flamboyant career structure, that the higher reaches of the art would be less in demand and that culinary thought would be pragmatic rather than theoretical (we have traditionally had cookery writers who collect recipes, whereas the French have devised systems). Once set, standards are more easily maintained in a framework in which there is some element of formality – as with the long French lunch break – and separate courses rather than food lumped together. It is noteworthy that the best British meals – breakfast and afternoon tea – are both approached by the British in a more ritualistic manner than lunch and dinner.

The difference in state religion mattered, too, I think; Protestantism tending to encourage a democratic plainness. A climate which can often produce better vegetables and – especially – wine must make a difference, as must Britain's relative isolation from the influences of other European countries. The odd curious recipe from the fringes of an empire is not a compensation for the lack of a proper culinary dialogue.

All these are reasons why the British should have a less developed culinary tradition than the French, but that in itself is not a disaster. Good British recipes exist – the cook books are full of them – but in our industrial society they have dropped out of use. British cooking has probably been getting worse since the enclosures and the industrial revolution, with generations of people separated from the land, living on adulterated food in towns. In France, many more people stayed closer to food-production, so that the society has kept in contact with basic quality.

A man who grows carrots must respect a good carrot.

A man who is a peasant, poor, but largely self-sufficient, will respect quality in many foods. No less important, those foods and standards will also be available to other people. The fact that in France you can buy very good quality basics and food sub-assemblies like *charcuterie* – an extension of the peasant's pig-based economy – is their biggest advantage over Britain in the way people generally eat. Every British chef I have ever talked to and a good number of cookery writers I have read have said that British ingredients are as good as any in the world. This is just not true, at least in many areas – and a quick comparison of the taste of the average French chicken, tomato or loaf of bread with the British equivalent will prove it. Variety, too, is much less in Britain – in some of the more far-flung regions, almost unbelievably so. In what British market can you buy two or three kinds of garlic, four or five of onions? In France, food sells on flavour (soft fruit, for instance, is sold and eaten much riper) but in Britain a more commercial system sells appearance, ease of distribution and ability to make a profit out of people who couldn't care less and buy convenience foods where their forefathers bought adulterations.

Locality hardly exists in our mass-distribution system: Cheddar is Irish, Scottish, Dutch, New Zealand, West Country – and frequently a mockery of the fine cheese it should be. Though our hard cheeses are good, and the best of our blues equal or surpass any French, there is no English soft cheese, though Scotland has Caboc: slip-coat is a name in the history books. Modern transport killed off the folk-song and the local cheeses simultaneously – bringing commercial entertainment in and taking the milk out to the big factories. Alas, there was no Cecil Sharp of cheese, to collect prize specimens before they disappeared.

So, except in certain genres as, for example, cakes and puddings, we have a tradition that until recently has tended to encourage things to get worse; though travel, consumerism, interest in self-sufficiency, and a few enlightened caterers and writers make it look as if our goose may not be cooked to a cinder just yet. At home, in particular, a lot of family cooking can be excellent, borrowing recipes and techniques from all over the world. In the generality of public cooking, however, we have a long way to go before we can even get rid of lousy food, let alone remove those tell-tales of an inferiority complex – a prissy concern with garnishes, over-sized portions, mammoth menus (the French system of variations on a set menu served over a limited period is much more sensible).

We do not need the obsessional hierarchy of the French restaurant guides, with suicides if an establishment loses its place: we do need people to demand and complain, and to cultivate a pride in our traditional and local food. We do not need to be the same as the French, good though their cooking is; we have lots of things to keep us happy in our own way.

L'ALLEGRO – Things to throw in French teeth on the principle that we must have something worth eating that they don't. Probably by John Milton.

> Hence, loathed Instant Coffee!
> Avaunt, ye digit of the scaly tribe!
> Such suit not my inside:
> I've had enough.
> Junk food is junk: fingers are better lickin'
> Than patent chicken;
> Burger me no more burgers that lie dead
> In wrapped-up bread;
> And, sweaty slivers of sliced ham – sog off!
>
> But come, thou goddess *Kedgeree*
> And sing our national food with me,
> Our British dishes with the art
> To glad the gut, and cheer the heart:

Praise we now the grub that's good
(For instance, STEAK AND KIDNEY PUD).

Other sorts of PUD that please
Are SUMMER, YORKSHIRE, BREAD, and PEASE;
QUAKING PUDDING gently wobbles,
Giving all the collygobbles –
And th'Eldorado of the PUD
STEAMS golden 'neath the CUSTARD flood.
(E'en humble CRUMBLE has its place
For such as these have formed our race.)
Eve's curious sin in Paradise
Means that we now eat APPLE PIES:
With crust and CREAM and clove and lemon
They're each an Eden, never venom'd.
(Though this will make another song –
Quite likely, formidably long,
How Satan helped the human family,
By introducing COX and BRAMLEY.)

BREAKFAST! What heroes have you made
With BACON and with MARMALADE?
With eggs that spatter as they fry
And blame their cook with yellow eye;
With KIPPERS poaching in their jug,
And eggs that, boiling, go *glug-glug*.
ARBROATH SMOKIES, FINNAN HADDIE,
BLOATERS toughen up a laddie;
While boys from Aberdeen to Norwich
Grow stout and stoic eating PORAGE.

Never doth the Frankish eye
Glance upon STARGAZEY PIE,
Nor find relief, when life gets nasty,
In an initialled CORNISH PASTY:
No French chef did ever pluck
The feathers from a SAVOURY DUCK,
Yet modest Britishers are braggart

Singing the praises of the FAGGOT.
Rustic HAGGIS, IRISH STEW,
NORFOLK DUMPLINGS, HOT POT too,
RAREBIT rarely touched with ale,
CAERPHILLY CHEESE and WENSLEYDALE,
CHEDDAR, STILTON, DERBY, LEICESTER,
VINNEY's legend from Dorchester,
CHESHIRE blue and CHESHIRE white,
BUTTIES to cheer th'unsleeping night,
BUBBLE AND SQUEAK, TOAD, SHEPHERD'S PIE,
SALT BEEF, CURRY that makes you cry,
PORK PIE, HAM in PARSLEY SAUCE,
ONION STUFFING (with SAGE, of course),
COCK-A-LEEKIE, BEEF IN ALE,
BITTER, STOUT, and INDIA PALE,
Suave and smoky SINGLE MALT,
MACKEREL SMOKED and YORK HAM salt,
MULLIGATAWNY soup, SHRIMP TEAS,
TIZER, CABOC, ORKNEY CHEESE,
ELVERS, pies of VEAL AND HAM,
RUNNER BEANS and BRAMBLE JAM,
CUMBERLAND SAUSAGE, CHRISTMAS PUD,
MINCE PIES – all of them are good.

(Also in Britain, the country bristles
With people crazy about RISSOLES.)
In simple tastes this honest land's
Virtues – and its pleasures – stand:
Happy the lass that homeward trips
Towards TWO SAUSAGE, EGG and CHIPS;
Lucky the lad whose blushing bride
Loves COD with WALLY on the side.
(Such things all youthful lusts entice
With vinegar for added spice.)

True, subtle is the mayonnaise,
But SALAD CREAM too, has its days,
For everything that's really tart
Goes straightaway to the British heart –

Not subtle p'raps, and rather strange,
But causing a substantial range
Of feelings (that begin with tickles
And end in agonies) – from PICKLES:
INDIAN CHUTNEYS by adoption,
ONIONS a more usual option;
ENGLISH MUSTARD, sour RED CABBAGE
Ride o'er the tongue with rape and ravage:
MINT SAUCE (a one-and-only treat)
Leaves you no need to taste the meat;
WALNUTS black as bogs of hell,
They sourly twist the tongue as well,
Jelly of CRAB, jelly of ROWAN
One makes you grin, the other groan.
(The same effect occurs, of course,
With too much BROWN or WORCESTERSHIRE
sauce.)

Haste thee, nymph, and bring with thee
That decent matron, British TEA:
Bring SPONGES, FRUITCAKES without number,
That Queen of Sandwiches, CUCUMBER,
Buns of CHELSEA, buns of BATH,
DRIPPING TOAST upon the hearth,
BUTTERED TOAST with ANCHOVY,
ECCLES CAKES and BANBURY,
ROCK CAKES, LARDY CAKE and SCONES,
BARMBRACK, SHORTBREAD, HOT CROSS BUNS,
CRUMPETS, TEACAKES, WHOLE-MEAL BREAD,
PARKIN, men of GINGERBREAD,
Then – to stop baby getting restive
A pound of CHOCOLATE DIGESTIVES.
Note: ne'er distressed, what'er may hap
Is he who owns a BRANDYSNAP.

For, innocent, the British tongue
Keeps its delights forever young:
Sugared taste the tongue seduces,
Maketh flow the gastric juices:

Dull is the wife who is not quick
To seize upon the SPOTTED DICK;
Never maid so chaste and holy,
She rejects a ROLY POLY.
When TIPSY CAKE and SHERRY TRIFLE
Make her swain feel bright and blitheful;
For no seducer has the art
Of words more sweet than TREACLE TART.

These are the things that shall enhance
Our Fame, and not be found in France:
These are the foods the British can
Boast, softly, they have given Man.

CHAPTER 6

A Sancerre Enthusiasm

THE TENTH DAY

I left the Baudoins waving at their art nouveau gate and
cycled through the grey, still town, bearing an important
international communication between the youngest
Baudoin of Montargis and the youngest Vernon of
Muswell Hill: a pink envelope addressed very carefully in
a large round hand, and confided to me at the instant of
departure. The grass was wet from the storm of the night
before, but it was a warm morning so that a smell of mint
distilled from the verge of the harmless-looking hayfield
labelled 'Vipères' at which I turned off the main road,
heading for wine country by way of St-Firmin-des-Vignes.
The evening I arrived in Montargis, I had come upon the
first vineyard of my trip – no more than a patch, not to be
compared with my destination, Sancerre, sixty miles away
on the Loire.

Grasshoppers whirred away like tiny machines by the
side of the road (brought out by the rain, I wondered, like
the smell of mint?); there was an eternal cooing of wood
pigeons. I passed a field of onions in flower, as if an
impi were about to spring from the soil armed with knob-
kerries. There was no menhir to avoid along this road,
but there were some Gallo-Roman ruins just before
Montbouy, so I missed those instead.

Whereas a garden is like a poem in that it can afford
to hit out at you with concentrated sensations, landscape
is like a book – it flows, it is a journey of diffused
incident, and its quality is the sum of its impressions.
The view from the bridge at Montbouy is one of the

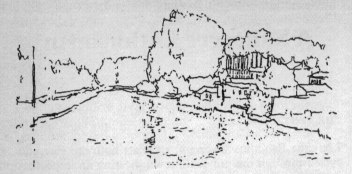

most striking examples I know of the perfection of the
unremarkable – a sleepy, pretty, untidy village snoozing in
harmony with itself. It was the sort of place Toad's
friend Ratty might have returned to if he had not been so
thoroughly English. Nothing was striking: everything was
essence of village. Canal and river came together here, with
a double bridge over them. The canal had a no-nonsense
hair-do of pollarded trees as if it saw its moral character
as threatened by a situation of dangerous fluidity and
was resolved to turn itself into a street, while the river
wandered like a drunken grandmother, waving golden
waterlilies in its stream and rambling off through a
tussocky meadow, half-rush, half-hayfield, past a rickety
little wooden wash-house with a lichened tile roof that
looked far from steady and was leaning further and further
into the water.

At one end of the bridge, a warm grey church, with
rather more buttresses than seemed reasonable, aspired to
a dumpy steeple. There were stone houses with old red
roofs and geraniums at the windows running motley
gardens down to the river. One had an unattended fishing
rod stuck out over the back wall: it looked as if it had
been leaning there every day for years for something to
do, but was not really expecting anything to occur in the
way of fish. Downstream, a high clump of trees made clear

shadows in the water, and a line of poplars crossed the horizon, as regular as harp-strings. There was silence and stillness apart from a small rush of white water from a canal sluice coming into the river: two small boys came shrieking and panting across the bridge in a bicycle race. Then there was silence and stillness again: a sun shower made patterns round the waterlilies.

At the town of Châtillon-Coligny, the main road crosses back over the canal again, but on Michèle's instructions, I kept to the east to Dammarie-sur-Loing, so that I could see the village where she was born. Dammarie showed little sign of having participated in such a momentous event: there was not even a winkle stall. Over the crossroads, past a dilapidated church with a rusty clockface was a rise which brought me up on to the side of a gentle valley, with green declining to the canal like a tufted lawn, and darker patches of trees. It started to rain – the road was wet already – there was a faint boom of thunder and as the valley went misty at the edges I sheltered from the shower for ten minutes in a nettley wood. That was the only rain that fell on me while cycling during the entire month's trip. I carried my cape almost 1000 miles for nothing: in fact, later I calculated that my energy expenditure on needless precautions against rain amounted to 5,272,745.2 foot lbs., which just goes to show that you can be too careful (though not if you aren't): however, doubtless it would have worked out less in the metric system.

At Rogny, a village either clustered round its church on the hillside, or spread out along the canal like a watery coaching-town, the Loing went in one direction, the canal in another – with seven locks to help it on its way – and I went off between them. It was afternoon now, and I had fallen victim to the great hazard of French cycling: thinking that, when you get to one town, you will be at the next in time to buy lunch before the shops shut. But fleecy clouds and sun came out, over a road which kept leaving the open fields for patches of woodland – in one of which, distant, but clear in a dapple of sun, I thought I saw a wild-cat. It was certainly a cat, and certainly ran like a wild beast when it saw me coming. Would that the midges I kept having to wipe out of my eyes had done the same. The country became more and more like England except that among the few houses of my second Dammarie of the day – Dammarie-en-Puisaye – I came unexpectedly on a splendid medieval castle or fortified farm with twin round towers with roofs like chinamen's hats at its gate and crumbling walls tree-shaded at the back. There were small fields with hedges, and a range of hills in the distance beyond the church spire of Bonny-sur-Loire.

Down I came to the great river of France. I was very unimpressed the first time I saw it, until I discovered that the dirty ditch I was rumbling over was in fact part of the flood-prevention system, which now depends as much on channelling off excess water as attempting to keep it within bounds: though the twentieth century has been quiet, the Loire has drowned a good many tens-of-thousands in its time. To get to this great sprawling yokel of a river, you must first cross a swamp-land of ditches, then spreading beaches, and at last there is the stream itself, a psycho-path of a river with all its currents twisted up underneath and just a hypocritical ripple on the surface: tearing at its islands and sandbanks, even in the blue of a summer day.

With all the whirlpools, quicksands, floods, and the moving silt from the tributaries, they gave up navigating this mighty, but unpredictable river and built instead a parallel canal for the barges – the Canal Latéral à la Loire – at the end of the last century. I found that everything ran more or less parallel with the river: the main road invisible and inaudible on the far side; the deserted road on mine; the canal and the towpath.

'Take the towpath,' Joy had said, that morning. 'The man in the local tourist office recommends it.'

Perhaps he meant some other bit. Or recommended it for a horse. Or a Sherman tank. The surroundings were beautiful, even the deserted road out of sight: the towpath was a grassy bank, and that was the trouble. Bicycle wheels do not travel well through even medium-length grass, and the only alternative to that was a double rut which something motorized had been along when the ground was soft. There was no chance of looking at anything else but the rut when – if your wheel wandered from it – a thousand mini-octopuses hiding in the grass immediately reached up to pull you down. It was like being an inexperienced tight-rope walker with DTs, except that there was a constant decision-making process to keep track of as well: which of the ruts was the smoother, what patches of crevasse ahead necessitated evasive action and a quick career across the octupuses? This added to the sensations of being a drunken tight-rope walker the problems of executive stress.

A full-breasted black barge appeared ahead, driven by a pinafored lady of considerable draught herself. She kept her bicycle in the cabin and her washing on the foremast (unless it was a new system of signalling): a domestic mariner afloat but only just, a compromise between Admiral Lord Nelson and Mrs Beeton. We eyed each other, the fat lady and I: alone on the canal we were obviously going to have a relationship (albeit briefly, on account of the fact that we were going opposite directions). We approached each other. We exchanged smiles. We each moistened the lips and adjusted the larynx preparatory to engaging in intercourse. They were simple things we had to say to each other (I think): eternal verities about the complex meteorology of our planet and its psychological effects upon the inhabitants, philosophical speculations upon the destinies of man and woman who – following the same path – may yet travel in different directions. (I had in mind something along the lines of '*Il fait beau maintenant*' followed up with the quick riposte '*Où allez-vous?*') Unfortunately, at that moment, I became aware of a stinging on the backs of my legs. Looking down, I discovered myself to be on the outskirts of a pile of sand dumped on the towpath.

Flag Communication for Barge Admirals.

.... I have a television set ...

I have starched my bra ...

I invite you to come aboard ......

I am not inviting.

Put a sock in it!

I have independent suspenders inside my waders.

A beret is a very good saucepan lid, but you have to wash it out afterwards

I bent to gear-changing and evasive manoeuvres. By the time I looked up again, the barge was yards downriver and a beautiful relationship had ended before it began. Then I ran into a pile of dredgings and the chain came off. It was probably that experience, as much as the old manure heap through which I had to ride shortly afterwards, that decided me to return to the road at Belleville-sur-Loire. I went up five gears immediately.

It was only slightly less rural since at that point the canal and road began to run side by side. Sometimes I would see a figure in a garden of one of the scattering of little houses and smallholdings; very occasionally a car hooted behind me to warn me it was coming past (among French drivers, a sign of helpfulness rather than aggression); or a barge would pass, its honking exhaust seeming totally disconnected from the smoothness of its passage.

Once, near Boulleret, there was the elaborate slate roof of a château, with its more humbly red-tiled barns clustered round; once, the surprise of a rainbow darting up over the meadows from a far-off sprinkling of white buildings across the river. An angler at the lock where I stopped to rest told me it was Cosne, once famous for its iron-work – including ships' cannon – which went by water downstream to the Atlantic coast until river transport declined in the 1870s. The angler seemed to be sitting there as much for the society of the lock-keeper and his family as anything: he caught nothing, though occasionally a fish would rise somewhere else. None of us thought it really necessary to do anything or say much. The evening sun was undemanding gold, and it took the buzz of a car going past to remind me that dinner was waiting elsewhere.

There was a pleasant rhythm of gentle weariness that comes with cycling at the end of the day – along the edge of a wood, past shadowy poplars by the water at St-Satur, and then the contours of a molehill-shaped mountain trespassed down the water's edge. There on the very top (where the moles were sticking their noses out and pretending to be houses) was Sancerre. At that point in the day, the long steep climb round the molehill was a bit hard. I arrived puffing, blowing, red-faced and steaming, to the amusement of a young mopedalist at the top.

THE ELEVENTH DAY

Among the more celebrated scions of Sancerre are a Constable of medieval France; a Napoleonic general (Maréchal MacDonald, whose father was one of the group of Scots who settled in the town after the Jacobite rebellions); and a scientist, E. H. Amagat – 'universally known', as the town guide-book told me in a spirit of some optimism, 'for his work on fluid statics'. Doubtless inspired by his example, those of enquiring mind flock to Sancerre to conduct their own experiments, which are usually performed with the apparatus of an *appellation contrôlée* bottle of the local wine, a corkscrew and a glass (ideally tulip-shaped, to concentrate the bouquet). The common conclusion of these natural scientists is that the level in a bottle of Sancerre, once opened, is anything but static, though it is often necessary to verify this result by conducting a control experiment with a second bottle. So I did.

The rain was back next morning, misting the panorama of vine-slopes, dripping from the trees that stand between the Hôtel des Remparts and the edge of the view. It was not a morning for bikes but it was good for sounds, with the drip-drip and a twittering of rain-resistant birds in front, a drain gurgling over to the left and on the other side the occasional car grinding up the hill and rounding the bend at the top with a swish of wet tyres. In sound snap-shots, as in photography, you have to take your opportunities, even though at any moment I was expecting the man from the tourist office. I was just recording the drain with one hand and trying to keep the drips off the microphones with the other (apart from being bad for them, a drop of rain can produce a noise rather like the sound of the obliteration of the City of London by a meteorite of strawberry jam) when the mayor arrived. He had never seen anybody recording a drain before, but he took it in his stride.

'*Ah, oui, le vélo est la,*' said the mayor, who had obviously been tipped off that I was coming. 'You'll have to do the Tour de France next year. Came up the hill, did you? 350 metres up and look at that!' He waved a lean brown hand at the view: 'You can't see a thing. The only panoramas round here are the cellars. Yes, the *caves* are a possibility today – you might say recommended.' M. Laporte smiled for a moment, and his face relapsed. He had an aristocratic dome to his forehead that gave him a certain gravity and, it was whispered to me, it was only

months since his wife had died, so his natural good humour would surface in a gentle melancholy and then go under again.

We made up a party to view the panoramas in the *caves*. There was M. Fabre from the Syndicat d'Initiative, the office for the promotion of local business and tourism that is invaluable in every French town; M. Farrugia who, having been a consul in North Africa, spoke English and had come along to translate in tones almost as piping as the birds I had been trying to record, for he was somewhat shrunk into the Sixth Age of Man; me, and M. Laporte, who turned out to be President of the Wine Growers of Sancerre as well as Mayor of St-Satur, lying at the foot of the hill within a spectacular curve of the railway viaduct.

St-Satur was also the scene of a particularly frightful atrocity by the English in 1420, when the local colony of Augustinian monks were tortured and burnt alive or tied up in sacks and thrown into the river in pursuit of an outrageous ransom. The monks looked prosperous because they had almost completed a fine Gothic church, but it was not a sign of wealth as much as their entire capital turned into stone for the greater glory of God, so there was nothing to pay a ransom with anyway. To this day the church is out of proportion, for what few monks did escape never managed to gather either the resources or the heart to add the church tower.

We approached the *caves* by way of an educational and titillating visit to the vineyards, bumping along a rutty track through rows of dwarfish vines planted with mathematical precision in fields of stones in which soil was scarcely visible. The vines are grown low – no higher than a tomato plant – to take maximum advantage of the heat reflected from the ground. The slopes folded away into the mist, which was shivery in T-shirt and shorts; the green of the vines was dulled and quickly faded into grey. With the white stones, the landscape was almost monochrome. At that stage of the year, the grapes were clusters of green lead shot: it was hard to imagine they would ever produce red wine – for there is red, and even a little *rosé*, Sancerre as well as the more famous white, and the grapes before me were Pinot Noir. Indeed, most Sancerre has been red throughout the history of the vineyards, which are recorded as far back as AD 583 and – since Pliny mentions the wines of the Loire – very likely go back centuries before that, though there is no need to go to the lengths of the bishop who declared in his sermon on the miracle at Cana: 'The water that was turned to wine was, without doubt, turned to Sancerre – and I defy anyone to prove otherwise!' The Sauvignon grape which now predominates almost five to one only replaced the red variety after phylloxera laid waste the French vineyards towards the end of the last century. There is very little that threatens the vine apart from wet weather leading to mildew or dropping of the flowers, and frost (which flows easily off the same slopes that open the vines to the sun: in Pouilly, across the river, the land is flatter, and frost a greater danger); so it was all the more shattering when phylloxera arrived from America like a vinicultural Black Death. At home on the roots, the *phylloxera vastatrix* is a grape-louse less than a millimetre long, yellowish brown with a long snout and little red eyes, an aphid sucking the sap from roots or leaves according to the stage of its life cycle and capable of increasing to 25 million in one summer from a single parthenogenic female. There is a rhyme on the Loire:

> On parle des assassins,
> Des voleurs et des coquins,
> Mais le plus grand scélérat
> C'est le phylloxera.

This biggest rogue of all was the second gift from the state of Colorado to the rest of the world, the first being the famous potato beetle. Fortunately, there was a third: disease-resistant American vines on to which French varieties could be grafted. So the Sauvignon grape took over, for in the soil of Sancerre it is capable of greater finesse – though it was not until the coming of mechanization in the years after the Second War that the big expansion of the vineyards began. M. Laporte told me that production had tripled in twenty years, with a quarter of the wine going to Britain: he himself was among the biggest of the *vignerons*, with 18 hectares of land (about 44 acres). Most of the Sancerre wine-growers have about four or five hectares split up into small plots scattered over the slopes – indeed, over different villages – for the French laws of inheritance tend to the continual division of property. The list of *vignerons* reveals an extraordinary tangle of family names spread over the different communes, boding ill for the chances of any outsider with a yen to buy himself into what seemed to me an unobtrusively profitable business. Indeed, I was told that if ever a vineyard did come up for sale, it was always bought by the other *vignerons*. I counted only 215 different surnames in the 600-strong list of people who own the Sancerre vineyards – producing between 6 and 7½ million bottles a year.

Looking out over the countryside, I could see nothing to indicate where one of the area's 8000 plots ended and another began. Every vine seemed to be the standard 1·25 metres from its neighbour, every row the standard

1·3 metres from the next. It was not until I talked to Pascal Gitton that I began to have some idea of how different the results might be. Pascal – who had travelled widely in his studies of wine-making, so that he spoke English with a Californian accent – was bearded and friendly, the son of Marcel Gitton, who was sinewy with having worked the vineyards from the age of nine.

They lived at Ménétréol, to the south of Sancerre, in a long old house with the neighbour's goats and chickens fussing in the nearby barns, and ancient cellars which had once served 100 acres of vines, until wine-making ceased with the First War. The cellars lay unused for almost half a century: it was not until another world war had come and gone that Marcel Gitton started putting the barrels back. He began with half an acre of vines and multiplied it a hundredfold – but not through any compromise of the quality produced by traditional methods. The Gittons have no modern wine-press into which you can dump a whole day's pick by fifty harvesters, press the button and forget about it. Instead, they have a brand new, old-fashioned press, a wooden monster with a great screw in its middle twisted by capstan bars. Taking delivery of it in 1978 caused the same sort of sensation locally that you might find in Grimsby if a trawlerman ordered a paddle-steamer.

'With old presses, the must is very clear,' Pascal told me. 'With a modern press, it makes like mushed grapes and people are tempted to press quicker. We do the opposite, because the wine is better, I think. But it takes so long: often in the harvest we finish at 2.30 in the morning, and start again at half-past six.'

The grape juice runs from the press into a V-shaped concrete chamber beneath the floor, and is left for a few hours to deposit any rubbish in the bottom of the V before being run into barrels where it spends most of its life, only being put into stainless steel tanks for bottling anything from eight to ten months later.

Meanwhile, there is pruning in late autumn: winter, as always on the land, is the time for repairs and preparations, cutting vine stakes and so on: with March comes more pruning and the start of care of the vines, tractor work and spraying against mildew (anything up to nine or ten times a year according to the weather). Bottling starts in June and goes on to September with some 112,000 bottles to fill in combination with other work; the *vendange* is a month's work in the fields for twenty-five people, for on this holding the numbers that can be hired are limited by the capacity of the press. They may end the *vendange* as late as mid-November, for the Gittons are always the last ones to harvest. Then it all begins again. 'Wine is a living thing,' said Pascal, 'and you have to follow its life all the year round.'

Lackadaisical ways born of over-confidence in the French reputation for wine-making are not for the Gittons, who now also have a small vineyard across the river producing Pouilly Fumé, so called after the smoky bloom on the Sauvignon grape, and whose meticulousness has made them pre-eminent among Sancerre *vignerons*. Their grapes are not thrown into a large wheeled tub, the *bain de vendange*, and left to squash all day in the sun. They harvest in small trays. They never use chemical fertilizers: 'They are like a whip to the fields – too much in one go,' said Pascal. 'Vines like to be in not too rich a soil – to make good wine, you don't need much vine. We've only fertilized twice in nineteen years.'

The Gittons bottle much later than many other growers, who may start in January. The Gittons begin in June in time to end just before the harvest, so that the wine stays as long as possible in bulk in the barrel. A side advantage of this is that, afterwards, they can simply wash their barrels out, put a quart of wine back in the bottom, and leave them ready for the new vintage within a few weeks: there is none of the burning sulphur inside to keep them sweet which would otherwise be needed. Their wine is the perfection of a natural and traditional process, the only ingredients being the grapes and the wild yeast that blooms them.

'These are old cellars,' said Pascal, as we walked along the side of the farmyard containing the neighbour's goats (good neighbours – cellars and goats – since the local goat cheese *crottin* is considered to go particularly well with white Sancerre). 'Four hundred years ago they built them better than they do now. In a modern cellar, you have to top up the barrels all the time because of evaporation. Not here; the humidity is balanced – unless you drink too much out of a barrel, like we're going to do now.'

M. Farrugia and I shared a little frisson of excitement: this was what we had been waiting for. The cellars were a consistory of great black barrels ranged along the walls like a very neatly kept mausoleum of abbots, an arched cata- comb of wine, living but lying in state. The cellar had obviously been built barrel-size: there was one row on one wall, one on the other; a couple back to back in the middle and space to walk between.

Our steps echoed among the arches: I felt I ought to have a cowl, and long sleeves in which to hide my hands.

'It takes a month to rack the wine when the cellar is full,' said Pascal. 'With stainless steel, of course, *soutirage* would take two days. We don't use pumps – just jugs: there are 117 barrels here, 30 at that end, 800 bottles in each.'

I began to feel that I was in the presence of someone who was either a great artist or a commercial masochist.

'But isn't it an awful job to sterilize them?' I was thinking of the horrible infections that are apt to overspread my own Château Muswell, and the constant chemical warfare waged with campden tablets.

'Sterilize? What for?'

'But in England, when we make wine –'

From somewhere in the depths of the cellar came a discreet but tremendous chuckle, as if a gout of gas had just been released somewhere at the bottom of a barrel. I abandoned the subject.

There was a weak electric light that cast shadows in the corners. Out of them came a black monk which, as it came closer, turned out to be Marcel Gitton bearing a tray of glasses and a twinkling pipette. We approached a fat black barrel and removed the wooden bung on its midriff (to approving noises from the direction of M. Laporte to the effect that plastic bungs were not the same). In went the pipette and into the light rose a straw-coloured ichor, sparkling as if a small portion of summer had got trapped inside. There was a reverent hush, a gentle trickling as the pipette moved over glass to glass, a little subdued clearing of throats ... Then the silence was broken by the most tremendous sucking noises, as if one of us were concealing a stirrup pump about his person. It was Marcel Gitton tasting, sucking the air through the wine as one might call a cat; swooping the glass back and forth beneath his nose with a critical but content expression on his countenance.

'I'd just as soon smell my wine as taste it,' said Marcel Gitton proudly.

'*La couleur est typique – ni blanc, ni jaune,*' from somebody else.

'We don't blend,' Pascal told me. 'This is a wine from a chalky soil. Ninety-five per cent of the vineyards in Sancerre are on chalk.'

A fragrance came out of the glass. It was surprisingly difficult to imitate the sucking noises, which seemed to be the correct thing to do, and which now echoed through the shadows like a relay race running round the cellar in soggy shoes. The wine tasted fresh, provocative, obviously of considerable class. I was apprehensive lest I should be expected to spit it out. Where? But looking round, nobody else was: I was glad, it would have been sacrilege.

'The chalky soil's got more nose, it's a bit shorter in the mouth – we call it a feminine wine. That was a ten-year-old vineyard looking west.'

Before I knew it we had advanced to a second barrel and I had to swig the remains of my glass in a hurry.

'Now this is from twenty-year-old vines facing east. But this too is chalky soil. Les Montachins is our best chalky soil wine: in the archives at Bourges, they talk about this very vineyard since 1490. You'll see the taste is real different.'

I felt honoured, but apprehensive, since when I make my wines, the principal preoccupation with regard to age is the shelf-life of grape concentrate. They don't say how old the vines are on that, and they usually forget to mention the soil. Even when it comes to buying the ready-made bottle, I felt myself unaccustomed to distinguishing between east and west-facing plonk. So, it was a revelation. As he said, the taste was 'real different': not better or worse, but different.

More sucking occurred: the vital thing, as far as I could see, was to build up a negative pressure in the mouth and start the intake before allowing the lips to part slightly, so that you did not dribble.

'Les Belles Dames is our best flinty soil wine – grown on the slopes of Ménétréol, where it's so flinty you can't see the ground.'

That again was different: all were delightful. I was really getting the hang of rolling the booze round the tongue like a connoisseur.

'I prefer the Montachins,' said Pascal. 'The flinty soil is longer in the mouth, but not so smelly. Of course we have all types of chalk . . .'

We moved on through the gloom, acolytes of ever-increasing devotion, with a fine sense of mysticism coming upon us – slurping as if we were all kissing each other.

The drizzle had stopped as we drove towards M. Laporte's establishment – not his winery, since we had just seen one of them, but his *cave de dégustation*. This tasting establishment, the Caves de la Cresle at St-Satur, was a combination of Swiss chalet and warehouse, built alongside a large car park, making it a kind of high-class drive-in wine-bar. I am generally nervous of such places, which are common along the highways in wine-producing areas, for they seem to offer only two alternatives: go in, taste, and risk assault from an infuriated *vigneron* if you say you don't like it; or go in, taste, and come out staggering under a couple of crates of bottles. On this occasion I had no apprehensions: I went *in* staggering.

M. Farrugia, M. Fabre and I fetched up against the bar. M. Laporte stepped behind it as if he had been a prince of the blood playing at bar-tenders. He went to the refrigerator.

'*Ce n'est pas un réfrigérateur*,' M. Laporte said severely. '*C'est une glacière: il ne faut pas casser le vin.*'

'It breaks itself if it goes into a refrigerator,' piped M. Farrugia, who was becoming chatty. M. Laporte drew out one bottle after another and ranged them before us.

'*Voilà*,' said M. Laporte with dignity: '*Voilà la richesse des vignobles français.*' It might not have been quite all the *richesse*, but it looked as if it might well be most of it. There was a musical glugging noise followed by the reverberant sucking.

'The taste of stone,' explained M. Laporte. 'We have travelled less than eight kilometres from Ménétréol and already the taste is not the same. Here is another from three kilometres further on.'

The conversation took on a quality of ritual intonation, voices rising and falling like plainsong in praise of bottles, and M. Laporte's gold medals.

'The great white wines are of the North,' said M. Laporte, sonorously. 'Wines of the Midi are strong, full-bodied, of the sun, but they do not have our vivacity. Our wine must not be too strong, 12° or 12·5°: if it is 14°, it is no longer Sancerre. Nor must there be too much of it: wine has more character in a low-yield year, fruity, dry.'

'It is most fruited,' said M. Farrugia, cheerfully.

The great enemy of the vineyards of Sancerre is hail which is one reason why the *vigneron* is glad to have his land in widely separated parcels. They know when to harvest because the grapes' acidity stops falling and the

sugar content ceases to rise. Then the race is to gather
the grapes at their peak, and the hope that it will not
rain, for then the water that clings to them dilutes the
must.

The voices rose and fell: we held communion with a
bottle of Clos de la Terre des Anges, and pronounced it
angelic.

'This wine is not fruited,' said M. Farrugia of whatever
it was he held in his hand at the time. 'When you eat to
the fish, it is fat.'

'*Les fruités avec un poisson qui est maigre*,' explained M.
Fabre.

'*Un poisson gras – non fruité*,' agreed M. Laporte.

'This wine is not fruited – requires fat fish,' said M.
Farrugia, with the air of one who has said it all before. We
rolled our palates to the car, and drove to see Roland
Fleuriet at Verdigny.

Like M. Laporte, who had two sons at work (and a
third temporarily tied up in military service) as well as
nine workmen for his 18 hectares and shipping business,
M. Fleuriet's was an *entreprise familiale*. Unaccountably,
we seemed to have got behind schedule, and committed the
cardinal discourtesy of dragging him from his lunch.
He had a farmyard, with hens scratching in the ruts and
roosting in the barn on the leggy tractor that rides high over
the vines. It all looked as if the most the farm would ever
produce in the way of beverage was a glass of warm
milk – but there in the barns was a modern bottling
plant, a brand new wine-press looking like a gigantic green
fish-and-chip fryer, shining steel vats and oak barrels
almost big enough to walk into.

'Diogène,' said M. Farrugia, 'Diogène lived in a barrel.
Happy man.'

M. Fleuriet, small, brown and sinewy like Marcel
Gitton, set up another demonstration of the equation:

$$\frac{\text{(Wine from here)}}{\text{(Wine from there)}} = \frac{\text{(these tastes)}^2}{\text{(those tastes)}^2} = (????)^{16}$$

I began a conversation with M. Fleuriet in an attempt to discover whether vineyards had been made everywhere possible, or whether they ever broke new ground, and my trusty tape machine captured it all for posterity.

'*Mais, mais ... er ... mais,*' said I, breaking into the conversation: '*er ... au centre du limitation on trouve ... er ... er on trouve pas ...?*'

'*Meilleur?*' asked M. Fleuriet, helpfully.

'*Non, non,*' I said, eleven times (I cannot think what had got into me): '*Er ... er ... non ... mais ... au ... au ... centre du ...*'

'*Au centre des vignobles?*'

'*On trouve peut-être les champs qui n'ont pas les vignes ... er ... mais,*' (three times).

'*Peut-être vous avez raison.*'

'*Mais,*' (twice) '*je voudrais savoir si ...*'

'*C'est totale,*' said M. Fleuriet, in answer to heaven knows what.

'*... si c'est possible de créer nouveau vignoble, ou si tous les champs sont employés,*' triumphantly.

'*Non,*' said M. Fleuriet.

'*Tres fruité,*' said M. Farrugia, who was becoming increasingly bilingual. 'Fleuriet wine good for *poisson*, not fat.'

I gave up talking and just listened. M. Fleuriet told me that when he started everything was done by hand. He was just coming to the end of bottling, he said. Forty-five thousand bottles had gone out, three-quarters to individuals, one quarter to Parisian restaurants, and only 6000 remained. He took me to see them, stacked head to tail against the walls, without racks – *tête-bêche* he called it – and made his bottler go mumpety-clickety for me so that I could have a sound effect.

Fleuriet *fils* told me he was happy at the prospect of following in his father's footsteps. 'It is a much respected job,' he said.

'It is perpetual – from generation to generation – and if a man dies and has no children we all club together to buy a little piece of the land,' added M. Fleuriet. 'To be a *vigneron*, it is a religion: but the *vigneron* is happy, because he is free.'

M. Farrugia became poetic, and a trifle daring. 'When we talk of wine,' he said, 'it is like the words we use when we see a woman. "*Il y a de la robe*": it has on a nice garment. "*Il est plein*".' (He left that untranslated.) '"*Longue en bouche*": there is a word called "long in the mouth".'

'Ah,' I said, 'in England we have an expression "long in the tooth", but that's different.'

We went to lunch and M. Laporte brought the wine, offering with his touch of gravity a light red that was nevertheless mellow and confident – and a delicious white which may or may not have been fruity but certainly went well with the crayfish, shellfish vol-au-vent and fish steaks with sorrel sauce or hollandaise served by the Hôtel des Remparts to us all at a large, jocular table. The chef-proprietor, M. Decreuse, then brought on coq au vin – marinaded for four days, cooked with the blood, and *un vrai coq* (which was most important).

'Talking of importance,' I said to M. Fabre, 'which is the most important in a meal – the food or the wine?'

'You ask me a question very difficult for a Frenchman

to answer,' replied M. Fabre. 'There are two functions of wine – the first to add taste to a sauce – you must always use a good wine, or you spoil the dish whether you are using it as *vin de sauce* or *vin d'arrosage*' (spraying it on as they do in Dijon to *andouillettes*): 'and the second is as a *boisson* – when you eat, you can't drink lemonade or Coca-Cola, you'll ruin everything. You must suit it to the dish.'

'Sancerre stands up well to *daurade*,' said M. Farrugia. *Daurade*, it turned out, was carp, though whether fat or thin remained unspecified. We went on to *crottin*, the local goat cheese, eaten fresh – almost as soft as yoghurt – with chopped shallot, parsley, salt and pepper.

After lunch, M. Decreuse came and sat with us, and insisted we take a glass of his plum liqueur in which the plums were macerated all winter. He was a little man, M. Decreuse, with sleepy eyes, so that it was rather like sitting at the tea table in *Alice in Wonderland*. It was not until 4.45 that I made my warm farewells, and took unathletically to my bicycle. To this day, Sancerre above all is the wine whose taste brings back memories of my trip: there may be other greater, but none fresher, none more fragrant, none that so roll out the landscape of France inside the head as they roll out the taste of summer upon the tongue. Best of all, I now have an infallible method of judging sea-food: you simply ask a passing connoisseur whether a fruité or non-fruité wine would be best with it. From his answer you may distinguish immediately whether you are in the presence of a fat or thin fish, a distinction with which I had previously found it difficult to cope.

WHAT TO DO WITH YOUR BOTTLE OF SANCERRE, ACCORDING TO THE LOCALS

1. LE TREMPE – cut-up bread, soaked in Sancerre (white or red), sweetened and served chilled.

2. LE TREMPE BOUILLI – cut-up toast soaked for two hours in sweetened red Sancerre and served hot.

3. STOMACHE ACHE. In the case of *la grippe*, the Sancerrois are supposed to take a medicinal draught of wine, mulled and sugared, though they are probably the only people prepared to do this with Sancerre.

ACCORDING TO ME

1. Why not just drink it?

It was fortunate that the road led downwards. I paused for a moment because, when it is clear – and there was sun now in a blue and white sky with the rain-clouds disappearing on the far side of the Loire – the view from Sancerre is not one to abandon without a thought. Then I swooped down – all the more swooping for the lunch – on the land that folded below like a bath chap that had somehow managed to get itself covered with woods and fields instead of breadcrumbs. Descending at first through houses, then among the ranks of vines, whose established rows were bouffant with green, the new planting sparse and twiggy, I came through the pretty village of St-Bouize (could it be, I wondered, a corruption of St Boozy?), and the plane-shaded little town of Herry.

I took once more the long, samey road by the long,

samey canal, a pleasant monotony in the pale gold sun that, at the tiny la Chappelle-Montlinard, poured upon an immense field of sunflowers. They were too big to add to the bulging wild-flower collection in my dictionary, but wild sweet peas of a peculiarly vivid puce grow all along the canal, and there were vetches flowering in pink and a dark blue that struck the eye as a triangle strikes the ear. The road was dead flat with humps leading up to bridges over the canal – up for a bridge, down again and speed on, up for a bridge, down for a bridge and speed on. I passed a fine golden teddy-bear lying on his back by the roadside with his legs in the air, waiting for his friends to come and set him upright again: I reflected that, having partaken of Sancerre hospitality, I knew just how he felt.

The shadows lengthened, the fish began to rise, people came out and sat before their houses. In one tiny village there were flags up – for the next day was the Fourteenth of July – and the villagers were gathered at a few trestle tables by the canal with playing cards, glasses and music from a radio. At another place, the village children were being dragooned through celebratory games in the village square by a man with a megaphone. Shortly after Marseille-les-Aubigny, an inland port where English cabin-cruisers like the ones on the Norfolk Broads ride high on the canal as the road sinks below it, I turned off through Cours-les-Barres and Givry, to trundle across the Loire once more on to a road that got bigger and bigger until I found myself riding on a cycle track through a subtopian flatscape surrounding an old city, just as the light was going. I was almost 400 miles from London.

THE TWELFTH DAY

There are three celebrated examples of purity in Nevers. The first is Saint Bernadette of Lourdes who spent the last dozen years of her life in the convent of St Gildard and was buried there in 1879, only to be exhumed no less than three times and discovered to be – if not exactly as fresh as the proverbial daisy – at least in remarkably good condition considering the circumstances. Decently attired in black habit and only the thinnest layer of cosmetic wax, she now lies in state in the convent chapel in a golden casket with glass sides, looking rather like a monochrome Snow White.

Coming a poor second to Bernadette in terms of holiness is Vert-Vert, a parrot. The religious equivalent of a regimental mascot, this sagacious bird is said to have lived in the convent during the eighteenth century, where it learned to pronounce on so many points of doctrine that its fame spread to the monks of Nantes who asked to borrow it, though for what purpose it is difficult to imagine. Unfortunately, Vert-Vert went by water and, sailors being what they are, picked up so much bawdy that by the time he got to the end of the Loire he was so foul-beaked he had to be shut up alone for fear of currupting the brethren. He died, in solitary confinement, of indigestion – or so the story goes.

The other conspicuous example of regional purity was grazing over the tussocks of the meadow in front of the hotel when I woke early the next morning – white Charolais cattle, whose parchment skin and compact, though substantial, shape makes them quite unlike the galumphing, udder-swinging milch cow I usually expect to see chewing over the gate. Perhaps a lot of its charm comes from it being the colour of milk, which is appropriate for a cow. Many virtues are claimed for the Charolais, notably that of exceptionally rapid growth. Although the breed is now to be found all over the place, and in the first instance came from Burgundy, it belongs to this part of the country by adoption as the result of the success of Claude Mathieu, a late eighteenth-century stock-breeder who came to live in the Nivernais. The herd is kept at Nevers, and from the steak I had enjoyed the night before, it seemed that standards were being maintained. Good beef is a local speciality, along with nougatines, a round honey-flavoured sweet originally created in honour of the Empress Eugénie.

I have always wanted to know how the French occupy themselves on the Fourteenth of July since we have nothing equivalent, having chosen to ignore St George's Day. Dancing in the streets I understood to be obligatory, but surely they could hardly do that non-stop for twelve hours? When Joy got up, which was – as it tends to be with Joy – later rather than earlier, I learned that the celebrations had already started, and that I had been part of them.

About the time when I had been rumbling over the Loire, somewhat delayed by lunch, a group of anxious people had gathered with champagne bottles in their hands at the local Syndicat d'Initiative, waiting to celebrate my arrival, before leading me on to a *Sonnerie de Cloches*, a *Prise d'Armes*, some *Salves d'Artillerie* and a *Defile Militaire* in front of the Ducal Palace followed by a *Retraite aux Flambeaux*. Since I had not arrived, they had put the champagne aside until the morning and gone on with the rest. I said I had heard a sort of grumpling bonging noise as I came into the city, with a superimposed clank. Yes, said Joy, that was the *Sonnerie de Cloches*, and the clank the *carillon*. It had been due to clank again to an accompaniment of artillery at eight o'clock that morning: had I heard it? No? And the other thing I'd missed was the Great Nocturnal Cycle Race. Good, I said. Never mind, said Joy, there's another one this afternoon.

The Syndicat d'Initiative of Nevers is rather efficient, I thought, as I listened to the speech of welcome being delivered to me by its President, Jean-Paul Harris (or 'Arreece', as the name had become since his paternal ancestor settled in France): for to open up an office building and set up a champagne reception for thirty people on a Bank Holiday morning at less than ten hours' notice was impressive. But this part of the country can hardly fail to be competent and lavish, having had so much in the way of wealth and aristocratic connections for centuries. Nevers is solid history, solid France – which was one reason why Alain Resnais and Marguerite Duras used it to typify their country in the film *Hiroshima Mon Amour*.

It lies not very far from the centre-point of France, at a cross-roads and at the junction of two great rivers; it has its roots deep in the soil, its bourgeoisie was famous for its manufactures (it was the iron-making capital of France in the nineteenth century), and its aristocracy as aristocratic as one could wish – members of the houses of Bourbon, Burgundy and Cleves. A leading French revolutionary, Chaumette, came from Nevers; it was a military centre for Julius Caesar, for the Americans in the First World War and for the Germans in the Second – suffering heavy bombing by allied forces as a result. Its motley cathedral is a collage of French architectural styles; the eleventh-century Eglise St Etienne combines a touch of the lush living of Burgundy with the severity of the poorer lands to the south – the Auvergne.

Nothing could be more thoroughly French than Nevers, no place could be more fitting for a foreigner to pass the Fourteenth of July in – even if the presentation plate which M. Harris put into my hands owed its origin to Italy. In Nevers, you can buy pottery ornamented with oriental delicacy after Persian and Chinese models; you can find plates such as mine in the popular style, bearing coats of arms or symbols of the Revolution; or there are scenes from classical Italy. The techniques of glazing earthenware at a very high temperature came to Nevers as the result of the marriage of the heiress of Cleves with Ludovic of the family of the Gonzagas, Dukes of Mantua. Not only did Nevers gain the techniques of *faience* from the Italian craftsmen he brought with him, it has a chapel in pure Italian baroque, Ste Marie.

Nevers has one more claim to celebrity: some sort of boot is named after it. (So it said in the town guide-book, but close inspection of the footwear of the inhabitants during the course of the afternoon failed to reveal any characteristic pattern – and, indeed, hardly any boots at all.)

The first thing the inhabitants of Nevers did to celebrate the storming of the Bastille in 1789 was to have the military parade I had missed the night before. It had been somewhat thinly attended, I gathered, by a preponderance of elderly people of conservative tendency, and there was a substantial feeling in the town that it was not an appropriate form of celebration, ought not to have been re-introduced that year, and ought not to be tried again.

The French have a great leaning towards formalized structure in their public enjoyments: that is to say, they all want to be the one who tells everyone else what to do. In the afternoon, there was the cycle race arranged by the shopkeepers and businessmen of the Rue de la 14 Juillet. Round and round the block went the cyclists – with a little one superbly equipped, intensely serious, and very, very last at the back. Their gears buzzed like paper bees and every time the little one came round the crowd cheered and a group of youths chanted something which sounded like *'Allez, bouillon!'* but was probably something else.

But there were two really lucky people at this cycle race, and neither of them were on bicycles. They were the man who was the one to drive furiously round the course in a little old Renault, skidding round the bends and hooting imperiously at every corner; and the man who shouted at everyone else over the public address system. Frenchmen really love this (I have never heard a Frenchwoman do it) and they do it very well, as if they have been practising showing off all their lives.

But on the bandstand in the park the Batterie et Philharmonie Municipales were modesty itself. The park was thronged with comfortable families of comfortable people, many of whom seemed to have to move only a short distance between the chat with one acquaintance and the chat with the next, and to take even those few steps at a leisurely pace. It was as if there were concealed patches of glue in the grass: promenaders would suddenly stop dead, and stand contentedly observing the others, listening to the music that drifted down the hill from the bandstand, which was like all bandstands in the world – i.e. the sort of construction you might expect if you asked a professional erector of pergolas and garden fences in Wigan to design you a Chinese pagoda. In the same way, performers and performance evinced a quality of compromise.

The Batterie and the Philharmonie were divided into two camps, front and back, the front being concerned mainly with noises of a vaguely continuous character, the back being devoted to bangs. Since there was less to do at

the back, time hung heavy on the music stands of the
Batterie, the more so because most of them were teenagers
in apprehension of being considered traitors to their kind
by any of their hip contemporaries who might have happened to be passing. A blonde to the left of the bass
drum with no visible instrument herself (though possibly
she had a triangle concealed about her person) was
demonstrating her independence by sucking a cigarette and
causing chaos in the back row by her demands on the
attentions of two attendant admirers. An unkind fate, or
possibly the conductor, had positioned a third admirer at
the far end of the row, from which he darted sultry and
menacing glances at the happy trio. Most of the Batterie
seemed to be suffering from that muscular affliction of the
young which makes it impossible to stand equally upon two
legs, and were transferring their weight from side to side in
a spasmodic series of lurches.

In front of the younger generation, the Philharmonie
soared phlegmatically into a heaven of popular overtures,
like a squadron of air-borne dromedaries under instruction. Thick necks were sweating into shirt collars under
the strain of the twiddly bits: in their blue suits and sun-
glasses the players looked intensely serious. Middle-aged
fingers hopped heavily among the intricacies of the Boëhm
system of fingering: ageing embouchures shaped themselves stiffly to interminable introductions, and when they
got to a march or an oompah bit with a good tune, all
of them showed their delight by frisking solidly over it
with the enthusiasm of lambs who are lying about their
age. After every number, the crowds broke off their conversations for a ripple of respectable applause. It might not
have been considered a rock-star's ovation, but all of us in
the park felt that when the Batterie et Philharmonie de
Nevers had mounted its bandstand, a peg had been put into
the universe to hold our little piece of creation together;
that being what they were, where they were, was in-
dubitably right – from the rather fast blonde to the rather
slow tuba, to the conductor swaying like a dreaming

dervish, half-way between his soul and the fact that they were coming up to bar 29, where the clarinet always got the F sharp wrong. Such people inherit the earth, and a little bit more.

That night I met another kind of music, after the *Grand Feu d'Artifice sur les sables de la Loire*: that is to say, by the centipede of a bridge that stretches its many arches across the river. Fireworks are differently institutionalized in France, being geared much more to public display, and the principal private initiative was the throwing of firecrackers among the crowd. In Britain, fireworks start in the back garden, with sparklers, a brief shower of golden rain, a catherine wheel that gets stuck and a couple of tiddly rockets. At the other end of the scale, there is the big municipal display in which the crowd is kept so far back that it is practically on the horizon.

The French are not as over-protective towards their citizens as we are – an attitude which must result in a great deal less self-righteous busy-bodying, a good deal less dispensable legislation, rather more self-reliance and probably very few extra casualties. They have developed the intimate municipal display to a fine art, with fireworks that, to the foreigner, seem gratifyingly dangerous from the number of bangs (great use seems to be made of maroons), though they are probably perfectly safe, but are much more fun because you are closer to them. As usual, there are plum jobs for people who want to run around self-importantly with a glowing taper. Not being institutionalized to a single night of the year, fireworks are taken more casually and hence, I suspect, are less of a disappointment and perhaps less of a treat. The great difference between a British crowd and the one along the Quai des Mariniers was that the French one didn't say 'oooh' at the rockets like we do. They clapped, they even cheered a little, but that child-like sound did not escape from them.

As the fireworks felt different, so did the fair – a roundabout and a couple of vans set up on the gravel walk across the road. Where British fairs have an air of gaudiness and dirty paintwork about them, the neat vans that travel from village fête to village fête in France have a formica quality of regimented enjoyment, though the shooting galleries – which are full of crack shots in this land of *la chasse* and compulsory military service – necessarily have a familiar shot-to-pieces feel to them. For the toddlers who had survived the *course en sac, course à l'oeuf, enveloppes surprises, course à la brouette* (wheel-barrow race) and the greasy pole (*mât de cocagne*) in the afternoon, there was the standard enjoyment of such fairs. A screaming roundabout of police cars, spaceships, racing cars, motor-bikes and boats, turned sedately in a frenzy of hooting and flashing lights – tots with glowing faces parodying a grimly adult dimension, a mixture of Donald Duck and sudden death, with a supervisory proprietress automatically bobbing a large ball with a tassel over the infant heads (if you catch it you get a free ride). You find such a device all over France: I call it 'The Machine for Teaching French Children to Drive'.

Nobody was doing much driving after the fireworks, with the cars nose to tail among the pedestrians up towards the park for the *Bal Populaire Gratuit*. At last, I thought, dancing in the streets (or almost). But when I got there, there was a band with very loud amplifiers on a dais and a large gentleman in spectacles swaying and sweating over his accordion. A very thick crowd milled around: a pressure-group of local youth perched on the bandstand barracking for rock music, and on the available tarmac gyrated a seething mass of dancers into which it was impossible to penetrate.

I was just setting about recording the barracking when a hand tugged at my sleeve. Whirling round somewhat guiltily – for there was music in the background, and musicians and friends of musicians are apt to be, quite rightly, obstreperous with people waving microphones near their performances (though I have heard of a man who goes to the opera in a wheel chair with microphones in the arm-rests to overcome this problem) – I recognized a press photographer from the reception that morning. This press photographer delivered a long and complicated sentence extremely fast, ending with the word 'photo'.

'*Volontiers*,' I said, to the word 'photo'.

In an instant, I found myself taken round to the back of the platform and dragged into the spotlights between the musicians, who looked surprised but went on playing. The crowd looked curious, but went on dancing. The photographer motioned to me to hold out my microphone to the man with the accordion: he had obviously decided that a picture of two fat men was better than one and that I should pretend to be interviewing the *chef d'orchestre* in the middle of his concert (which, for all I know, may indeed be customary among French broadcasters). There was a pause of inexplicability as we faced each other. I could not explain, the accordionist was busy with a complicated succession of arpeggios, but he eyed me, all the same. The photographer shouted something. 'Bravo,' called someone in the crowd. The man with the accordion nodded. Photographs took place with our expressions fixed in a rictus of professional delight, staring into each other's eyes like lovers with a conversation that we could not have. I'm sure the people in the crowd must have been saying: 'I know the fat one on the right, but who's the fat one on the left?' Nobody answered them. Then it was over.

'*Merci*,' said the photographer.

'*Merci beaucoup*,' said I. The man with the accordion bowed his head politely and went on with his arpeggios. I stumbled from the platform to a brief catcall, stage right, from the bandstand.

'You were very good,' said Joy.

At the next number, the bandstand faction got their way and the singer came on.

'Why is he singing in Turkish?' I said to Joy.

'He's not,' said Joy.

SINGING IN THE ENGLISH

The following words of a young singer from Nevers were transcribed from my tape: it has not proved possible to trace their precise meaning, but it is clear that the folk-process has been at work upon a mid-Atlantic original.

I wanna know, I wanna know, wanna nohnar,
I won a noh, won a noh, won a nohnar,
Ar ah ar ha ar ah ar ah – aahh,
A whalean ate you,
So I throw my guts on your tibbles.

CHAPTER 7

Rich Borders

THE THIRTEENTH DAY

The celebrations had left no debris behind them the next morning, though it was after ten when I set off, so there would have been time to clear it up: there was one solitary bottle in the gutter by the Machine for Teaching French Children to Drive, and that was all. From the far side of the many-arched bridge, I looked back at the straight-up-and-down houses on the river with their random graph of slate roofs and the tower of the cathedral peaking behind. In the morning sun, it all looked as clean and detached as a painting of riverside houses.

Then I followed the main road south to the turn-off to Bourges, which takes you across the Allier, a livelier river than the Loire, so that salmon traditionally reject the upper reaches of the great river for the faster currents of its tributary. Here, on the way to the rusty iron suspension bridge over the Allier, I returned to the Canal Latéral again, but a canal subtly different – somehow more rural with the frivolity of a twist or two in it to relieve the long straight stretches with only the bridges and the flowery lock-keepers' houses to break the monotony. Indeed, the canal has every excuse for skittishness, having had to go up and down stairs to get over the Allier and its associated wilderness of sand and willow, which it crosses on an aqueduct with three locks at either end. I came by them at Le Guétin: they were each one as massive as the mouth of Moloch, with silhouettes of children scampering along the railings against silver clouds, watching the boats come through.

Shortly after, I turned south once more, by a corner restaurant with nut-brown shutters and a smell of onions and french beans coming from the kitchen window, taking the wooded road that coasts the river until Apremont-sur-Allier, where a butter-coloured château on the hill-top commands both road and water. From the distance, it appears as an elegant mansion, all style and windows but, closer to, you see old walls and medieval towers: five now remain from the fourteen of the English fortress that was conquered by Louis XI at the end of the Hundred Years' War. There is a local legend that a cannonball fired by Joan of Arc is lodged in the walls – and only a few points of circumstantial evidence suggest that it is not true, viz: that Joan was probably somewhere else at the time; that metal cannonballs had not then been invented, nor had the Great Tower been built either.

Apremont was a revelation: at any moment I expected Richard Tauber to fling back the shutters and let loose on a top C to an innkeeper's daughter in a tight-laced bodice below. The verges were neatly mown, the street lamps were lanterns hung from conscientiously curly wrought-iron gibbets; the geraniumed houses were of the same golden stone as the château, with tall red roofs of old tiles, high chimneys and odd little towers and dormers. It all looked far too charming and far too authentic to be true, as if it had been built, with some refinement, for the tourist trade, but they had forgotten to put in a ticket kiosk.

I was about two-thirds of the way through this medieval Welwyn Garden City when I came upon the ticket kiosk. It lived in a medieval souvenir shop with the now familiar high-tiled roof and swallows under the eaves, who seemed undisturbed by the thunderings of the ticket machine, which were infrequent at the time, since it was coming up to Sunday lunch. There was one French family trying to decide between the delights of the Musée de Calèches and the Parc Floral, though the cost of both together was very reasonable by French standards, since admission prices – like fairs – tend to be high. They seemed to be sure about the Coach Museum but the Parc Floral had them worried: 'What was it, what could they expect from it?' Madame was asking, eyeing the ticket machine rather as Joan of Arc is said to have eyed the butter-coloured château. She seemed to be implying that it was not at all the sort of thing a patriotic French matron was used to. Nor was it: Parc Floral is what M. Gilles de Brissac calls his English garden, an interesting combination of personal enthusiasm and sales technique more easily associated with a hard-up British stately home than with a prosperous estate on the banks of the Allier.

The family made up their minds, paid their money, and went clickety-click inside. The friendly lad behind the counter said he hardly spoke English well enough for the BBC – sometimes he did the ticket machine, sometimes he did the gardening, and he preferred gardening – but he would phone M. Gilles who would explain all.

I lounged in the quiet of the hot midday: the martins twittered under the eaves; hardly anything went past to disturb the dust on the sunny road outside; sometimes there would be the click of the ticket machine as visitors went in, occasionally a scrunching of gravel as they came out. Among them were two comfortable women with husbands in flat hats, as if they had come from some French equivalent of Coventry: their wives were exploring the souvenirs – plates decorated with herbs, fruit, flowers and improving mottos; seeds, cushions, bangles, aprons, and generally a better class of dispensables than you find in England. Meanwhile, the husbands advanced on my bicycle and me, which aroused their interest and curiosity, respectively. They were most impressed by the gears, they said, which must surely indicate an intention to travel up the North Face of the Eiger, or something similar. I had come from London, I was going to the Mediterranean? – *Formidable!* I must have a souvenir of this encounter and one of them took out his wallet and from it a postcard of the longest bicycle I have ever seen. We parted with effusive international goodwill. They could not stop, they said: they had to have lunch, and then they were going fishing, as soon as they could dump their wives. They bundled up the comfortable ladies and drove away.

Gilles de Brissac came down from his butter-coloured château in an old Renault 4 which looked as if it had been actively involved in the construction of the garden – which had taken seven years, M. Gilles told me (no one on the estate ever calls him M. de Brissac or M. le Comte). A slight, spare man with bone-china English, he wore jeans, a check shirt, a gardener's tan and an air of aristocratic competence.

The story of Apremont is not the one we usually hear in Britain – of the stately home trying to make ends meet by exploiting tourism: the estate was viable in itself, I learned from M. Gilles. His aim was to give the local society back some life – which, like many another part of the countryside, it was in danger of losing – and to put to some use what M. Gilles found around him. The coaches in the museum for instance were not a special collection. They were simply almost two centuries of family transport left to moulder in the barns, from the Marquis de Saint-Sauveur's dog cart to the carriage which used to trundle to Paris with two gendarmes sitting on the box on behalf of Eugène Schneider, iron-master of Le Creusot, to bring back the wages in hidden compartments. (Le Creusot lies some 100 km to the west: the Schneider industrial dynasty built it up to the greatest iron town in France during the course of the last century.) When M. Gilles decided to add a toy collection to the museum, he simply opened a cupboard and pulled out the boxes which the Grand-Duchess Vladimir brought as a present from St Petersburg just before the First War – dolls of Edward VII, his friends and entourage grouse-shooting; M. Fallières, then President of the French Republic, out with a gun after rabbits. M. Gilles comes at the end of a long line of acquisitors: his library, for instance, contains 40,000 books.

But the thing that cried out loudest to be made some use

of was the village itself, and the making of a show-garden was in a family tradition of embellishment dating back eighty years – to the day when Eugène Schneider, third of his dynasty, married into the incredibly well-connected family of aristocrats who had passed down Apremont in the female line since 1722 (despite the cutting-short of one of M. Gilles' ancestors during the French Revolution). The family centred their lives on Paris, which was traditionally rather more of an attraction to the French aristocrats than London was to the British, and would come to Apremont perhaps for two months in the summer. M. Gilles became the first of his family to live in the château all the time. But it irked his grand-father, who was very keen on architecture, to see beautiful country, a beautiful château, a beautiful river and some beautiful fifteenth-century houses in the village. He wanted nothing but beautiful fifteenth-century houses – a theatre set *à la berrichon*, the local style. So one by one he bought up all the buildings that disturbed his ensemble, pulled them down, and built new fifteenth-century houses in their place, using the same butter-coloured stone as had been dug locally for generations and sent off down-river in flat-bottomed boats to build religious establish-ments at Orléans and St-Benoît-sur-Loire, among other things.

So, given the extent of the re-modelling that had already taken place (and it is not to be thought that steel-magnate's Berrichon has anything at all in common with stock-broker's Tudor, for it is most splendidly done), there was really nothing surprising in M. Gilles bringing in the bulldozers to dam a valley into a series of ponds, importing trees weighing up to three and four tons apiece, and turning old quarry land and cow-pasture into lawns, gravel walks, rose-beds, herbaceous borders, and a garden for each season of the year.

'Very logical: France is the country of Descartes,' said M. Gilles, 'but you see the influence of Sissinghurst, Sheffield Park, Hidcote in the Cotswolds – all those

famous gardens.' He still remembered, he said, the first
time he went to Sissinghurst – he could put a date to
it, July 6, and a time – it was coming on towards
evening – when he first saw the White Garden. 'It was a
shock: I had never dreamed that anything could be so
subtle.' Now there is a white garden at Apremont, offering
its own delicate homage to the original. As that is English,
so are the herbaceous borders, so are a majority of the
names in the garden's plant catalogue that are not simply
Latin; so is the rock garden and waterfall, for which 650
tons of stone had to be imported even though it is on the
site of an old quarry – for the quarry was worked out.

What M. Gilles began in 1971 was something quite new
in France, where gardening has been a great formality at
the top end of the social scale, and flowers and vegetables
in rows at the other. But his work, which took six years
in its first stage, was luckily timed since it coincided with
an upsurge of enthusiasm for gardening and nature in
general, sometimes even extending to an act strange to the
traditional French character – walking on the grass.

'It is always forbidden, but I wanted to prove that it is
quite possible after all,' said M. Gilles. 'Everybody told me
I was quite mad, that the garden would be ruined. But if
you put notices all over the place – "You mustn't pick
flowers", "Keep off the grass", "You mustn't pull the
branches off the trees" – it gives exactly that idea to the
people. The very fact of nothing being forbidden makes
the public more respectful.'

It certainly seemed to be true of his visitors of the
day before; the garden had not been tidied after them –
as I saw, there was no need. Though he might be
engaging in the tourist trade with rather more elegance and
refinement than some of his peers across the Channel,
nevertheless, since he had a show-garden, a coach museum,
a souvenir shop and a two-coach-load size self-service
cafeteria, I wondered whether he had any plans to open
the château itself to the public.

M. Gilles replied that it would be very difficult; he would

have to clear all his knick-knacks away. 'I think this is the only case of a castle in this region of France which is not open to the public. But I am living in it: if you have a mass of people visiting the house it would be less personal. I know quite well the Duke and Duchess of Bedford, and I've been at Woburn to spend some weekends there. I must say, it was dreadful. At five to two, we all had to leave the dining-room and rush up to our rooms: people came pouring through all those drawing-rooms, and we had to go somewhere else. It's not really very pleasant when you live in a place.'

As I cycled away below the butter-coloured château, I reflected that peaceful lunchtimes are more than coronets, a bicycle more than Norman blood.

HOW THE GARDEN GROWS: THE PLANTS AT APREMONT

M. Gilles gave me a list of his cherished plants before I could tell him that I was only a flower gardener. From my wife, Sally, I understand that this is a vulgar taste, and that proper gardeners who go round talking Latin at each other are more for leaves, barks and similar constructional elements. So I gave her the list and asked her to pick out anything she thought particularly interesting to British gardeners, though, since it is an English garden, it is by definition made up of things we know already.

TREES

There seems to be a fine collection, including many especially good for autumn colour: obviously, they will get more impressive as this baby garden grows up. They include:

Coniferous Trees such as Ginkgo, Taxodium, Cryptomeria, Metasequoia, Sequoia.

Broad-leaved Trees such as Liriodendron, Nyssa, Liquid-ambar, Pterocarya, Cercidiphyllum, Parrotia, Amelanchier, Cercis, *Pyrus salicifolia* 'pendula'; and many flowering fruit trees.

SHRUBS AND CLIMBERS

The collection includes lots of different roses (*Rosa filipes* 'Kiftsgate', *moyesii, rubrifolia* among them) though some of the interesting French names probably hide varieties known to us by different titles.

Shrubs (apart from roses) include interesting varieties of Caragana, Ceratostigma, Buddleia, Hibiscus, Hydrangea, Kolkwitzia, Viburnum, Romneya, Ceanothus, Camellia and Paeonia.

Climbers include the lovely Campsis.

HERBACEOUS PLANTS

These include various species of Convolvulus, Euphorbia, Primula, Phlox, Lychnix, Geum, Heuchera, Artemisia, Liatris, Lithospermum, Helianthemum.

OTHER

Bulbs (which the French call *oignons à fleur*) include Lilium and Fritillaria and lots of daffodils and tulips.

The Water Garden includes the Sacred Lotus.

It was a hot afternoon of birdsong and the officious buzz of blowflies. The road still took me along the course of the Allier with its tufted willows and sprawling sandbanks but moved away from the river itself, and the next water I saw was at Lorbat, where waterlily lakes lie below as the road winds up through woodland. Just before Lorbat there was a *parc animalier* listed at Château de St-Augustin but I had seen enough of tourist attractions for one day – and a very fat adder lying asleep in the road a few miles beyond Apremont at Neuvy-le-Barrois had temporarily sated my desire for close acquaintance with wild-life, it having been rather a narrow road and rather a long snake. I knew they didn't bite you unless you irritated them, but nobody had ever told me whether they considered wheels an irritation, or whether they were capable of running after bicycles (and if so, how fast and how far). But the creature stayed asleep, like the rest of the countryside, except the flies – which are the price you pay for cycling among livestock, for as well as the adder there were the Charolais and, shortly afterwards, sheep.

It is hobbit country here with some farmhouses that are not too small but none that is too large: the landscape *bocage*, small rough pastures and little woods (except that I crossed the forest of Bagnolet, through long straight canyons of green, the feathery line of blue between the tree tops becoming even thinner in the far perspective of the avenue). After the forest, the land became fit for planting, and there were crops again (I had made my way up from river level to a modest plateau) but the most famous growth from this soil was a crop of kings. Not half-a-dozen miles away was Bourbon-l'Archambault, a surprisingly small town considering its family connections, which extend not only to the great dukes who were rivals to the French crown and a bastion against the English, nor just to the branch of the family that took over the monarchy in later centuries, but right back to a minor deity.

Today Bourbon-l'Archambault has two principal tourist resources: the white shell of the castle that stands above the lake with its towers only moderately nibbled by time and a red-roofed cottage nestling under its walls; and hot springs which attract such of the sick as are convinced of the importance of such things as the equilibrium of the thermal micro-climate as related to the co-efficient of the electrical field of the air. The original inhabitants, who were less scientific than we are today, and had never even thought of making *un profil bio-électro-climatique* of the area, were credulous enough to attribute the springs to the underground workings of Borvo, protector of springs and god of subterranean fire. Hence Bourbon-l'Archambault, and the name of the kings of France, who may thus be allowed the claim of being in line of descent from a warm puddle.

Like any self-respecting and expansive puddle, this one watered the surrounding territory, so now that the Bourbons are gone you come upon the traces of magnificence among the fields. At Moulins, some twelve miles away across the river on the other side of a centipedal bridge, there is reason to expect magnificence since it was the capital of the Bourbonnais (as it is now the county-town of the Allier Department) and, for a time at least, the court of what is today not a great deal more than a market town outshone any other in the land, and has left behind one of the greatest altar-paintings in France for us to remember it by: Le Triptyque du Maître de Moulins, very colourful, very precise and very devout in the sacristy of the four-spired cathedral.

It seems, however, that the Bourbons did not belong to Bourbon-l'Archambault, but took their name from it after they had conquered its fortress and dispossessed the Vicomtes de Bourges who had got there first. Aimand is the first of whom we know anything, and what we know is that he lived at the beginning of the tenth century and had estates a little to the south in what is now Châtel-de-Neuvre and the little town of Souvigny, lying midway between Bourbon-l'Archambault and Moulins.

It was to Souvigny that I went in the expectation of putting up at the Auberge des Tilleuls, a pretty little hotel-restaurant of pretensions looking out over a lime-tree garden, but the chef, who was taking the afternoon sun on the bench outside, said he was full up with a marriage and redirected me to the Hôtel de la Poste. The old part of Souvigny (which is most of it) lies on the side of a steep hill with a quiet main road running along the bottom of the escarpment. I was just preparing to go bouncing down the cobbles when I was suddenly aware of an excess of architecture – a long building with giant-economy pillars and an over-size gateway which looked as if the architect had been left with a quantity of stone and a small corps of ornamental masons on his hands, and had had to find something to do with them. Behind that, much older, plainer and a deal more impressive were the twin towers and Gothic front of a church which seemed to have stopped short of becoming a cathedral only because it might have been a shade pretentious to call a town of just over two thousand a city.

The Cluniac monks who built the priory church of St Denis des Bourbons seem to have had a taste for substantial churches, having begun with one in Cluny, the home of their order in Burgundy, which remained the largest ecclesiastical building in Europe until the construction of St Peter's in Rome. Churches were a particularly good investment for them since they were an order of Benedictines who were characterized by almost non-stop religious services. Scarcely had they founded their order than the first of the Bourbons gave them land in Souvigny, and the fortunes of the efficient, highly organized Cluniacs and the competent, ambitious Bourbons thereafter followed parallel paths to success until the fifteenth century when the dukes chose this priory church as their family resting-place.

There I found them in a soaring Gothic nave, as tall and cool as the trees in the Forêt de Bagnolet; that is to say, I found part of them, for during the French Revolution a good number of royal heads were cut off the effigies here, just as the living ones tumbled on the guillotine, and the effigies of Charles I and his wife Agnes, lying in state on their slab of speckled marble, have both lost a nose. Discounting the relics of St Odilon and St Mayeul, which live in painted wooden cupboards in the walls – for these particular saints were simply two great

Cluniac abbots and venerating them is rather like venerating successful businessmen – I found three surprises in the priory church: a fine twelfth-century calendar of the months of the year with grotesque little figures such as we know from the Luttrell Psalter (and which surely must represent what many people actually looked like in those times of unchecked disease and poor food); a tablet to an unexpectedly recent Bourbon: '*Ici repose son altesse royale le prince SIXTE DE BOURBON 1886–1934*'; and a charming hotchpotch of a monastery garden beyond the cloisters, which was not as grand as Apremont will be one day, but there was the peace of centuries about it.

THE FOURTEENTH DAY

The Hôtel de la Poste was an opening through the formal façade of a small shopping street into the back-door panorama of Souvigny. One of the cheapest hotels of the trip, it seemed at first no more than a cavernous bar among the shops with the obligatory espresso machine glinting at the back like a cross between the Golden Calf and Robbie the Robot, and the local young men looking only slightly less bored than usual by reason of being in a place where they were supposed to enjoy themselves.

To get to the rooms you negotiated a long, dark passage or went round by an arched gateway into a little gravel courtyard where there was a cage of cooing doves, and a growling boxer in the garden next door who was perpetually irritated by them. Then you climbed a little open-air staircase twisting up the wall with geraniums growing all over it, and there was a room with a wrought-iron balcony and a view over an expanse of back gardens – with flowers and vegetables planted in rows, just as M. Gilles had said French gardens traditionally were. There were asters and dahlias, and from the direction of the priory came a not entirely sonorous, but exceedingly atmospheric bell, striking the hour twice. (This is extremely convenient for the sound recordist, who otherwise tends to always miss the first note, so that when he gets back home to his studio he has to copy an extra one out of the middle, cut it out with a razor blade and join it on to the front of the original with sticky tape. By this means, you only need three bells from your clock plus a certain amount of patience, and your finished recording may strike anything you choose until the tape runs out, which is usually about 2000 o'clock.)

I recorded the tinpot clock rather late in the morning, in company with the chambermaid who had come in to do out the room – an excellently co-operative lady who consented to stand stock still, and apparently without breathing, until the last reverberation had died away.

In the bar the pinball machine and even the juke-box were silent: in the yard the doves made contented noises, the boxer prowled furiously next door, the house dog leapt up in its little pen at a chain link fence sparsely covered by roses, with incessant yaps of boredom. Grandma came out to feed the chickens, which lived in a small stone dungeon by the corner of the barn: she had silver hair and a respectable granny's dress of dark blue with little white stars on it. She walked with heavy steps as if she were so close to the earth her feet had become part of it.

It was hotter where I was going, in company with the Mayor of Souvigny, Henri Coque. I had met him the night before, with a Pakistani lorry-driver whom he had brought along to translate. M. Coque was a small farmer in a baggy suit – 'paysan' is how he described himself – with large brown hands that hung out of his rumpled sleeves as if the fingers were waiting to be milked: but there was a natural dignity in his manner, a simplicity, an interest in other people that many a smarter politician might envy (if smarter politicians did envy such things). He was so simple that he was a mayor without political affiliations – which was very unusual, especially in country like the Bourbonnais where, he told me, politics were polarized between the low-paid and unemployed and the wealthy landowners.

Yet he was plainly devoted to the welfare of his commune, and very proud of the local industry.

At a meal at the Auberge des Tilleuls, where they do excellent compote of rabbit and a refined duckling with peaches, I had noticed that the three glasses before me (red, white and a large one for water) were bells of an unusual elegance. I suspect that all over Souvigny, in the humblest backparlour, people drink their *ordinaire* from fine crystal, for there has been a glassworks in the town for three centuries and more.

From the outside, the works looked deserted, a mixture of old and newer buildings with tufts of grass growing in the dusty paths. Inside, it soon became clear that this was no place to work if you did not like heat since the only cool jobs in the place belonged to the women, packing and chattering; to the engravers, whose room sounded like a jungle of angry grasshoppers doing a war-dance; and to the little man in the cellar who spent his life moulding identical clay retorts, lined up in rows like a cross between Russian dolls with a design fault and funeral urns. Nor was it a place to work, I thought, if you were scared by the sight of blood. I saw no bandages, but there were the most horrifying barrow-loads of glittering jaggedness waiting to go back into the furnaces, having failed to reach perfection in their previous existences. The glassworks had an interesting quality of medieval damnation about it: it was a marriage of heaven and hell, with a railway angel operating a kind of celestial shunting engine along a track in the roof to feed the rumbling, revolving cones that mixed the ingredients in one workshop, and in the next a dais of insatiable furnaces, roaring with a bustle of black figures around.

The glass-blowers lived in the dark like demons, crouched over their little pots of flame. To each blower there was an apprentice demon to bring the blob of molten glass like red treacle from the main furnace, heat it up again in the demon's private fire-pot when required and pass the demon the scissors to trim round the base. The making of the glass itself was black magic: the demon blowing through a black tube into a black mould which opened to reveal a fiery goblet to be rolled and trimmed until it cooled sufficiently to be taken off with tongs. In-between times, the apprentice demons ran to and fro bringing cool water from the old tap in the yard in crystal glasses that brought back a flash of daylight brightness with them into the gloom and grime. In the same way, the craftsmanship in this factory illuminated the sleepy country town with a fragile remembrance of the refinement of the Bourbons.

It was noon when I left Souvigny, and the glass-blowers had almost finished their day's work, having begun at five that morning. My road led past the Forêt Dominiale des Prieurés-Moladier – most of the woods around remember the monks in their names, as the architecture remembers them in outbreaks of ornament, after the style they brought from Burgundy. I made good speed trying to out-run the flies (who, however, always seemed to telegraph an alert to others ahead of me) for this was still livestock country, often hedged and quite English-looking. This made it all the more startling to come over a rise and run full tilt into a sight of the fifteenth-century Château de Fourchaud, standing lonely and untenanted in the fields, with barbed wire on its old iron gate to keep out such tourists as might happen along the deserted country road.

It was a tall fortified house with tiny windows and round towers of suede-coloured stone. The high red-tiled roofs and tall chimneys were in perfect repair: it looked as if its men-at-arms had just popped out to fight a quick war, had been kept a little longer than they had anticipated, but would be back shortly. I rode on to St-Pourçain.

St-Pourçain-sur-Sioule is a town that has never quite made it. Though it has a charmingly named tributary, la Bouble, the Sioule does not move quite fast enough to make itself interesting; the church is undeniably large, but a rag-bag of any style you fancy from the eleventh century on: great quantities of V.D.Q.S. wine flow from a vineyard which was in production in pre-Christian times, but it is pleasant, not special: the countryside nearby is also pleasant, but not more than an agricultural monotony; St Pourçain himself is remembered as a 'pious hermit', which is a terribly boring way to be remembered.

The atmosphere of 'not-quite' affected me, even in the

short time I was there, by causing the lunchtime rendezvous I had arranged with Joy to disappear from the face of
the earth – unless we mis-read the guide-book, and there
really was no Relais du Centre, as seven people, including a
shop-keeper, a hotelier, a gendarme and a man who said he
had lived there all his life affirmed when I asked them.
Certainly it was not among the line of cafés strung out along
the main road to cater for the hungry traveller to Clermont-
Ferrand; nor was it in the town centre itself at the top of a
steep hill which I climbed three times in an extremely low
gear in case I might have missed something.

St-Pourçain then put it into my head to ride several miles
on out of town so that Joy could catch me up, while at
the same time putting it into her head that she should go
back towards Souvigny in case I had broken down at an
early stage; and by the time she had gone back, and I had
gone back and we had encountered each other by chance

as I rode up and down the main road cafés peering into the interiors like a fat waif at a delicatessen, it was too late for lunch. This was sad, because the night before M. Coque had strongly recommended a regional speciality, *Pâté aux tartouffes*, which he said was a pie of potatoes and cream, and I had been in hope of finding it on the menu, possibly along with *oyonnade*, which is the local goose stew.

'So there you are,' said Joy.

'So there *you* are,' I said, asserting myself.

I left St-Pourçain to muddle through before he got at my bicycle, in which a disquieting click had established itself in the region of the bottom bracket, and set off on the peaceful ride towards the forest of Marcenat. It was flat, crop country – none the more interesting for my having been over several miles of it twice already, though at one point I came across an electric pylon sizzling to itself like fury, with a tremendous zizz of grasshoppers round its base as if they had come on pilgrimage to worship it. But St Pourçain had spread his mantle of pernicious mediocrity over the forest, and at St-Rémy-en-Rollat I hit the main road and heavy traffic, so that I was quite glad to fumble my way over the town-plan of Vichy to my hotel in a street of hotels. The one opposite the Hôtel de la Poste was called the Hôtel des Archers but, though there were a good many people around of the right sort of generation (i.e. about as old as Walter Gabriel's grandparents), Vichy did not feel at all like Ambridge. Thank heaven.

THE FIFTEENTH DAY

Vichy is a magic town, and the magic is that it is built upon water which bubbles up out of the ground and turns into money on contact with the air. (In Britain we are used to our spas being rather down-at-the-heel, and it was a surprise for me to come upon one which is still big business.) Vichy is also built on the river Allier, and that is the water that comes out of the hotel taps.

Both kinds of water attract visitors. The Allier had been dammed to make a two-mile-long boating lake as part of a vast sports complex, whose aficionados are young, bronzed and firm of step. They are also the ones who seem to get their pictures in the tourist brochures and on the glossy stand-ups in the smart chemists' windows, which are temples of publicity to expensive super-cosmetics and pseudo-medicaments.

The French *pharmacien* surrounds himself with a very posh mystique indeed: he is no simple dispenser, but prescribes much more for minor ailments than his British counterpart. He keeps his marble floor spotless, his prices high and his nose in the air: and, like many other things in Vichy, the pharmacies have a Parisian *chic*.

Most of those who go in and out of the *pharmacies*, however, and take the waters in the Halle des Sources, or attend for treatment at the Bain Callou or Le Grand Etablissement Thermal (which I translate as THE GREAT HOT WATER ESTABLISHMENT) are neither bronzed nor firm of step, but slow and shuffling. Sagging people, indigested people, arthritics, hypochondriacs; people who ought to have an operation but are afraid, people who have had an operation and are still afraid; grey-faced people, fat-faced people; the unseasonably-disastered young and the middle-aged who are running rough; the worn-out old, taking the sun on the curly white chairs in the Parc des Sources and watching the bronzed ones go by to tennis or canoeing wondering – with that mute incomprehension of old age – how it has come about that youth and health have passed on to others, and they are now the ones with stiff joints and desiccated sinews.

Vichy, queen of the spas, takes all into her bed-and-breakfast embrace, as she took Marshal Pétain and his equivocating government during the war. She is far from being a virgin queen and her comforts are rather commercial, but she will give you a lively time while you are with her, according to your abilities: from Baby-foot (whatever that is) in the Parc des Enfants to bullfighting;

from Rigoletto to a trip round a Chilean beaver farm; from a Meeting de Trot at the race course to an Occultiste-Médium, Astrologie, Radiesthésie, Etude de Mains, Graphologie, Grands Tarots, Librairie Esotérique; from the Grand Casino and the Missionary Museum to the Nouveau Sex-Shop. (*'Films: Gadgets: Lingerie Sexy: Repartez avec un cadeau insolite!'*)

My entertainment came unexpectedly as I was enjoying a *café-cognac* after dinner before one of the three cafés on the cross-roads at the bottom of the Rue de Paris. A small brass band (made up of music students, I learned when they passed the hat round) appeared from nowhere and set up on the opposite corner, playing jolly favourites very fast to the delight of everybody except the proprietor of that particular café. It was led by a young man in a tiny bowler hat waving his silver trumpet in the air as if he had got the mouthpiece stuck in his teeth and was trying to get it out. A plump young gentleman was very intense about being humorous with a Swanee Whistle, and the euphonium bobbed brightly over the heads of the little crowd that gathered round, with the café lights reflecting off its dents. When enough people had gathered to make that corner totally impossible, the café proprietor called the police, and the band were good-humouredly moved on, much to the relief of the miserable-looking man who had been occupying the table next to the bass drum. Everyone else had been much entertained, and there was a wild applause as they left.

The truth is that there is a desperate need for distraction if you are taking the waters, which must be one of the most boring activities known to humankind, and has always been so, if one can judge by Mme de Sévigné, who came to Vichy for a rheumatic hand.

'I've taken the waters,' wrote that defatigable correspondent. 'They're quite awful, and they taste terrible. You come, you go, you go somewhere else, you wander about. Then it's time for lunch, then you go and see somebody, then you dine, then you go to bed: and that's the cure.' And so it still is, as a rule, and you do it for three weeks.

'They drink the water from the spring: they go each morning to have showers or baths, and some of them with rheumatism they have also mertz,' I learned from Jean-Louis Bourdier, a cheerful young doctor who drove me down to the Parc des Sources in his Jaguar while my bottom bracket was taking the cure in the local bike shop (unnecessarily as it turned out: bottom brackets seem to be my particular hypochondria).

'Sorry?'

'You know what means mertz?'

'No.'

'It's written M.U.D.S.'

'Oh, mud.'

'Yes, muds,' said Dr Bourdier helpfully. 'A kind of earth, very hot: you put it on the joints.' Though his accent occasionally betrayed him, he spoke smooth, relaxed English. He was a splendid advertisement for Vichy: he glowed with health and good living and displayed the most engaging and friendly bath-side manner. As a sceptical patient, among the things which I exclude from my unhealthy life are *bains minéral à action sédative, bain avec douche sous-marine, bain carbo-gazeux (procure une sensation d'euphorie et de détente nerveuse), bain oxy-gazeux (l'oxygène a une action tonique générale et excite la circulation veineuse), bain de vapeur individuel (avec nébulisation d'eau ionisée de la source Boussange), douche mixte (action tonique ou sédative suivant la technique), douche intestinale simple,* and *douche intestinale speciale,* but so agreeable was Dr Bourdier that at his bidding I thought I would quite happily sit up to my neck in strawberry jam. He was also frank when I asked him how he had come to be a specialist in Vichy.

'I came to Vichy because I heard it was good for migraine. I had fantastic migraine when I was a student: I couldn't work a day a week. I would have tried anything, even go to Lourdes and pray. I see a doctor, he give me water, I had never any more migraine. He had a nice daughter – you know what happens – and when I married my wife, he wanted to stop working and asked me to take over: so I stayed. It's a nice town, well-known for its flowers: half of it is parks. Now I prescribe water: I'm an ecologist – no drug, only water.'

'And you didn't have even a single migraine?'

'Never more, and you know I'm a gastronome: I eat much, and always with cream and spices. I don't remember any migraine – perhaps one in twenty years. I believe in Vichy myself. With migraine we have good results on seventy-five per cent of people – that's a good result.'

Drinking water and bathing water cost between 400 and 600 francs for three weeks for the standard treatment, Dr Bourdier told me. People can come to Vichy, fares paid, on the French National Health: the hotel bill is their own business, whether it be for a little *pension* or the 3-star hotel whose corridors connect directly with those of THE GREAT HOT WATER ESTABLISHMENT. I understood from Dr Bourdier that, should I ever need to recuperate from viral hepatitis or give myself a rest from anti-rheumatic drugs (which tend to be bad for the stomach), Vichy would be a good place to come to. There seemed to be two classes of patient: the genuinely sick, and the self-indulgent.

'It's a gastronomical nation that eats much, generally too much: and they have trouble with their levver,' said Dr Bourdier, introducing me to an organ that in Britain comes with bacon, but in France is a centre of anatomical mysticism. 'They like to eat the cream and sauce, and they have trouble for that: trouble with their levver, gall-bladder, intestines, stowmarch. Also, it's a country where people drink much alcohol, and they have sometimes the beginnings of cirrhoses. They have trouble like diabetts and goat, and trouble with cholesterol and lippitz. That's why they come to Vichy.' ('Goat' I understood to be gout: that 'lippitz' were lipids I was told later.)

'What do they do afterwards?' I asked.

'Of course they start eating again!' said Dr Bourdier.

While a small part of Vichy is selling medicinal waters, the rest of the town is all set to undo the good work. There is an extraordinary number of pastry cooks and *bonbon* shops in Vichy: and every encouragement is given to stuff yourself with the local speciality, Vichy-Etat pastilles in blue and white boxes. Since Vichy water's main constituent is bicarbonate of soda, it would presumably be good for boiling cabbage, if you like your cabbage boiled that way, but its only use in cookery that I could discover is in Vichy carrots, which are cooked with a small quantity of water plus sugar and butter, so that you end up with a sweet glaze. The inducement however is generally to nibble: there must be good cooking in Vichy somewhere but, with thousands of lodging-houses and hotels to choose from, the odds on finding it are extremely long. You just have to be thankful that culinary mediocrity in France can hardly compete with the British.

We went to see the waters, which lived in a glass pavilion at one end of the Parc des Sources, with the Arabian Nights dome of the Grand Casino shining golden at the other. It was still early: there was the faintest of mists in the air and the sun flowed down the walks between the shadows of the trees. Scrunch across the gravel, tip-tap down the paths came the curists: the smart bearing glasses done up in a little wicker basket like a button-up wine cradle, the slow stopping to rest on the curly white chairs dotted among the lawns. They moved through a lost age: around them Vichy itself remembered leg-of-mutton sleeves and man-servants, and how the best people would arrive in July after the racing at Deauville, and go on to Carlsbad or Baden-Baden before returning to Paris. Napoleon III was a great enthusiast for the waters.

'The funny thing was it was a mistake: the illness for which he came is not treated by Vichy water,' Dr Bourdier told me, but Vichy entered high society at Napoleon's coat-tails in the 1860s. That society had mostly disappeared by the end of the Second World War, so the historical feel of the spa is an amalgam of those eighty years of high capitalism, centred on the prime of the early 1900s.

The Halle des Sources, the glass pavilion, was a cross between a grove of water-nymphs and a self-service bar, the head nymph a young woman who issued season tickets and charged the casual visitor 3F 90 at the gate. The grove was of fluted pillars of white cast iron which fanned out at the top into palmetto arcades around the waters, which bubbled below floor-level amid the splendour of art nouveau glass and marble in the centre of the hall. Though there was at least one barmaid nymph (dressed up to look medical) down below with the waters, filling thermos flasks, most curists served themselves at perpetually trickling spouts in blue terrazzo self-service counters. We homed in on one of the original springs and Dr Bourdier hung over the wall to point out the line of Roman brickwork, announcing that the volcanic waters were coming from 300 metres down with as much satisfaction as if he had put them there himself. The temperature went up one degree centigrade for every 30 metres of depth, he said, so you could tell the origins of every one of the 250 separate springs which make the ground at Vichy a hot spot in France.

We headed for the self-service counter to try the waters, and I was about to put 20 centimes into the automatic cup-vendor when there was an American accent behind me.

'I have a lousy doctor,' said a short, wide old lady with a moustache on her voice.

'Hello, madame,' Dr Bourdier greeted his patient politely.

'Don't forget you've got an appointment with me at 3.15. I have a lousy doctor,' said the old lady, belabouring the point. She was, I saw, a winkler, but Dr Bourdier was un-winkled and introduced me as a man riding from London to the Mediterranean on a bicycle.

'How does the bicycle feel?' demanded the old lady rhetorically.

'Have you really come all the way from America for water?' I asked. 'What does it do for you?'

'I've been coming here for fifty years, son. Look at my age: you should be as spry at my age.'

'Her name is Methusalum,' said Dr Bourdier, getting his own back.

'He means Methusalah. I'm seventy-four,' bawled the old lady. 'You get my energy at seventy-four and you'll be all right, son. And this is notwithstanding the water and notwithstanding my doctor.'

Other curists in the neighbourhood began to show signs that they detected an interesting happening, even if it was in a foreign language.

The old lady dropped her voice and relented. 'He happens to be one of the finest physicians here,' she said confidentially, so that it appeared to those around that she had embarked on a recital of allegations too terrible to mention above a whisper. 'He's not only a good physical man, he's a good psychologist. Old people need some sort of personal treatment.' It was her birthday the next day, she told me. She was going to have a cocktail party in THE GREAT HOT WATER ESTABLISHMENT: they would provide the champagne, she was bringing the ice and glasses.

'I happen to have a gall-stone problem, son. I have three great big gall-stones like that.' She cupped her hands to indicate something to score a goal with. 'Everyone says I should be operated on but I've been coming here and eating everything, and drinking more than *you* ever drink.' Her voice had worked up again. 'I'm the biggest old souse you've ever met,' bellowed the old lady to the Halle des Sources. 'I have my drinks at noon – *and* in the evening; when you have gall-stones you *shouldn't* touch anything, and I believe the water does it for you. Notwithstanding the doctor. Come over here: I'll give you a glass. I haven't had a venereal disease in twenty years, so you don't risk anything!'

There were five waters on tap and, thanks to my education in wine-tasting at Sancerre, I knew how to savour them professionally. I rolled them round my tongue, made the obligatory sucking noises, and swallowed. Chomel was warm and velvety with a heavy sulphurous bouquet and plenty of bicarb to give it body; Grillettes was cool with an aniseedy sort of flavour; Célestins light and slightly bubbly, just like the Vichy water you get in bottles.

Dr Bourdier was slightly astonished to hear that the British hardly drink bottled water. The taste of tap water, he said, spoilt the wine, thereby – I think – putting his finger on the reason why the French drink bottled water and the British do not. Wine and water drinking are necessarily related because you cannot quench your thirst properly with wine without getting drunk, and water is practically the only thing possible that can be drunk with it.

Since it is natural to discriminate between wines, it becomes natural to discriminate between waters. Even the terminology is sometimes the same. In one supermarket I found nine different brands of water, and Vittel ('thanks to its hint of sodium it easily penetrates the cells') and Volvic ('dissolves powdered milk perfectly, recommended for babies') were both *Grand Eau*, like a *Grand Vin*. Apart from Perrier and Vichy waters, there were Source Badoit ('optimal for preventing tooth decay'); Vals (which was just 'delicious'); Evian ('fresh from its long journey through the icy sands of the Alps, recommended for pregnant women'); Eau de France and Val Cristal whose bottles bore no claims and therefore may presumably be described as non-vintage; and Contrexéville ('contributes to the elimination of excess uric acid by its diuretic action'). Most waters claim this 'diuretic action': indeed, I have heard it whispered that such an effect may actually occur sometimes in Britain with ordinary tap water, but that, no doubt, is just boasting.

'This is ancient First-class Bath,' Dr Bourdier told me, ushering me into THE GREAT HOT WATER ESTABLISHMENT, explaining that treatment was no longer divided into social categories as if it were a railway train. 'We shall see the swimming pool for people with arthritis; mecano-therapy, a lot of machines with which you do all joints; and then we shall see mertz. Is that right?'

'Mud.'

'Mud.'

THE GREAT HOT WATER ESTABLISHMENT was echoey with hushed voices and nurses' heels: in the lofty entrance hall, an electronic cash-register broke into loud chattering whenever anybody wanted a bill. It was a place of great contrasts in movement: the brisk walks of the attendants against the old woman in the warm pool inching her thin limbs so little and so slowly, it was painful to watch. Mecano-therapy was like Frankenstein's engine-room, with human beings strapped to machines that moved them like lay-figures. The machines had great black cast-iron frames, shining steel shafts, beautifully turned brass fittings and were ornamented with gold lining as if they had been state carriages.

'They are the oldest you can find in Europe now,' said Dr Bourdier. 'I think they are the last ones still working. When they stop, I think they must be sold at Thosaby, no?'

'Sotheby's, yes,' I said.

'You see, you put the arms here ...' (He spread-eagled himself against a black monster with straps for the wrists) 'and the back here ...' (against a velvet cushion). 'It is to make you breathing' (he started the motor and the cushion went in and out in the region of the small of the back). 'It is a kind of torture,' said Dr Bourdier, genially.

There was the hum of electric motors and the click of escapements: the lay-figures on the machines were silent except, now and again, there was a painful breath. A Senegalese in blue pyjamas was being vibrated from the wrists, shaking like a dog out of water. Opposite, a pair of limp white hands went flip-flop, flip-flop on yellow velvet cushions.

We luckier ones took to the corridors again, clip-clop, clip-clop, Dr Bourdier explaining the star attraction of the place, the Douche de Vichy.

'It's a very soft shower given for three minutes on the levver. When the skin becomes red, we stop the shower, the people go a bit far away, and we give a strong shower, like a fireman.' It sounded fascinating; I wondered to myself whether the Nouveau Sex-Shop had heard about it. We came to a row of cubicles with little arched doors, like hobbit-holes. We stopped. I waited, agoggish.

'Here are ze mud,' said Dr Bourdier proudly. 'We say myhrrrd: it's a kind of earth from the Allier river, with Vichy water. It needs a year to do mud. It's made in the open air with special plankton; it's always mixèd, mixèd, mixèd every week, the sun come and we have a special effect of éleo-chimie – sun is working in the water. And when the mud is good for use, it comes to the Establishment by truck and is kept here all the season.' It was on the tip of my tongue to ask him whether it got dirty and, if it did, how they could tell that the end of the season was the right time to throw it out.

'We can't go, because people is in now,' said Dr Bourdier. So I never met the mud: it was most disappointing.

As I wandered away from THE GREAT HOT WATER

ESTABLISHMENT, Vichy suddenly went into convulsions. There was a tidal wave of people on the pavements and an eruption of traffic, peremptorily directed by policemen in pith helmets. It was the Vichy rush-hour, which occurs just before lunchtime. After about a quarter of an hour, everything vanished, and the policemen went home. I sat and picnicked in the park, so utterly alone that I thought I was very probably illegal. As far as the eye could see were throngs of little white curly chairs, some solitary, some in conversational circles, all waiting to be sat upon by elderly bottoms.

BEER AND TEA, WINE AND WATER: YOU ARE WHAT YOU DRINK, THANK HEAVEN – a Scientific Note for the Chauvinist Reader by Bulwer Wellington-Ffoulkes

'Oh, minerale!' you may cry, but it is a health hazard not to be ignored. The British probably had water before the french did, and time has taught us to treat it with caution.

Water has its place in the garden and bathroom, is useful in nurturing fish, washing the car, facilitating certain industrial processes and rehabilitating the turf at Lord's; but none of these activities is relevant to the human stomach. There are three kinds of water: clean water, dirty water and soda water. Dirty water is obviously dangerous, taken internally; clean water may be dirty water recycled; and the toxicity of soda water in excess is acknowledged by the fact that it is traditionally sold in a special container in the manner of a fluted poison bottle.

We do not paint a wall which we wish to be yellow with blue paint, and, in the same way, only brown fluids are wholesome to a brown liver: that is why the British drink tea, beer and whisky, whose pigments maintain a physiological colour balance.

Let me take you inside a frenchman, however, and I shall show you a wanton irrigation with contrasting liquids. Down the hatch go 73 centilitres of Beaujolais; the liver turns quite puce and jostles truculently with the duodenum. Immediately, in a subconscious attempt to re-establish chromatic equilibrium, the french throat opens once more, and a gush of water follows, washing the wretched lobes into a pallid self-parody, and thumping the gall-bladder against its palpitating fellow-organs. The consequence of green and yellow chartreuse I leave to the imagination.

How can a nation have healthy livers whose interior decoration is a riot of colour? Let them be brown, let them be moderate, and – if they wish to undo the effects of past indulgence – rub themselves with old fruit cake, cold cocoa or good honest gravy.

B.W.-Ff.

CHAPTER 8

Bleu d'Auvergne

THE SIXTEENTH DAY

I crossed my third frontier when I left Vichy. The first had been the clanking gang-planks of the Channel ferry which led to Normandy and the country round the Seine; the second was the little stretch of bone-rattling *pavé* outside Etampes, the boundary of the flatlands of France, provinces of wheat, beef and wine; now I climbed the valley of the Sichon into the foothills of the Auvergne, and the world was suddenly wilder.

I had been bowed out of the hotel by the pale Portuguese chambermaid who came to Vichy to work every summer so that she could give her children a good start in life, but missed them terribly, she said; and by the little mute who kept the keys of the garage. Together, he and I looked like something out of a circus, the fat man and the dwarf, grinning and gesturing at each other in uncommunicable goodwill.

I crossed over the railway, past the peeling blue and white sweet factory. Vichy, that is so smart along the river, bids a tatty farewell to those who leave it to the east: but in the suburb of Cusset there was a dusty square with round-topped plane trees taking the sun, and two shirt-sleeved gendarmes taking the shade as if they had no intention of doing anything else for the rest of the summer and out of it all came a sense of southern timelessness. I was not yet in the south: but not very far ahead were the borders of Occitania, the Mediterranean half of France. Instead of hedges in the roadside gardens, there were vines. On my left, the hill-slopes grew scrubby and rocky, as if they were trying to make out a case for being some sort of mountain; on my right ran the Sichon, rushing and glittering over brown stones. It was quite unlike the sleepy rivers of the plains whose company I had kept for the last few hundred miles: it trilled over a succession of rapids, whose notes changed as the last one faded and the next came within ear-shot. The valley narrowed to no more than road, one field, river and a trim of sloe bushes, nut trees and ferns. There was the flick of a lizard scuttling off his warm place on the road ahead too fast to see: the next one, however, was too big to be so limber – a gigantic eight inches long, and bright green.

Under the cloudless sky along the deserted road behind came a slow convoy of Dutch cars of decently muted northern colours, the tourists inside looking at the hills as if they were so surprised to see them that their necks had got stuck at a permanently obtuse angle. They stopped to read a riverside notice which told them that they might not bathe, canoe or wash cars in the river: considered it seriously for a moment and drove deliberately on – after which the road was empty again.

The only other living things on the road were the lizards, an importunate horse-fly (the little flies of the Allier water-meadows had copied the landscape and gone wilder) and a ferocious Alsatian slavering at me on the other side of a rather low chain-link fence. There was a human being at the little village of Aronnes: a pale, wide-toothed old man in blue peasant trousers tucked up to his knees, leaving a pair of scrawny white legs to make what connection they could with a pair of clogs. They only just managed it. He had an ancient circular saw with an ornate cast-iron frame like the people-stretchers I had seen at Vichy and a curly-spoked flywheel that hummed above him in his cool work-shop as he methodically cut handfuls of twigs into firing. Like his legs, he was a creature of the dark, but when I peered into his doorway he blinked his way into the sun for long enough to tell me that it was all uphill ahead, but there was a café at Ferrières-sur-Sichon: then he went back to his twigs, cutting them in a regular zizz-zizz on his splendid saw.

Up the hill, it was hot enough for me to take care to ride through each patch of shade, for I had left Vichy without bringing any water. I passed the Dutch convoy at bivouac by the side of the road in their modestly coloured cars – pale orange, pastel green and beige. The beige tourists were walking beigely by the roadside, looking as if they did not know what to do with all this countryside, and extremely out-of-place.

At Ferrières-sur-Sichon all the shops were at lunch, but the café was open and turned out to be the Central Hotel, run by a chatty man in his forties who told me over a glass or two of cool beer that he had dropped out from running a club in Paris only seven months previously to find tranquillity in the Montagne Bourbonnaise: I judged that he would probably find as much as anybody could cope with, from our lone conversation in his shady bar looking out on an absolutely empty cross-roads. Ferrières was a little town of 2000 people, five football teams and seven cafés, he said. When I remarked that, leaving aside football teams, it seemed rather a lot of cafés for such a small population and that it must be rather difficult to stay in business, he said that there had been twenty-seven: cafés were what kept a place alive, but Ferrières was falling into a coma.

Since this was still the fringe of the Bourbonnais and not yet the Auvergne, people around raised Charolais, and some kept a few sheep or grew a few vegetables for market. There weren't many tourists, though Ferrières had a little grotto to show off to them. There was a waterfall at l'Ardoisière half-way to Vichy, and did I realize that I had missed a prehistoric museum just down the road at Glozel? I must have failed to look properly contrite, since I am almost as keen on missing museums of prehistory as I am about missing menhirs, for he thereupon went into detail. He told me that 300 burials of ancient personages – who were ancient Scots if they were not ancient Danes, and clay-miners if they were not something else – had been dis-

covered, originally nosed out by a cow: the cow's attendants at that time had set up the museum, which contained
all manner of carvings. I expressed admiration, especially
for the cow, and concealed my intention of not going back
downhill to see it. I have read since (in *Fastness of France*,
Bryan Morgan's book about the Massif Central) that the
exhibits are bogus, so perhaps I should have made the
effort.

There were no visitors to any of these attractions that
afternoon, unless the beige tourists went there, for the only
people who came into the Central Hotel that lunchtime
were Joy, bearing our picnic lunch, and a tall man in a
boater who, on being questioned as to whether this was a
breakaway movement from the beret, said he thought not,
but couldn't be sure because he was from East Anglia himself. He had come unexpectedly into a little money, he said,
and was following a leisurely road south, taking photo-
graphs of curiosities along the way. He produced a
complicated-looking camera to prove it and, when he
understood that I was from the BBC, eyed me as if he
thought I might be suitable. He was a languid man of good
humour and a courtly manner. His camera, which was an
expensive profusion of knobs and flashing lights, was really
wrong for him: he should have had something gentlemanly
of mahogany and brass with a bulb to press and a tripod to
stand it on. Perhaps we would run into each other again, he
said, for he was travelling very slowly. We invited him to
lunch.

Lunch was in the corner of a pasture looking across hills
that folded little furry woods and fields over each other like
the limbs of a family of sleeping bears. Joy never buys
enough food for two people if there is the possibility of
catering lavishly for four, so there was the local *jambon cru*
which is as different from our cooked ham as sirloin is to
scrag end, cheeses that began to run in the sun and had to be
prevented by being eaten, and perfect peaches. Of all the
pleasures of France there is none greater than the picnic:
picnics in the early morning with hot crusty loaves from an

early baker, apple juice and a slight shiver; picnics by the river with the wine cooling in the water; picnics in the forest, picnics in the shade of a hot day. The French travel with tables, chairs, canteens of cutlery, ice-boxes, barbecues, sunshades, several courses and a lot of family to eat them: they take possession of nature, but I prefer to sit in a corner of it.

The man in the boater had one bottle of Pelure d'Oignon, that forthright *rosé* which they drink a lot in the south: Joy had a Languedoc red, Corbeilles. When I left them both comparing guide-books and routes in the corner of the field, I tottered off with a sense of sunny beatitude. There were horse-flies around and, when swatting them, I noticed a tendency for my front wheel to finish up in the hedge. Obliging it, I stopped and gathered a dessert of wild strawberries. Wooziness, however, does not last long when you are cycling continuously uphill – and it was seven miles to the top of the Col de la Plantade: it pours out in rivulets which attract more horse-flies, which spur you to greater efforts, which cause more rivulets, which attract . . .

The countryside roused itself to a fitful snooze: occasional cars came past, including Joy and then the man in the boater. But I would not have swopped places to ride more easily, though I was glad of every walnut tree to shade a patch in the road: even uphill it was pleasant, just slower.

I stopped and picked stocks, purple and white, that had escaped to the verge from an overgrown garden; I passed beneath a tree, and the road was dotted with little red cherries. As I approached the top of the climb, I became aware of a svelte figure in flannels ahead: it had a straw boater cocked over one eye and a camera at the other. It photographed sadistically and continuously as I toiled to the summit.

'Splendid pictures: you looked quite awful,' said the man in the boater. 'I'll send you a print – if they come out: I only bought this machine for the trip, and it's a bit complicated. See you again, I hope, along the way.' He strolled to his car, and was off.

The road wound gently downhill through groves of beech trees and larches with little streams running between their spindly trunks; after them, pine forest, as black as its name, Les Bois Noirs, so that I felt as if I had already climbed to the mountains; but then hayfields, farmlands and villages appeared, and at Paluduc – a sleepy, dusty place with all the house mailboxes lumped together in the centre – I reached a panorama over smiling country, unbroken except by a lake in the middle distance. This was the best distance to see it from, as I discovered when I rounded the hillside above and it made itself heard as well as seen with a fuzz of cheap pop music from the *camping* of St-Rémy-sur-Durolle. The lake had been made artificially, complete with swimming pool and fairground, its purpose being to pull some of the tourists from Thiers, downriver in the valley, which is a place of French pilgrimage on account of the fact that it makes knives.

It is difficult to imagine British tourists flocking to Sheffield to purchase cutlery on the spot, but no doubt the French food mystique accounts for Thiers being full of expensive knife shops, all doing a good trade when I saw them. It is undeniable that Thiers is very much more attractive than Sheffield, with steep streets and half-timbered houses. Thiers' cutlery industry, which is said to be based on technology brought back from the First Crusade (though there is also a legend that the first knives made there were Druids' sickles for cutting mistletoe), depended on the swift Durolle for power. The grinders used to work lying face down on a plank over the torrent that whirled the wheel below, with their dog crouched on top of their feet for warmth – a picturesque manner of working, now, thank heaven, lost for ever, though people were still plying that uncomfortable trade as recently as 1939. Twenty-two paper mills once lined the river as well. They are long gone, but the coming of electric power hardly detracted from Thiers' position as a cutlery capital producing more knives than the rest of France put together: hundreds of tiny workshops each employing no more than a handful of craftsmen.

It feels rather odd being surrounded by so many knife shops. The place is not all picturesque, by any means, but Thiers is admirable in that it does not dwarf its workers, yet is the seat of a major industry whose history knew hardship but not the humiliating regimentation of the big factory or the grime of the steam-engine. It is a place that harks back directly to the older, water-powered industrial revolution and the dignity of individual labour. Nor is it a town that has spread out too much in the way of subtopian tentacles. St-Rémy-sur-Durolle, in which I stopped at the Hôtel des Voyageurs, has its *camping* well removed from the town proper and, that apart, is completely small-town rural.

'Very good, you going up all those hills,' said Joy when she arrived, somewhat after I did. 'Hard, was it?'

'It was only thirty-seven miles,' I said, modestly, failing to mention that the Cyclists' Touring Club recommended average was fifty. I had begun to question Vernon's First Principle of Physical Geography (see page 23) but had decided to replace it with Vernon's First Principle of Physical Activity, viz: that when cycling through France to the Mediterranean, the tough bits are at the end, so you get into training. However, it is not as bad as it would be were the Massif Central bordering on the English Channel.

'I've bought you something for tomorrow,' said Joy. 'I went into a chemist in Vichy and asked him if he had something for a fat, unfit man cycling into the mountains.'

'What did he say?'

'He said, "Oh-la-la, very dangerous," and called everyone else in and they all went into a huddle and agreed that this stuff called Coramine-Glucose should stop you having a heart attack.'

Joy handed over a packet of pills each big enough to dose a cart-horse. Like the health-giving waters, they seemed to be of fairly general application, being recommended for 'states of fatigue, troubles due to the altitude and predisposition towards faintings': at that moment, if I had been going to have anything medicinal from Vichy, I would rather have had some muds for the joints.

THE SEVENTEENTH DAY

St-Rémy has a plain church just across the little square from the hotel and it tolled me down to breakfast at a workmanlike hour. Indeed, while I was drinking my coffee, a succession of men in check shirts briskly drew up outside, knocked back a *verre rouge* at the bar in a business-like manner and went off back to work. Madame helped me to get my bicycle out of the barn at the back, acting as long-stop for the fawning cohort of *chiens de chasse* with which it had spent the night, and pointed me down a horribly steep hill, which in a couple of minutes lost me most of the altitude I had gained on the previous day. I went under the motorway bridge at the bottom and began the long climb up to Vernières, dogged by a little yellow post-van which was always rushing past me in a howl of low gears,

dashing off on side-tracks like a terrier after rabbits, and re-appearing behind me again.

Where trees shaded the road, there were patches of coolness left over from the dawn, but the sun, though still low, was already hot. I passed an apple orchard where tall grasses were flowering with a pink fuzz in which the dew caught the light and broke it into a shower of glitters; then a paddock of rangy walnut trees. The road wound and wound; so did my legs, in bottom gear. My progress was slow but dignified, apart from a tendency to heavy breathing. I thought I had achieved something when I got to the top, and a nearby bird thought so too, for it broke into a fanfare of chirps: I attempted to record it, but the song was drowned in panting noises. The road curved round the side of the hill. I came to the crest of the last rise to see miles and miles of green Auvergne spread out before me, and a single lark above the wheat on my own hill-top.

There was a feeling about the hills that life there had a hard edge to it – even on that summer's day when the roadsides were full of wild marjoram with fragrant leaves and long stems topped by bursts of pink flowers crawling with bees. The walnut trees were laden with fruit, which the people thereabouts eat simply, press for oil, add to a local cheese, or make into walnut paste: none of the French I had talked to had ever heard of pickling them, and viewed the concept with great suspicion. Vernières had been a tiny straggle of derelict buildings, roofs caved in among the brambles, with a couple of new houses standing contemptuously trim nearby: now I came upon more and more tumbledown corners among the scattered farms – signs that, in the struggle between the place and the people, the place often won. Each farm had its vast log-pile as a reminder of the severity of the winter when keen winds sweep even a little snow into a wall, called a *congère*, and roads are often impassable. These farms were not like the establishments of easy prosperity I had left on the Allier. There were still some signs of the old peasant way of life, self-sufficient and poverty-stricken, growing a bit of this and a bit of that. I passed straggly, one-family-sized vineyards as I bowled through the hamlet of Escoutoux, where the village women were gossiping on the dusty ground before the church: a tumbledown house further on sported a great oak wine-barrel in its yard, surrounded by a jumble of firewood and rubbish. A little girl in a swim-suit played in the dirt; her mother, a youngish woman in a blue overall with a yellowish, deeply lined face, was doing the washing in a lean-to with a tin bowl and an old tap. The floors of the house were plain concrete, the curtains ragged.

The Auvergnat peasant was described to me as close with hard-earned money, obstinate and conservative by nature so that water and electricity took ages to come to some places because the people considered such things frivolous luxuries. But new generations could see the contrast between rural poverty with a few acres and two or three cows, and the easy life of the town. The twentieth century brought a general drift away from the slavery of the land, a loss of men to work it after the First World War; and in the years after the Second War, the face of the Auvergne changed. They call it the land of blue and green – blue for the mountains and forests, green for the fields and grass. As more and more peasants left for the towns and sold their farms for forestry, the landscape became more and more blue, and the few simple-livers who dropped out of the city and went back to the land did little to redress the colour balance. Solidity is the characteristic of the countrymen and women who are left, as it has been since the days of Vercingetorix of the tribe of the Avernii who stood so firm against Caesar. The people I saw on the tractors in the fields looked as if they were auditioning for the part of Grade-1-Ethnic-Rural-French with their peasant-blue trousers, check shirts, berets and apple cheeks. The brown and white cows of these substantial-looking people were substantial too, and I thought I picked out a typical sort of local dog, a stolid sandy-brown creature, unless some local bitch had been phenomenally active.

There was a buzzard over the blue hills as I came down the long descent into the valley of the Dore, feeling rather like a somewhat ponderous hawk myself – experiencing the same rush of air, the same twisting and banking as I bent to the road with the scrunch of gravel under the tyres. Shortly after, a second buzzard with a three-foot wing span soared up out of a field and flapped heavily into the sky, only just above my head. At the foot of the hill, there were poplars and a tiny stream in a field of meadowsweet: against the backdrop of humpy blue mountains was the hill-top town of Vollore-Ville with its château, all round tower and high rampart, watching over the valley as if it were still the middle ages.

At this point there was a break in the idyll, for I missed the minor road I had intended to take along the side of the valley and came instead to the Dore itself at Courpière, at the scrubby end of the town strung out along a main road. There was a 6-kilometre hill out of Courpière and, being a Route Nationale, it was built for engines and not for legs, unlike older roads that wind uphill at a pace suitable for a walker or a horse and cart. The gradient was uncomfortable, there was no shade from a furious midday sun, and I had once more run out of anything to drink in the place they call the *château d'eau*, the waterworks of France. I was tired, and bethought myself of the tablets recommended by the Vichy *pharmacien*. I stopped some five kilometres up the hill and took one: at the end of the sixth kilometre I felt awful and took another. Then I really felt bad, as if I had been working on a chain-gang for the previous fortnight. Nor were the surroundings especially healthful, particularly in comparison with the charming, peaceful lanes of the morning.

The road came down to river level again, and twisted along the banks through a steep, wooded valley which was also occupied by the railway. Then came some messy factories, then roadworks, then a landslide of rubbish tipped down the river bank next to a notice 'Décharge Interdite sous peine de P.V.', whatever P.V. was: a chemical effluvia rose from the river. Another hill followed, more factories – one issuing clouds of red dust as if it were a plant for grinding up old bricks very fine – and more roadworks. Olliergues was a pretty, higgledy-piggledy cluster of tall houses crowding the river bank, but the shops were shut and there was no water to be had.

The miles went slowly, torridly and painfully by as I crept along the map, which I took to consulting every couple of miles to know how it could possibly be that the journey was still going on. After Vertolaye, where there is a chemical industry, the river got smaller and cleaner, the valley opened out once more into green and blue farmland and forest, but I was in no condition to appreciate it – and the avenue into Ambert gave me two tremendous thumps in the front wheel that luckily failed to buckle anything except most of my bone structure. I arrived at the Hôtel du Livradois in Ambert after a journey of forty-four miles that felt like eighty. Feet, limbs, palms and psychology were in a bad way, and I took to bath, beer and bed for the rest of the afternoon.

I woke up to find the sun gone, the sky sulking and the hills rumbling with distant thunder, all of which were in the best local tradition of unpredictable weather. Downstairs, Joy was entertaining a reception committee of a couple of local newspapermen and M. Miolane from the Ambert Syndicat d'Initiative. There was another member of the party – a teacher of English, Georges Crouzet. He looked clean-cut and very much fitter than I felt.

'I used to be a racing cyclist,' Georges told me.

'Oh?' I said, not quite enthusiastically.

'I can't now: my doctor says not too much, because I have some problems with my heart.'

'I'm not surprised, round here,' I said. But I cheered up: in fact, I cheered up a lot. Georges was such an enthusiast: doctor or no doctor, he told me, he cycled into the mountains for a dose of contact with the countryside which he could not do without. He was Auvergnat through and through. Crouzet is a common name in the Auvergne, both for people and villages; he had been born some miles to the south, at Le Puy, which is almost, but not quite the true South, the Midi (or, as they say, '*Le Midi moins quart*'). As a teacher he might have been posted anywhere, so he counted himself lucky to have got a job in Ambert, in the country he loved. But all language teachers have secondary nationalities, and he told me that the other corner of the world that would suit him very well was England, on account of the fact that the English were kind, sociable and easy-going – qualities which he did not always find in the French, especially in the North.

'It's a question of individuals,' Georges told me. 'But as you move south, you'll meet a lot of people who'll speak to you as if they'd known you since a young baby.'

The process seemed to have started in Ambert. We sat round and drank beer, and were jolly.

The Hôtel du Livradois was a trim white building with dark blue awnings looking out over a little square decorated with a piece of modern sculpture in granite; while just over the road stood an ancient fountain surmounted by four heads of Neptune with pipes in their mouths like copper cigarettes, dribbling water out of the ends in contempt. The name of the proprietors of the hotel was Joyeux, who had been there since 1946 (when it was only a *petite auberge*, said Madame Joyeux) and they ran their business to suit with their name. Below the dark blue blinds were tubs of petunias to delight the eye and a few little white tables at which a parched throat might be comforted. There was a maid who comforted British prejudices by offering pillows as an alternative to the cherished French bolster; but the greatest joy came from the kitchen of the chef-proprietor himself. Delicious ham pancakes in a creamy sauce, grilled salmon with excellent tartare sauce, and the sweet speciality of the house – ice-cream with extravagant adornments including meringues, Grand Marnier and bitter chocolate sauce. All this cost £5 a head not including the wine: St Pourçain was still the standard white, and Châteaugay turned out to be a smooth red *vin du pays* with a touch of acidity, most agreeable. The cheeses were splendid, one of them being the most beautiful looking cheese that I have ever seen, the Fourme d'Ambert, which is named after its tall, cylindrical shape and is said to date back to before Julius Caesar. The mountains of the Auvergne produce according to a tough existence: St Nectaire, the most delicate of their cheeses, is still substantial and sourish; Cantal is rather like an extremely good and fairly powerful Cheddar; Bleu d'Auvergne is positively ferocious; Fourme d'Ambert is a much smoother blue within a heavy rind like Stilton, but sometimes much more colourful.

___

A SONG TO MUSIC BY BUTTERWORTH

Loveliest of cheese, the Fourme d'Ambert
Is clothed in rind without compare:
A craggy surface, seamed with ruts
And bloomed with orange on the crust.

Now, as the land is blue and green,
Within that cheese is blue and cream;
The cream to soothe, the blue to bite,
The orange rind to cheer the sight.

Then let us all make Mardi Gras
Upon the hills of Livradois;
Upon the mountains of Forez
Let's eat the cheese, and live the day.

___

Ambert and the Auvergne not only nurture fine cheeses, but also artists. Ambert's most famous writer is Henri Pourrat, who wrote *Gaspard des Montagnes* in the 1920s;

a half-century or so earlier, Emmanuel Chabrier was less locally committed and went off to Paris, first to be a civil servant and then to ascend the light classical top twenty with music such as the Spanish Rhapsody. But if ever countryside deserved to be rhapsodized, it is the Auvergne, for it is an essence of rural France as Shropshire is an essence of rural England. For us, the nostalgic Housman put the twilight of an ancient pastoral into words, and the Butterworth and Vaughan Williams settings of *A Shropshire Lad* are the embodiment of the not-quite-nature, the landscape with figures that is England. Granted, the lyrics are the romantic genteel view of a professor of Latin who used to write them while he was shaving, and the Shropshire lads and lasses are the same swains and shepherdesses whose uncharacteristically elegant ardours have been chronicled since Horace. But it is only those who do not till the soil themselves who can afford to be romantic about the country: folk-song itself is almost always about people.

In the same way, the most loving musical evocation of the French countryside is apparently simple but full of artistry, though based on folk-song and written in dialect. It is the collection 'Songs of the Auvergne' by Joseph Canteloube who actually came from further south, in the Ardèche, but was nevertheless an Auvergne lad. He was almost an exact contemporary of Vaughan Williams, and the two men were collecting folk-songs in their respective countries at about the same time. Canteloube was much the lesser of the two and remained tied to a region, like Housman. His operas are *Le Mas* (a *mas*, pronounced with the *s*, is the southern name for a jumble of buildings and families making up a farm unit – a cross between an individual house and a village) and *Vercingetorix* (which I would love to see, to discover whether the characters are required to appear in a costume of woad); but his songs call across the orchestra like voices across the hills.

Georges Crouzet told me that there were still folk-groups in many Auvergnat towns, though I imagine that what the folk actually prefer, as elsewhere, is the travelling accordion band or pop-group. I could not find anybody in the Auvergne who had ever heard of Joseph Canteloube, but I did not ask many people, and perhaps I picked ones who did not like music. We all have our preferences: at Boisseyre for example, a hamlet about a mile east of Ambert, there is a particularly fine dolmen, but fortunately I managed to miss it.

THE EIGHTEENTH DAY

I was glad not to have to rush for my bike the next morning, being somewhat stiff from the previous day's cycling and in a fair state of collapse from the evening's *menu gastronomique*. Having a moment to contemplate my navel, I noted objectively that I did not seem to be losing any weight: in fact, the said navel was even less easily visible than usual. Heigh-ho. I went down to breakfast.

Though in conversation, the French go bananas on bacon, eggs and marmalade (which are usually the only nice things they can find to say about English cooking, apart from Yorkshire pudding – which, I am told, is translatable into French as *un auvergne*), they do not carry this enthusiasm into everyday life, which is just as well, because if they did they would most likely elevate breakfast into a ceremony occupying some hours. But *petit déjeuner*, though *petit*, has its charm and that charm is that it is a coffee festival, with the crusty bread fresh from the baker, the hot croissant, the pat of unsalted, slightly sour Normandy butter and the pot of apricot or bilberry jam all assembled to do honour to that fragrant beverage. This hierarchy is clear from the utensils provided to consume it with.

Though great play is made in school French lessons of the household practice of keeping the same knife and fork during a meal, I found this hardly noticeable among families and totally contradicted in restaurants, where the dignity of waiters requires that plates, knives, forks, spoons should appear like something out of *The Sorcerer's Apprentice*, be whipped away and replaced with other, identical knives and forks, and be provided even for someone at the table who is not eating (a custom which makes French restaurants even better value than they already are, since you can share meals).

But at breakfast there is not even a plate: you must eat as best you can off the saucer of the cup, the saucer carrying the butter and jam, the bread-basket and the tablecloth, which is usually protected with an impervious napkin. Crumbs get everywhere. At the same time, you have a teaspoon too small to raise a ripple in the coffee cup, and a dessertspoon too large to go into the jam pot – which in the best establishments is mini-glass instead of mini-plastic. The only utensil whose use is clear is the knife – which has to be for the butter, unless it is also for getting the jam out of the jam pot and stirring the coffee. But, eaten in company with a brood of shiny copper pans on the wall for decoration, a grandmother clock (I could tell it was a grandmother by its bulbous bottom), a grandfatherly, ponderous, twisty-curly old sideboard and rows of very upright chairs sitting at table like obedient children, and begonias in the window boxes beneath the blue awnings, *petit déjeuner* can be exceedingly pleasant, even if the cutlery is obscure.

It was a cool morning, with a grey sky and the mountains hidden in mist, as I left the Hôtel du Livradois for my morning appointment. Ambert thinks of itself as part of the Livradois, though strictly speaking most of it, including the official seat of local government (an extraordinary round *mairie* like a little Albert Hall with a light-house on top), are on the other side of the river Dore which runs between the Monts du Livradois and the Monts du Forez. The name Livradois comes either from a dialect word meaning 'flooded' or, more likely, *liberatus ab aquis* the freedom of the waters, so it is appropriate to the town for, as the Durolle brought wealth and craft to Thiers, so did the Dore to Ambert; and both towns celebrate great technologists.

To Thiers came a young apprentice, Fernand Forest, who made the first four-cylinder car and the first petrol-driven boat in 1890, and ten years later was sold up for debt because he had not safe-guarded his patents properly (indeed, for some years he could not afford to have any at all); out from Ambert went the Montgolfier brothers, the great balloonists. Whereas Thiers lost its papermills but remained an industrial town by virtue of its cutlery, Ambert used the river exclusively for sawmills and paper. There were 300 mills, now gone, which allowed it to claim the title of 'the cradle of French paper-making'. Paper profits made Ambert the third town in the Auvergne after Clermont-Ferrand and Riom, and built the late Gothic church of St Jean with its proud and pretentious six-teenth-century bell-tower, which still sounds over some of the same narrow streets and jettied timber houses that it did when it was new. The papermill of Richard de Bas remains, making the finest paper in the traditional laborious manner, with water-powered hammers thump-ing rags to a paste all day, so that the tourists can go there and see how they did it in 1326. In more recent times, however, the town's major industry came to be the making of religious objects, though – as I was not surprised to learn from Georges Crouzet – that line of business 'had its problems', and there was more hope for the future in a small plant building electric cars. Generally, manu-facturers do not care to penetrate too far into the Auvergne, on account of the winding roads and difficult travelling in winter.

Ambert is a Catholic town, but its choice of a holy bauble industry is somewhat ironic since it was the wars of religion that ruined it: though for the delectation of future tourists, they also produced a celebrated exploit by a famous Protestant leader, Captain Merle, who held the town against Catholic forces by taking the statues from the church and dressing them as soldiers along the ramparts.

Since those days, most buchery in the Auvergne has been carried on in the name of the stomach, and performed on pigs, for this is a land famous for its hams and sausages, and it was to a *charcutier* I was going that morning. Joy had investigated some 900 miles' worth of pork butchers along our route before we left London, and in all the journey had not found one who spoke English, so M. Miolane had brought along Georges Crouzet again to translate any technical terms we might encounter.

'*C'est une très grosse affaire*,' said M. Miolane with a bravura that would have done credit to the stage of the Comedie Française. He was tall, with a slight stoop, a brown, geologically lined face, and great good humour, a cross between George Robey and Tollund Man.

M. Bernard, his butcher's shop, his family and his *charcuterie* lived opposite the church in a tiny village under the very edge of the Monts du Forez – he and his family upstairs, the rest down. He was not an ordinary *charcutier*, but a considerable success story of a progress from the little shop his father left him to a business that, if not quite a meat empire, was at least a sausage dukedom. Zeros in French money are not my strong point – I am never quite sure whether people have slipped into old francs without my noticing it, and there are far too many noughts in the metric system anyway – but millions of francs tinkled through our conversation that morning like the gold and jewels falling from the mouth of the good girl in *Grimm's Fairy Tales*. I understood that M. Bernard had a capital investment that year of £2 million: no, that couldn't be right, not with only sixteen other *charcutiers* on the staff; there was machinery that cost 17 million francs, £170,000: or, if it was old francs, £1,700 (which sounded better): unless it was £170: or £17,000. Whichever it was . . .

'*C'est français*,' said M. Miolane, proudly.

I gave up a detailed audit of M. Bernard in favour of the general proposition that he was doing very nicely, thank you. There was a white pantechnicon outside with his name on it in blood-red letters – as was a livery only fitting to someone whose success, like many another's, was built on the slaughter of innocents. Yet the millionaire himself still worked on the shop floor with his men, in a white apron that went over one shoulder like a toga.

The shop had a new front in rigidly geometric patent grey stone. It was guarded outside by a pair of golden cypress trees in pots, and within by the head of an enormous yellow-toothed wild boar, scowling at the *Filet de boeuf 45 F, Rumpsteck 40 F, Gigot entier 38 F le kilo*, the hams hung up in muslin bags and bunches of salamis like the udders of over-developed cows. There was one customer, an ordinary housewife doing a little shopping – she said that she had popped in for some dripping and a bit of meat for the dog, plus sausages, ham, chicken, steak and veal. We left her to her modest purchase.

Through the shop was a marble hall: slabs piled high with chickens and ducks, butcher's benches dying the death of a hundred thousand cuts, sides of pork hanging in racks like suits in a wardrobe. A stout gentleman in a maroon pullover, plastic apron and a little white cap like a sun-hat made out of knotted handkerchief was working out his psychology on half a pig – slash, chop and bang. It was like Bluebeard's honeymoon, if Bluebeard had had a harem. Nearby was a large plastic tub of tripes soaking in water, with a litre of *vin rouge* keeping cool among them. Trolleys rumbled over the tiles between machines, shining steel monsters: one mixer eight feet high lifted up hoppers of meat and tipped them into itself in a nonchalant gobble, and then stood around waiting for more, its appetite only briefly satisfied. A meat grinder swallowed 100 kilos of meat every two minutes, slurping. A single-minded little device in a corner was a skinner – squeezing sides of meat between knobbed plastic rollers, dropping the meat on to a conveyor belt and the skins into a tub so that they could be sent off to make gelatine.

'*C'est formidable*,' said M. Miolane with respect: '*très rapide.*'

No waste in a pig, M. Bernard told me: everything was used, from head to tail. Everything? I wondered.

'How about the ears?'

'With the ears you can make a pie,' said M. Bernard. 'We use sixty tonnes of meat every month: we can make two tonnes of sausages in an hour ...' He went off into more zeros: enough to make an entire piggery turn in its sty.

The pork was local, usually from the same three or four farms, though before the EEC standardized prices, pigs had been imported from Holland because they were cheaper. He would like to export to Britain, said M. Bernard, but he could not yet cope with the regulations. He sold his products locally to small butchers and grocers, not to supermarkets, and specialized in sausages and hams. The hams were not smoked, but lay cheek to cheek by the hundred in tubs of salt, pepper and thyme for twenty-five days: they also had to be boned, the cavity sewn up to keep the air out of the inside, and pressurized in moulds at five tonnes per square inch (well, something like that;

it was zeros again and possibly not inches anyway); whatever it was, a fat man with a little moustache was doing it with a compressor like a tyre-pump in a garage.

The final part of the process was the drying – as with the *saucissons*, the salamis. *Saucisses* were fresh meat, about nine inches long, with garlic, salt and pepper added. The same kind of meat went into the *saucissons*, either pure pork (in which case they were tied with red string) or a mixture of pork and beef (which were bound with grey). The other ingredient, I learned, was the mountain air, and that was what made Auvergne hams and *saucissons* so good. The *saucissons* were made in two shapes. *Rosette* was a standard salami-shape; the other sort bulged out in the middle and had to be restrained with a string corset.

'*Jésus, jésus,*' said M. Miolane and, when asked why it was so called, '*C'est comme ça,*' in tones implying that the sausage was at least a cosmic inevitability, if not an act of direct intervention by God. The shape affected the drying and this produced the individual flavour. Once, I learned, sausages made of the family pig and hams smoked up the chimney hung in the attic of every small farm, dried by the mountain winds whistling through the crannies. M. Bernard's way of doing things was to hang the *saucissons* for one day at about 30°–40°C, so that the moisture drained from them, and they turned red; then he put them into his drying-room, where fans simulated the winds of heaven, and blew air at a constant 10°–12°C from a different direction every two hours.

'*J'aime le saucisson aillé,*' said M. Miolane, a touch wistfully, for it was drawing towards noon.

There was a lot to see at M. Bernard's, especially since it included an old factory building which he had bought and was fitting up as the next stage in his expansion. Also, by this time, I had dropped behind the main party to record the sounds of *charcuterie* and was being conducted by M. Bernard's little boy, who had a proper juvenile appreciation of machines with knobs on, and was anxious to help in such matters as opening and closing cold-room doors to make the sort of vault-like boom that would go down well in a horror film. And so would the scene beyond: the cold store looked like a back room in hell with dim yellow light and the cold misting over piles of dismembered pink sinners stuffed into shining plastic bags. Sitting in the middle was a great goat's head, the centre-piece for some special dinner, that eyed me like Satan through the swirling mist. The little boy said that one day he, too, would be a *charcutier*, and led me proudly into the drying-room which was built entirely of wood, like a sauna, with racks on which hung hundreds of rosy rows: a sausage forest laden with fruit, blowing gently in the artificial breeze as if the spirit of the pig still stirred within.

It being about lunchtime, we trooped up to the Bernard family home over the shop and into a parlour well-supplied with modern furniture featuring hygienic surfaces, as if M. Bernard could not quite separate his home life from his work – and, indeed, a fragrance of drying *saucissons* came up the stairs with us. There we took an aperitif, and conversed in an atmosphere of mutual respect. M. Bernard told me he had often tasted black pudding which English friends brought him as a present every year: it was pleasant enough, he said, but it was different. He presented me with a *jésus* corseted in red twine in case I should fall hungry upon my journey: in fact, he gave everybody one. That *jésus* made my staple picnic lunch for the rest of the trip, and – as it was blown by the winds of heaven (even if artificial ones) – so I judged it worthy to sit upon the right hand of the Greatest Charcutier of All.

'*Pauvre petits cochons*,' said M. Miolane, hypocritically.

It was still grey when I left Ambert at the start of the afternoon, by a route recommended by Georges as being considerably easier than that originally planned, on account of the fact that it had only one 10-kilometre hill. To begin with, the road ran level along the edge of the valley of the Dore, but just past Chadernolles – a hamlet with dirty roads and Auvergnat dogs so stolid that they refused to move even when hooted at and threatened with being run over – I began a long, slow climb into the mountains, and soon realized that the series of plateaux over which I had been climbing since Vichy were their foothills. But it was easier going than the blazing day before: a hazy sun appeared for a moment, and spent the rest of the afternoon dodging in and out of luminous grey clouds, but the air, cooled by the storm during the night, never became more than warm.

The road had been built by someone who appreciated that mountains are not to be rushed at, but taken gravely. At first it climbed between pines and rocks, with a stream running invisibly further and further below: I was not even in bottom gear, and the unidentified clicking had vanished from the nether regions of the bicycle, to be replaced by a gentle, but equally inscrutable clunking. There were just the three of us on the uphill: the bicycle, the clunking and me; except that some kilometres along I came upon a sonorous buzz by the side of the road – a gigantic and sweet-smelling lime tree, its flowers alive with little red bees. In some ways, it is actually more pleasant to cycle uphill than down: you are not jolted by speed, you have time to look around you and consider the smallest plant

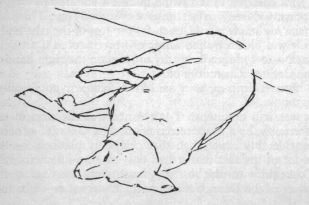

by the roadside. Best of all is the enforced self-indulgence in which you grind up to the top in the best Puritan ethic, and then have no choice but to squander all that hard-earned gravity in a prodigal burst down the other side.

But the pass did not come with the end of the pines, nor of the mixed woods that followed them, nor with the tiny grey roadside chapel of Vernadet, with a blue and white Virgin watching over a basket of shrivelled flowers above the lintel, and wooden eaves like the Great Western Railway. Instead, the road turned out to be a beanstalk leading to a succession of cloud-top countries, one at every clear view over the green slopes to wooded mountains going bluer and bluer into the distance. It seemed impossible that the road could continue to rise without taking to the air but the few red roofs and the grey spire of the village of Baffie appeared ahead over the folding meadows, and then they were below me, half-lit in a patch of sun, and the valley of the Dore was even more impossibly remote, somewhere beyond a wood, somewhere over the curve of a field, somewhere before a cloud.

At last came the Col du Chemintrand (which was hardly a pass in the accepted sense of the word, since there was not a great deal in the neighbourhood that was much higher): it had a prosaic sawmill and a great deal of associated timber on one side of the road and the Belle-Vue-Café-Restaurant-Pâtissier on the other, which was a 30-foot-long example of turn-of-the-century sign-writing with serifs like moustachios peeling from a long stone building which began with a barn, ended with a lean-to outhouse and had a little cottage in the middle. A less pretentious municipal sign in better repair certified that this was indeed 1028 metres' worth of *col*, and the road led down a little way on the other side into a country that had decided that it had had enough of going up in the world, and would lie flat instead, growing wheat and grass. The farms had that detached look of buildings that never expect to see a visitor, except occasionally in the summer.

The little town of Viverols, occupying the only available rise in the middle of the plain with the ruins of a castle among its trees, was not quite kempt, as if it too had been surprised without a chance to make itself presentable, but it was beautifully set overlooking pastureland with a bright stream rippling through it – the Ance, which flows due south to Pontempeyrat and by the time it passes below the terrace of the Hôtel Mistou, where I stayed the night, has become a river. But a cyclist has to go a longer way, turning at Usson-en-Forez on to a main road that gently switchbacks over the hills until it swoops upon the little town huddling in a hollow. By the time I got there, and had made my way up the exceedingly long side-road to the hotel, I had become quite blasé about the fact that the bed in which I had passed the previous night was many hundreds of feet below the one that was waiting for me.

The hotel was beautifully set in old mill buildings with a race rushing below them and a watery meander in the gardens before it. Perhaps it was the river that was responsible for the flies, but it was definitely the kitchen that was responsible for the worst dish of my trip – a *civet de canard* that tasted as if it had been undergoing prolonged obsequies in the form of ceremonial re-heatings. Like a good Englishman, I sat there and ate it without a murmur, for Madame who made out the bills was one of those ladies who ties her spectacles on to herself in case they should show impertinence. Joy meekly consumed her *lapin en papillotte*, which came to the table done up in half a yard of kitchen foil in an effort to pretend it was not dry (which nothing cooked in a packet should be) and was altogether not a pleasant experience. The trout in champagne sauce was nice, though a terribly pretentious way to waste champagne. Still, at £6 a menu, the meal was much cheaper than a British equivalent would have been: and if you can buy in a reasonable terrine from outside, and serve that first, and put Fourme d'Ambert, St Nectaire, Cantal and chèvre on the cheese-board, you have a great advantage over a bad British restaurant in the depths of the countryside, which must stand or fall by its own efforts, or go frozen. Nor do our restaurants have the natural advantage of French bread and wine – though the Mistou baked its own bread, which is unusual in a country whose love-affair with crustiness establishes one baker in a tiny village and six or more in a small town. French bread is like love – essentially transitory, and what lies at the heart may be rather lightweight: but the crackle of the crust is worth the long-time sog of the sliced loaf any day.

A DISSERTATION UPON SLICED BREAD

The philosopher is confronted by the following dilemma:

Sliced bread exists.
Sliced bread is not good for eating.

He must therefore ask himself: 'What, then, *is* sliced bread good for?' Here are some possibilities:

Cleaning your bicycle chain.
Building a garden wall.
Skimming through the air in a spirit of hilarity.
Filling up potholes as a socially useful gesture towards other cyclists.
Standing flower pots on.
As a substitute for acoustic tiles on the ceiling.
When cycling in tempests, for keeping the wind out of your ears.
As an impromptu cushion when you wish to smash your fist on the table in an authoritarian and emphatic manner.

For hanging from your handlebars in an effort
to attract the company of small birds.
For muffling oars.
For throwing at persons of low moral reputation
as a gesture of contempt.

However, the philosopher must reply to himself
that sliced bread is not good for any of these either.

The dilemma remains.

THE NINETEENTH DAY

Having sped down rapidly into Pontempeyrat, it was
inevitable that I should slowly wind out of it again. I was
passed half-way up by a small boy on a very large bicycle
who said '*Courage*' in a friendly but not quite respectful
manner before vanishing rapidly over the brow of the hill.
One thing I envied him: his proper racing shorts. Mine
were coming apart at the seams with the strain, as I had
been mentioning casually to Joy for some days past in the
hope that she would boast of being a wizz with a needle
and thread and put the matter right; but on this issue she
had maintained the attitude of those who have spells put
on them in the cradle by wicked fairies. I rode therefore
with a split short, as some ladies of an open-hearted
tendency wear a split skirt, and had added a couple of safety
pins to my luggage in case it got worse. Anyway, it hardly
mattered where I was going.

I turned off the main road and was in farmland that
rolled gently over the hills and broke into little pine-woods
on the crests, like Christopher Robin's private place at the
top of the forest, though the lad himself was elsewhere and
there was only a very loud blackbird echoing between the
trunks. In a meadow, a cow tinkled a solitary bell: a lonely
lark alternated its song between the plaintive and the pert.

The landscape was so deserted that it felt medieval, except that a distant light aircraft had cast its drone over all possible sections of the sky at once, like a very little insect edging its way across an enormous bowl. Though the lanes were fussy and friendly, there was the sense of a plateau, of being the last outpost of green below remoteness: in late July, the elderflower was still in blossom at this height. There was a sense, too, of man-made things existing in a state of siege. Dry-stone walls crumbled and were over-grown by flowers and grasses: the stones of the houses were rough as castle walls, with tiny windows as defences against the winter.

In the scattered hamlet of Fraisse, four brigandish black dogs slouched truculently out to guard the roadway, making me wonder what the cyclist should do when attacked by several animals simultaneously. Snapping, barking creatures that chase alongside you are no problem: they pretend to bite, you pretend to kick out, and by that time they are tired of the game and you only have to straighten out your wobble and proceed. Large creatures that wait are a more sinister thing entirely. I have read that one should ram one's bicycle pump down the throat of an attacking creature, which I understand to be a scaled-down version of the procedure for dragons, but if you have only one pump it must be difficult to decide how to dis-tribute it between several dogs – and, furthermore, must require a very good aim, which is probably only to be achieved by taking fencing lessons in advance. There are probably techniques worked out by the occupants of Russian sleighs speeding over the ice pursued by wolf-packs, but unfortunately knowledge of them seems to have died out, for one reason or another.

As I sailed gently towards the dogs, I reflected that a nineteenth-century cyclist in the mountains might well have been menaced by wolves, which were no respecters of any sort of privacy. Emilie Carles, a peasant school teacher who wrote a splendidly real autobiography under the title *Une Soupe aux Herbes Sauvages* records that her father used to tell of how his *arrière-grandpère* was visiting the *fosse d'aisance* (a pit with planks over it) when a wolf interrupted his meditations by jumping on his back. With considerable presence of mind the good man not only kept his balance but clasped the beast's forepaws tight round his neck and ran yelling to the house with his trousers round his ankles, whereupon everyone turned out and clubbed the beast to death.

As it was, I turned on my tape-recorder so that the Radio 4 audience would have an opportunity to enjoy the sound of one of their presenters being eaten alive; but the dogs were a great anti-climax, and simply slouched off as they had slouched on. Nor was I savaged by the flock of sheep I met being driven through St-Georges-Lagricol. There was only one street there to call a street, but it contained a fifteenth-century church and two bakers, who appeared to have been whiling away the time by holding a competition in ornamental breadwork. One had produced a loaf looking like an old-fashioned hand-saw, the other

a complex masterpiece with a strong resemblance to a model of an atom. There was also one of the smallest grocers in the world with the paint peeling off the sign 'Au Palais des Gourmets'.

As I rode over the hills I came to the conclusion that it is the little dips that are the most fun: on long descents you have to brake and concentrate too much. The ideal road lets you freewheel down as if you are flying, and mostly carries you up to the top on the other side. I sailed over such a rise near Vermoyal and suddenly there before me were the real mountains: the volcanoes of the Auvergne mist-shrouded in the distance even in the sun, layer upon layer of blue shapes stretching back like stage-mountains, cut-outs behind successive layers of gauze. There were daisies and wind in the grass on the crest of the hill, cornfields, pastures and woods spread out in the vale ahead like an aerial relief map, effulgent silver clouds, and sunlight mottling the landscape. Then the real downhill; the brakes would only just hold and the rims grew burning hot as I thundered down into the valley of the Haute-Loire, like a runaway pram with the baby drunk in charge.

At the base of the hill, the village of Vorey announced its presence at the confluence of the Arzon and the Loire with a cluster of red roofs and a stumpy church spire with martins wheeling over it. It is at Vorey that people from the two hamlets of Vertaure and Eyravazet vowed a mass in perpetuity for the soul of the leper woman they call Ste Juliette, who came begging in vain for food at their doors, and died of exhaustion and hunger in an old shed. In the years that followed, hailstorms blasted the harvests and the vines – except at Las Cabannas where she was buried – until her body was exhumed and carried to Vorey for burial in holy ground.

It is extraordinary how the world changes by taking one road rather than another. There had been breeze: now there was blazing sun. Over the hills where there was nowhere to go but other hills, I had hardly seen a soul: in the valley, on the route from Le Puy to St-Etienne,

Vorey was modestly bustling with tourists shopping for lunch. I shopped with them before I went on.

There were level fields by the river and a scattering of new houses along the road, until it began to twist and turn through the Gorges du Peyredeyre, where the river and road crowd into a rocky chasm, but which began modestly towards Lavoûte-sur-Loire with the pastures tilting into humps, and the wooded hills rearing into little mountains. Just after the town, there was a patch of grassy shade under the arch of a railway bridge over the river, and there I lunched, overlooked by a fairy-tale castle on a rock rising sheer from the water. From the riverside it appears little more than a round tower surmounted by a roof like a wizard's hat, but when you go back to the village and climb the winding road to the bluff, you discover that it is merely a trick of the angle, and that it is a long comfortable building with leaded windows looking out over what is now a garden of low box hedges patterned into an intricate fleur-de-lys, but was once a courtyard between wings of the château which were demolished during the French Revolution.

The Dukes of Polignac were great royalists, and were among the principal promoters of the court extravagance that encouraged the Revolution. The family traces its lineage back to the ninth century, but have only lived in the Château de la Voûte-Polignac, the second of their castles, since the thirteenth. One of them was still there, I learned when I visited the six rooms that are open to the public: his forebears would appear to have delighted in a great number of family portraits of people who liked being painted looking uncommonly po-faced and Aubusson tapestries of podgy characters doing biblical things. The most interesting Polignac there to me was the nineteenth-century Princess Armande Polignac, who was represented by her bust: it was inscribed to the effect that she was the first woman to conduct an orchestra. But from the river both castle and countryside are a dream.

This Loire was a very different stream from the sprawler

I had seen before, being recognizably still of the mountains
– shallow and rocky in parts – though that day the water
was murky, stirred up by storms of the day before, I was
told by an angler I met on the bank, who showed me
twenty-seven roach in his keep-net. He was a stocky man
with embarrassing trousers, but I could not point this out
to him because I had no idea of the French for 'zip'. As
we discussed England (he wanted to know whether it was
as hot in my country as it was in his, and whether we had
any mountains), a quartet of Dutch cyclists joined us, a
large bearded one, a little one and two pretty Indonesian
girls. They were on their way back to Amsterdam and the
Hague, they said, having been to Carcassonne and Avignon, but they would take the train at Paris, because
Belgium was so dull. They were laden with tents and
cooking pots: the Dutch, as a cycling nation, have remarkable stamina. I have met them in Tuscany on the last leg
of a trip to Rome and back, and whenever you see someone
attempting the mountains weighed down with tents and
a three-speed bike with a heavy chain guard, it is a hundred
to one he is a Dutchman. I told them I thought myself
lucky not to be carrying much in the way of luggage.

'Yes,' said the little one at the back sourly, staring at
my chest, 'and we don't have T-shirts with pictures of ourselves on, either.'

It was fair comment. After they had left, the fisherman
told me he had been on a cycling trip once, to Venice.

'First day, St-Etienne to Briançon – 280 kilometres,' the
fisherman told me. 'Climb the Alps, down to Susa; to
Milano, to Brescia, then Venice. Five days: a lot of kilometres.'

'I'm not *sportif*, myself,' I said.

Le Puy was still dozing after lunch when I dismounted
at my hotel in the Place Cadellade opposite the extraordinary art nouveau minaret surmounting the firm that
makes one of the things the town is famous for: Verveine
du Velay, a quite palatable liqueur, comes in green and
yellow strengths like Chartreuse (they also make fruit

liqueur in the Auvergne, particularly out of raspberries and bilberries). The Verveine recipe involves verbena, peppermint, thyme and some thirty other mountain herbs: green is the stronger.

It was a typically haphazard French square – all shutters, cars, awnings and sunshine – and I sat among the hotel geraniums looking up whatever-it-was they were advertising over the shop opposite in my dictionary (with some difficulty on account of my wild-flower collection therein). *Véritable dentelle du Puy* turned out not to be false teeth, as I had at first suspected, but lace. Though lace-makers are hardly less difficult to come by there than anywhere else nowadays, lace is a traditional product – indeed, at one time the common folk went about so finely tricked out with it that a law was passed to forbid them aping the aristocracy. But the principal industries of the town are religion and geology, both of which lend themselves to tourism.

The geology of the Auvergne is suppressed energy, which bubbles to the surface in hot springs and hides uranium in the rocks (as for instance at Bellevue-la-Montagne, near Vorey) but its power is most easily felt in its *puys*, which are just the opposite of *un puit*, a well, being volcanic peaks; and among the rocks on and around which Le Puy is built are two outstanding examples.

They rise from what was once the bed of a lake so that they are all the more striking for springing up in a hollow of the hills, rather than on top of them. But even more remarkable is the suddenness of their shape, for they are the basalt cores of volcanoes whose softer surrounding rocks have been eroded. One of them, the Rocher Corneille, is fairly large and clumsy, and bears on its summit an over-sized, over-pink madonna of saccharine sentimentality – 53 feet high, cast in 1860 from 112,000 kilogrammes of cannon captured from the Russians during the Crimean War, and with an observation platform on top of her head – a monument to what God's enthusiasts can do to God's creation in the name of piety and anything but an improvement on the ruined tower that was there before. The other rock is only some 270 feet above sea level, whereas the sole of the Virgin's foot (she would take a 1 metre 90 size in sandals) starts at 433 feet. But the Rocher St-Michel is a craggy needle with the eleventh-century oratory of St-Michel-d'Aiguille reaching to heaven with its pinnacled tower in what must be one of the most penitent situations of any church in the world – at the top of 268 tall steps. The first chapel was built there just over a century before the Battle of Hastings, and before that the rock was occupied by a temple to Mercury, for Le Puy's religious connection was made before Christianity.

At the original castle of Polignac on another extraordinary outcrop only three kilometres north-west of the town, there was once an oracle of Apollo: at the very doors of the exotic, almost oriental cathedral in the town lies a blue slab called 'the fever stone', which has the size and appearance of something prehistoric, and which will cure you of your sickness if you go to sleep on it. However, the greater miracle would be to go to sleep at all for it is the top step of the flight of five dozen leading up to the cathedral from the newer town below, and as the staircase is packed with tourists today, it was formerly packed with pilgrims, Le Puy being a particularly holy stop-off *en route* to Compostella, though in those days the celebrated Virgin of the town was not pink but black. The wooden image was said to have been brought from the East by Louis IX and may therefore have been an image of an older deity, rather than a statue which was simply black by reason of the smoke from the candles burnt before it. However, the original was itself burnt during the French Revolution, and the present-day black Virgin is a rough copy. Her pilgrims brought the town fame, prosperity and international influences, notably Moorish. That had been seen in Le Puy since one of its bishops was a leader in the First Crusade.

Having been accustomed to cater for tourists in one guise

or another for so many centuries, Le Puy has acquired a patina of the passing trade. I felt that it would be difficult to get involved with the place. The Hôtel de la Verveine was a box-like structure of box-like rooms, lit by fluorescent lights, above a restaurant at which guests were expected to eat and not go gallivanting off to somewhere more fancy on pain of the considerable displeasure of the manageress. However, since dinner was already arranged with a local family who refused to consider the possibility of eating tourist-class, there was no hope of pleasing her, and she was left to growl.

The Caroliaggi family were friends of friends and the paterfamilias, André, appeared to me as a man who would have been a cultured Renaissance nobleman (had he been noble and lived at the appropriate time); an equable monk (had he not been an atheist and a family man); a patriarch (had he not been considerately diffident); and a Paris intellectual (had he lived in Paris). As it was, he was a Corsican who had been a school-teacher in Le Puy for seventeen years – content, but, it seemed to me, only just.

We walked past cafés and bars crowded with tourists who had all hunted out together a little place off the beaten track where the other tourists don't go. We went straight to the last place any of them would have thought of looking, a forbidding grey-stone restaurant between the two principal squares. Inside, La Grande Brasserie du Velay was spacious, empty and excellent, with a very good Côtes du Rhône which happened to be the same one the Caroliaggis drank at home. It was also cheap and for 35F served herring fillets, veal with creole sauce which was creamy with a hint of curry and accompanied by rice and bananas, and apricot and almond tart. (What you are really supposed to eat in Le Puy is a traditional dish of lentils and sausages, but that is rather on the robust side.)

André the diffident began the meal until he saw that I did not know the etiquette of being a French host, whereupon he brought in André the patriarch to fulfil that function; he performed it so smoothly that the etiquette slipped by me, and I only noticed that it is good manners to pour a little wine for yourself first, to avoid giving your guests any fragment of cork which happens to be in the bottle. André the intellectual then told me that he was sceptical about my being able to gather true impressions of France on such a trip as mine. If I thought the French spoke aggressively, for instance, that was because I spoke the language imperfectly and everyone like me thinks native speakers talk too fast. He dismissed the idea that the French constantly talked about food – only to the British, he said, to flatter their prejudices. The British seemed to get their ideas about France from films: but films were not about France but about Parisians in the 16th *arrondissement*. It was much easier to make films about sex than about social problems and the British were left with the impression that the French were interested in two things, one of which was football. He then introduced me to André the atheist, who said that one of the things in particular that was ignored by the film-makers was the influence of the Church; he suggested that a Catholic country nourished different social taboos from a Protestant one. In France, the great unmentionable was money.

'People talk more easily about money in England. Nobody wants their income known here, because the poor are ashamed of being poor, and the rich are ashamed of being rich. In a Protestant land it is sex, the flesh, that is consciously or unconsciously considered as being dirty. To a Frenchman, because he is a Catholic, money is dirty.'

We went back to his house to meet André the connoisseur. He lived in a block of flats, and as a flat in England might have a glory-hole in which to keep coal, bicycles or a pram, he had a space in the cellar where he kept his wine, and from this he brought out one of his prize bottles, a fine, sweet Bordeaux. He drank good wine or he drank water, he said: never plonk. He had a particularly good source in the local wine-shop of Madame Molière, whose son we had dropped in to see on the way home. It was late at night, but M. Molière was still at work bottling a

Rhône wine which he had been at pains to seek out, a vintage which people could afford to buy but was of a quality far above the stuff in the supermarkets.

I had from André, the philosophical school-teacher of Le Puy, the sense of a quality of peaceful life continuing despite everything modern times could throw at it.

'You think they have put the clock back here,' André told me. 'People are friendly, there is no violence, the countryside is splendid. It's a quiet life: if you like reading, have a few friends, like Nature, it's not boring at all.'

'Do people feel anything special from the mountains, from all those centuries of religion?' I asked.

'Once, not now,' André replied. 'Perhaps you have a feeling of being protected or shut in.'

When I passed through Le Puy again, at the end of the summer, I stopped at the wine-shop of Mme Molière to buy a customs allowance of her excellent Côtes du Rhône. Out to greet me from the back of the little shop came André Caroliaggi, beaming. It occurred to me that perhaps a man so full of welcome should never have been confined in the coldly abstract world of the classroom, but should have made philosophy his hobby and his business being a wine-merchant.

CHAPTER 9

Le Bonheur

THE TWENTIETH DAY

After Le Puy, the land changed: the green was of a different
kind. In the valleys it was profuse and dark; above, there
was lushness to be found along the streams where the rest
of the uplands were sparse and yellowing, but nowhere
did the fields roll effortlessly verdant again, as they had
further north in the Auvergne. Perhaps one of the reasons
Le Puy was so famous a place of pilgrimage is that things
feel different either side of it: in a journey, as in a sentence,
it is always a relief to reach a semi-colon; it gives you the
hope of finding something different before the next full
stop.

I had seen the frontier on the morning of the previous
day, when I looked across from Vermoyal to the mountains. In the crossing it was vaguer: Le Puy gently sinking
into the folds of the hills as I followed the long, slow climb
out of town, until even the pink Virgin merged into the
anonymity of a huddle of red and white houses; the landscape ahead was beginning to show barer sometimes,
through tatters in its vegetation. There were also less
concrete differences coming in spirit and history for I was
across the numinous borderlands of Occitania, in which
flourished the ancient and courtly civilization which spoke
the *langue d'oc*, the language where *oc* means yes, and which
was overcome by the northern race who spoke the *langue
d'oïl*, the tongue in which they say *oui*.

Occitania was a culture that turned its face towards the
Mediterranean; it included not only what is now called
Languedoc but the lands to the north and lands to the east

257

of the Rhône. A peasant's patois would pass muster either side of the Alps: the troubadour could sing in a language which was not very good at abstract ideas but was closely in touch with life and nature, and capable of great refinement of meaning.

Today, the *langue d'oc* survives precariously among older people: at Ambert, Georges Crouzet had told me that his father spoke it fluently, but he hardly knew a word of it. There is also an intellectual revival, with university courses and even new writing in a standard version called Occitan. I was able to buy in an ordinary record shop a cassette of an Occitan singer/writer called Patric, whose songs were pleasant and impressively incomprehensible to me, though on the page you can easily see how the language works if you know French; you also detect correspondences with Latin, Italian and Spanish (sometimes it even seems closer to English than northern French, which has dropped syllables and letters which the *langue d'oc* has retained) – e.g., the English pilgrimage is *pèlerinage* in French, *pelegrinatge* in *langue d'oc*; other comparisons of words are water/*eau*/*aiga*; hen/*poule*/*galina*; house/*maison*/*oustal*; cold/*froid*/*frech*. I particularly like the word for 'wake up' or 'giddup': *arri-arri*. Following with a French translation is one thing, however; it must be quite another thing to speak a language with two dozen tenses, not counting subjunctives.

FRYING-PANS, ALMOST

This rhyme in the *langue d'oc* is traditional in the Cévennes, where they have *grillées*, long-handled pans exactly like frying-pans but with the bottoms perforated for roasting chestnuts over the fire.

LE BONHEUR

De gents Cevenas
Non faguetz padanas
Que traucadas son.

In the mountains, Cévenols
Make their frying-pans full of holes:
This must be the reason why
Cévennes' frying-pans do not fry.

There were a great many other people on the main road that fine, fleecy morning and all of them feeling the call of the South, for it was the second Sunday before August, and the tourists were in full cry to get quickly to their holiday in time to find a bar with a television set and watch the finale of the Tour de France. My own progress was somewhat slower, the hill out of Le Puy being over five miles long, with spasms of building along it, cheap housing estates naked of trees, corrugated sheds and warehouses, a builder's yard of pipes. The morning was afflicted with a severe attack of pre-fabrication. I passed a workshop with a graduated display of dog-kennels from which I learned that animals from the miniature poodle to the St Bernard come in eight standard sizes.

The caravans that passed me were anything but standard, except that most of them seemed to be over-optimistically named. A *Château* came by, followed by a slow *Spring* a d a lumbering *Sprite*: I preferred the relative modesty of one called *La Bohème*, a *KIP* and a do-it-yourself contrivance made by cutting a Renault 4 in half and throwing away the front end. However, we all travelled much more smoothly than Robert Louis Stevenson, whose *Travels With a Donkey in the Cévennes* crossed my route first at Bargettes beyond Costaros, for at that early stage in his journey he was still belabouring his obstinate but unfortunate Modestine every step of the way (two blows

259

to a step), having been driven to throw away a cherished egg-whisk and his leg of mutton so that he might have a whip-hand free. I noticed that the spirit of Modestine still lurked in that countryside, for one of the straps of my handlebar bag came loose, caught in the spokes and, stretching to hitherto unanticipated dimensions, finally parted with a loud twang and considerable danger to my left eye.

At Bargettes, neither I nor Stevenson were yet properly into the Cévennes, the mountains which lie to the south, but the French sense of place is confusing to the uninitiated since it includes not only the departments set up after the French Revolution (which are perfectly clearly defined) but also older political divisions of more than one kind and a hotch-potch of geographical features. Thus I was travelling from the *departement* of the Haute-Loire with the Margeride (*the* mountains of that name, not to be confused with any old *margeride* somewhere else) on my right; through Velay (the ancient territory of the Vellavi tribe). I was tending towards Gévaudan, though Gévaudan also covered Haute-Lozère, if not indeed Lozère proper, a *departement* lying to the south, not to be confused with Mont Lozère from which the *departement* takes its name and which is, of course, verging on the Cévennes mountains (though it is a mountain in its own right) – unless you take the term Cévennes to apply only to the country south of Meyrueis, or to include the whole caboodle – which is not strictly accurate, but may save a certain amount of trouble. (Since the re-organization of local government in Britain, we have been developing a similar multiple system ourselves of Avons, Somersets, Mendips and the like, but we have not yet had time to get the chaos really organized, as the French have.)

Whatever be the problems of geography, they are as nothing to the difficulties of donkeys. It is extraordinary that anyone who has read Stevenson's book should wish to involve themselves with such an animal in any circumstances whatever, but there has been a history of attempts to duplicate his miseries, one of which was by an English-woman, a Miss Singer, who is said to have been supplied with a donkey by the tourist office at Le Puy under the impression that she was a representative of the sewing machine company, and to have been nicknamed *la machine à coudre*. She was much fêted in the villages she passed through in 1949 – she assumed that this was because the country people were so bored they were glad to make the most of any distraction. In due course a mutual disenchant-ment appeared, but this too was in the Stevensonian tradition: the original notebook for the trip which was discovered in a Paris library during the run-up to the Stevenson centenary in 1978, turned out to be even more unpleasant about the local people than the edited version.

Since Stevenson had suffered with a donkey, and Miss Singer had suffered with a donkey, it was only logical that the centenary celebrations should include even more people suffering with donkeys. A lady reporter from the *National Geographic Magazine* covered the 200 kilometres of the walk in a shocking pink jumpsuit; other reporters rushed over the twelve-day hike in six days, succumbing to heat-stroke and exhaustion. A most appropriately un-comfortable time was had by all, not least by Pat and Pierre Vallette, a Scotswoman and her French husband, who were prime movers in what began as a small exhibition and snowballed, as those things do, into festivities with scho-lars, scouts and football teams flying back and forth between the two relevant countries in a frenzy of inter-national goodwill. But the most interesting permanent achievement of the Vallettes and their fellow-enthusiasts was to get Stevenson's route sign-posted and cleared so that anybody could follow it, which involved mobilizing all the villages along the way. Though a century had gone by, each village remembered Stevenson and roughly where he went, by oral tradition passed down from their great-grandfathers: they knew him often as l'Anglais, or M. Louis – or sometimes as Mr Singer, having mixed him up with *la machine à coudre*. Then, having established the route, the Vallettes went over the ground themselves to check the sign-posting, which varied from the informative to the enigmatic, and they took a donkey with them for one eight-mile stretch, in the course of which they were worn to a frazzle and ran out of sugar-lumps, so that they had to send the animal home.

The twentieth-century European seems to have lost the art of dealing with donkeys, which used to carry coal from the Cévennes to Nîmes without difficulty, and wine from the plains in skins on their backs to Le Puy: perhaps you have to know them intimately. They have the advantage over horses that they are not brought to a full stop by a cast shoe: the trouble is that recent-model donkeys seem to be brought to a full stop by practically everything else. As hikers and Stevensonians took to the Stevenson walk, a select group of donkey-entrepreneurs catered for those brave souls who were determined on authenticity. One donkey, however, would not cross a railway line; others hated water and would seize solid if they happened to look down when crossing a bridge and see the river between the planks, so that some walkers had to get a lorry to cart their beast across. Whether or not donkeys got used to the route, I did not discover: but a year after the celebrations, when I passed through on my more amenable bicycle, one donkey had already accomplished eight trips at £150 a time (the cost included the cattle-truck journey home). The route had other idiosyncrasies, I learned: it was possible to stay the night at the Trappist monastery of Our Lady of the Snows near La Bastide, but only men got cells – women had to sleep in the barn with the donkey.

Though hard, hot and prickly, however, the Cévennes are fine walking country for those with good legs, tough boots and rucksacks instead of donkeys. The Stevenson route, which is minutely catalogued in the bilingual *Topoguide de l'Itinéraire* (or Guide to his Journey), is only one among a remarkable network of trails and footpaths which have been similarly sign-posted for the hiker, but in any case continued to exist in their own right. In the

Cévennes proper, it can be quicker to climb an old path up the terraces than wind all round the mountain in a car: nor do paths easily fall into disuse in a stony land.

There is also a whole system of secret roads that the motoring tourist never notices – the *drailles*, *les routes de transhumance*, by which the flocks were brought from the arid lands of lower Languedoc up to mountain pastures for the summer. They are very ancient: the Draille du Gévaudan, which was to cross my route some miles ahead, is also known as le Chemin de César, and though nowadays the *drailles* may seem no more than a rocky line through the scrub or a shadow in the grass, they carried an immense traffic and were surrounded by an intricate complexity of grazing rights, often in dispute, with the shepherds paying a tithe to the villagers where they pastured according to the sizes of the flock and the village, and selling the dung from the animals in return. I learned that the hikers have not completely taken over, for 10,000 head of sheep still follow the Draille de Languedoc to Mont Lozère each year.

That fine morning outside Le Puy, the twentieth-century version of transhumance continued in the opposite direction, with herds of cars and caravans going my way. Their passage hardly touched the country – fields of cereals, clover, would-be maize far behind the crops I had seen a fortnight before and much further north in Beauce; a hayfield mown in a gigantic herring-bone pattern: dry-stone walls built of pitted volcanic rock, purple-black in colour and spotted with bright yellow lichen. Houses built in this stone had been crudely painted with daubings of mortar, so that the general effect was of a wall of prunes in custard.

Then there was a fork in the road: the tourists all streamed off like lemmings along the Route Nationale to the left, anxious to get to the sea and throw themselves in as quickly as possible. To the right was a lonely little railway-line and the by-road to Chapeauroux, absolutely empty – and that was for me.

At Landos I crossed Stevenson's path for the last time: he was going better at that point, having been introduced to the principle of the goad by a knowledgeable innkeeper on the evening of his first day, but he had gone round in a big circle in the vain hope of reaching the Lac du Bouchet, which is circular and rather dull but is said to be the work of Christ who punished a village that received him badly by submerging it along with all the inhabitants save for an old woman who had given him milk from her one goat. Stevenson had little to say of the lake, and nothing of the legend, preferring the story of the Beast of Gévaudan, which ate up quantities of locals in the 1760s, was itself killed more than once in the shape of a gigantic wolf, and inspired Stevenson to remark that he wished it had consumed more of the inhabitants.

From a cluster of farm buildings on the hill-top, the road wound downwards along the valley of a little brook fringed with rushes and silvery mint. There were grasses that shone fleetingly in the wind like moving lights stroked into the fur on a cat's back. A herd of respectable cows with bells tinkled at each other across the hoof-pocked banks of the stream. Then the rock neared the surface and the broom took hold: the valley sides became steeper, and turned to grey-and-orange rock speckled with frowsty lichens. At the bottom of the hill was a tumbling river, the infant Allier, that revealed a mineral wealth in the stones it rounded. There were black footballs that looked like polished coal, speckled rocks that flashed in spots in the sunlight. The whole cliff face had been quarried away at Le Nouveau Monde, which was now not so much *nouveau* as abandoned, with plants taking hold in the rock once more. Just across the river were the few houses and the Hôtel Beauséjour of Chapeauroux, set where the river Chapeauroux flows into the Allier at the end of a pine-clad valley. I was 670 miles from London, and had come only twenty-five from Le Puy, but the land of rock and forest had begun. The Chapeauroux is a trout-river, sparkling over the stones: on the hillside, where the pines

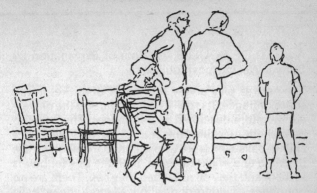

stopped, there were freshly mown hayfields, hummocky as if sculpted by a subterranean Henry Moore, and dotted with small ash trees.

I sat on the hotel terrace and ordered a Ricard before dinner (which Madame Dessauce, a white-haired governess-sort-of-lady with a good name for a hotel-keeper if ever there was one, insisted should be taken at 7.30 sharp): I do not care for *pastis*, but drank it in honour of the South, and a couple of lizards came out and switched back and forth over the stones, to affirm that I was indeed in the country of the sun. As I went to bed, there were the distant voices of villagers playing *pétanque*, the game of the Midi; it is a kind of three-dimensional bowls, in which you find a bit of road or any old reasonably level patch of ground, and throw three miniature cannonballs as near as you can get to a jack, which is known as 'the little pig'. It is said that the reason *pétanque* is popular in the south is because it never involves walking more than five yards at a time, which is rather unkind, but there are certainly few more peaceful ways of going to sleep than to the murmur of a river mingled with the far-off click of *boules*.

A LOAD OF BOULES – a Note of Explanation by Bulwer Wellington-Ffoulkes

The natives play a very funny sort of cricket in the south of france. It is called *pétanque*, and the players are therefore described as *pétomanes*. There are no permanent wickets: instead, there are two extra cricket balls which are thrown on to the pitch by the batsman and wicket-keeper, then the bowler bowls at them and they all run when they can. There are no boundaries, fielders or pavilion; all three cricket balls are made of metal so that they may also be fired from cannon in time of war; and everybody acts as an umpire. It is all extremely peculiar.

THE TWENTY-FIRST DAY

The day had begun at Chapeauroux well before the edge of the sunlight came creeping down the mountainsides. It began with loud birds by the river, the swish of an old man scything nettles round his beehives, and a float's gentle splash from an early morning fisherman. In the hotel, the chef was drinking coffee at the kitchen table as Madame prepared the *petit déjeuner*, which a pretty maid in a white apron far too small to be of any practical use served in a dining-room whose beams creaked as guests considered the possibilities of getting up in the rooms above.

I was on the road just after eight, a road which ran up the ravine-like valley of the Chapeauroux, which took to tumbling among rocks like the Allier the day before and had, in addition, wooded hillsides that tumbled down to it with silver birches mourning over the waters as if in disapproval of so much exuberance everywhere else.

The sun was still up among the pines and the air was cool: there were little springs falling out of the hills and mysterious conduits of water. There was no room in the valley for anything more than the road, the river and the occasional tiny meadow (in one of which was a story-book cow with a crumpled horn), and the village of St-Bonnet-de-Montauroux, even the graveyard was built in terraces.

I passed a one-man one-dog sawmill: the man was patiently pushing impossibly long planks past the blade and the dog – a little white Sealyham – was guarding him while he did it. A little further, and I found where his wood came from, for the ravine side was scattered with felled pines lying at every angle like a spilt box of matches.

But apart from that, the only works were down at the river where they were building a dam next to a scrawled slogan '*Les barrages sont la honte du pays*'. Dams are a particularly sensitive subject in that area, though it was difficult to say where the 'shame', if any, properly lay. Just over the hill at Naussac, the authorities were building a dam on the Allier to increase the flow of water down to the Loire in summer. There was great local ill-feeling about a fertile valley being submerged by order from Paris but, I was told, the reason that particular valley had been chosen was because the local inhabitants had been pretending for years in their tax returns that the land was poor and uncultivated, whereas in fact it was one of the richest parts of the area. Paris had never been to look. Several attempts had been made to blow up the dam: dynamite is relatively easy to come by in the mountains, where very often the only way of enlarging the road, or building a car-port, is to blast the rock apart: but the attempts had been unsuccessful, and the village would go under along with its fertile land.

The climb was gentle along the river, and I got to the point where the meadows started again just as the sun began to make short shadows. Near where the rocks smoothed out, even in the river bed, I came upon a drunken sign depicting an extremely iridescent fish and the name

L'Auberge de la Truite Enchantée: I didn't think it would sound quite so good in English, but that there must be a story behind it somewhere, as there are little fantasies waiting to be pulled out of all manner of everyday things.

Seen close to, rather than from a road above, the Chapeauroux was not quite a bathing river (I was still carrying a towel and swimming costume, and had been all the way from London, in the expectation of finding such a thing) for there were swirls of foam in the side-eddies. But it made that subtle hollow between pine woods into garden, winding through meadows as through lawns, fringed with rushes flashing in the wind. Though against the light it was peat-brown, it gleamed blue where it caught the sky and silver in the ripples. The light was extra-ordinarily clear. The fields suffered no unevenness other than the gentlest of knolls: the grasses were a rich stippling of greens, browns and purples. In one field four figures in wide-brimmed peasant hats were haymaking with wooden rakes, as if they had been posing for a picture postcard a hundred years ago. It was a place to hide away from a nuclear age.

But with every mile, the river grew smaller. It had lost its birch trees at the head of the valley: now its juicy rushes turned to hollow reeds, the lawns grew tussocks, yellowed, and the stone that had never been far beneath the soil began to appear above it. The roadside trees ended, and the road curved across the blazing plain, by the foot of a hill which swung up abruptly to Châteauneuf-de-Randon, a lonely watch-tower of a town set on a bluff surmounted by a ruined castle.

The tenth-century Tour des Anglais is no more now than the skeletons of two massive vaults set one above the other, with thin grasses growing peacefully among the stones, but it saw the rather humdrum death of probably the greatest soldier of medieval France, and the start of the strange story of his burial. As I would round the bottom of the hill, there was a sign to the Fontaine du Guesclin and, further on at the cross-roads, a massive dais of speckled stone on which lay the black figure of a slightly portly knight in full armour, with his feet couched on a dog with a half-human face that is by far the most interesting of the two, and made me wonder whether it was not the means which the stonemason had found to tactfully represent the true face of the man, for Bertrand du Guesclin described himself in these words: 'Large shoulders, short neck, the head of a monster; I was never welcome to woman; but I knew how to make myself feared by the enemies of my king,' and the features of his effigy are quite regular. This Constable of France inflicted defeat after defeat on the English during the Hundred Years' War before laying siege to the castle of Châteauneuf-du-Randon in the summer of 1380. It was occupied by the Sire de Roos and a Free Company who held out in hope of reinforcement from the English forces but, when weeks dragged by, set a date a fortnight ahead when they would deliver up the town if help did not come, coincidentally choosing a day which was to be significant again in French history – the 14th of July. On that day, there was no sign of relief and the keys were presented with all ceremony, but put into the hands of a dead man, for du Guesclin had fallen fatally ill with congestion of the lungs, caught, it was said, by drinking the icy waters of a spring. 'To no other man in France,' said de Roos, 'would I have given up the fortress.'

The dying wish of du Guesclin was that he should be buried in Brittany; but the way was long, and it was high summer. The body was taken to Le Puy, eviscerated and embalmed. The entrails were buried there in the Dominican church of St-Laurent, where they lie to this day with an effigy of the whole man above them. Meanwhile, a contest developed for the honour of providing the last resting-place for the rest of the hero, the king demanding it for the royal chapel of St-Denis. But by the time the corpse had arrived at Clermond-Ferrand, it was evident that the embalming had not been a success, and the flesh was cremated there, with the exception of the heart. The affair ended in a compromise, with the entrails in Le Puy, the heart at Dinan in Brittany, and the rest in St-Denis among the tombs of kings. (Strangely, just at this point on my route, I was passed by an estate car with a coffin on its roof, speeding like the entire Monte Carlo Rally put together. After a few miles I met it again, driving furiously in the opposite direction, still with the coffin: I could not help wondering whether it had been filled in the meantime and – even if it had – what all the hurry was about.)

I saw that time had overtaken Châteauneuf-de-Randon on this side of the hill, for a barrack of cream-coloured flats were taking advantage of the southern aspect and the effigy of du Guesclin now stood guard over a small hotel and a couple of garages. But the town centre above looked as if it had not changed for a century or more. It had an unreasonably vast square, made to hold the famous cattle fairs of this tiny place of a few hundred people: it was paved in patterns, with a bronze statue of du Guesclin being rather over-heroic in the middle, and a fringe of plain, jumbly houses. Yet everything one could need was there: a dusty hardware store which seemed to have accumulated by accident in somebody's front room; a grocer, two minuscule banks, one with a peeling wooden sign which – for a bank – indicates an extremity of drowsiness, a crusty-smelling baker and the Café de l'Union, Café du Guesclin, Café de la Poste, Café du Centre and Café du Midi, the last being guarded by a pert Alsatian in the upstairs room hanging its forepaws out of the window. The butcher sold milk straight from the churn.

There was a fresh breeze blowing that morning, and I made great speed over the Col de la Pierre Plantée and down past the pretty village of Laubert, with a three-pronged bell-tower to its church and bright orange lichen on its roofs. Here the stream of l'Esclancide made a fertile edge to the Plateau du Palais du Roi, which is so bleak that it is difficult to imagine any monarch even condescending to erect a tent, much less a palace. By my road there were meadows; cairns of great boulders showed how hard generations had had to work to clear the ground, though there were still a good many rocks too big to move, socketed into the turf. The plateau itself is sparse and yellow but for the bright pink of rose-bay willow-herb, with stunted oaks and dwarfish pines sometimes, granite outcrops and the peat-brown waters of the Lac du Charpal. These are hardly less featureless than the hills rising to the Signal du Randon, with its dominating red and white communications tower. There the road is marked by stone pillars, presumably to sign-post it in the snow, unless they are the boundaries of a *draille*.

I followed the Esclancide down into an increasingly hospitable countryside at ever-increasing speed until I was brought to a dead stop by the Monster. The Monster was crossing the road in a monster-like plod – that is, with great deliberation. It was built like the heads of two aard-varks joined at the ears and moved in a tottering gantry of grasshopper legs. It was bright green, like all the best monsters, and was almost four inches long. I was con-siderably impressed. I took it to be a cicada, down from its tree. I had not heard any shrilling along the way, but that might have been because of the cooling wind: as high fees are encouraging to stars of grand opera, so are high temperatures to cicadas, and neither species will let loose if the climate is insufficiently golden. At the rate the Monster was moving, it was not going to make the performance. I was unwilling to pick it up lest it should bite, or be venomous, but I banged my front wheel behind it to encourage it to get a move on before a car came along and squashed it. The Monster picked up speed by at least an extra six inches an hour. A car came along, swerved violently and hooted with great indignation at the idiot man standing with his bicycle in the middle of the road. Fortunately it was the only one in the next ten minutes, which was the time it took the Monster to get across. As it disappeared into the verge I noticed a movement on the other side of the road: a second Monster heading out across the tarmac. I left it to take its chance: I could have stayed there all day helping Monsters across the road. As I remounted, I discovered that the bicycle wheels had sunk into the hot road surface: I sped downhill rattling as the tar on the tyres attracted gobs of gravel that scraped in the mud-guards.

At Pelouse, a few white stone houses higgledy-piggledy over the hill, Joy came up in the car. There was a green stain on the front offside tyre.

'Road-hog!' I said to Joy.

'What?' said Joy.

There was a rutted lane leading into a wooden patch along the Esclancide, which was no more than a brook, running crystal over brown pebbles. There we lunched off picnic things including a *fromage de montagne* with holes like Gruyère and a pleasant dairy flavour, and Listel *rosé* – light, tart and delicious. It went straight to the legs: at the first hill of the afternoon I was passed by two cyclists – first a boy racing away with a speed that I had just finished ascribing to youthful vigour when an old man with grey hair and gold-rimmed spectacles whirred past after him.

On the arid hillside before Badaroux I passed the Ravine de la Tourette, where Gargantua the giant – who had already drunk so deeply of the Lot that he dried up the river – ate a carter, his team of oxen and a waggon loaded with brushwood at a single mouthful. But a rough stone on the hillside told a newer and grimmer story in its description: '*Passant, pour que tu vives libre: dans ce ravin le 29 Mai 1944 vingt-sept Maquisards du groupe Bir Hakeim ont été torturés et fusillés après que trente-trois de leur camarades eussent été tués au combat de la Parade.*' Alas, most passers-by were in cars and in a hurry.

I descended into Mende along the green valley of the Lot in a sobered frame of mind. In Mende I combed the bookshops for anything to tell me the history of the resistance in that area. There was nothing: in one shop, a woman knew of a book, but it had been out of print for years. Later I tried other shops in other towns, asked local people and tourist offices. There seemed to be a conspiracy to forget the twenty-seven who met so cruel a death that spring day in 1944 in the Ravine de la Tourette, to relegate them to a past as remote as that of du Guesclin. In one shop they asked me which war did I want – 1939 or 1702?

Eventually I turned up a sentence in a guide-book that had the day, the month and the year wrong, and a few paragraphs in a pamphlet dug out from behind the post-cards and the tourist leaflets in English, French and German. They told me what I already knew: that there was a battle at La Parade on the Causse Méjean: the next day there followed the ill-treatment and murder in the ravine. That was all there was to it.

The truth is that there has been so much blood spilt over Occitania, and particularly in Languedoc and the Cévennes, that in the panorama of history, the *maquis* shrinks to a pin-point, even in its greatest battle in June 1944 which is commemorated by the siting of its national monument at Mont Mouchet. The fight there was one to compare with Agincourt – for 10,000 *maquisards* faced 20,000 German troops supported by tanks and aircraft, and came out of it with casualties one-tenth of the enemy's. But the history of the south for century upon century staggered from revolt to war to bigotry to butchery to massacre – above all, in Languedoc and the Cévennes. Even Mende, a Barchester of a place if ever there was one, a drowsy county town whose only twentieth-century invaders are tourists, had its mass slaughter when the Protestant leader, the same Captain Mathieu Merle who held Ambert (and who pops up all over the region like a blood-stained jack-in-the-box), sacked the place in 1579. Now the human beings are forgotten: the episode is remembered by the fact that the cathedral was rebuilt with one tower shorter than the other, and that neither now contains the Nonpareil, the great bell which was so large they called it one of the wonders of Christendom, for the enterprising Captain melted it down to make cannon, leaving only the clapper.

But the episode of the most fervour, courage and brutality was the later War of the Camisards and the century and a half of oppression surrounding it. Not even the leaders of the Camisards could agree why they were so called by their enemies: perhaps it was because their followers went about in shirt sleeves so that they were free to fight; another suggestion was that the name began as an insult – 'shirt-stealers'. Their conflict was concentrated in the Cévennes for hardly more than two years, but its immediate causes went back half a century, and their theatre stretched from the borders of Catholic Auvergne to the sea – anywhere there were Huguenots to affront the authoritarian conformity of that vain and stupid monarch, Louis XIV, who began by whittling down the Protestants' civil rights, then removed them altogether, then sent in the soldiers to produce more immediate conversions.

The oppression extended over almost a century and a half up to the French Revolution, but it was after the coming of the soldiers with a licence to riot, and the razing of the principle of religious tolerance from the law-book in 1685 that the land went mad. For what else can it be but madness when a crowd is massacred after refusing to disperse in the belief that the protestant Holy Spirit would keep off the bullets: when a baby of three is roasted alive over a slow fire for being a Catholic: when men go into battle shouting 'Tartara!', a word having the power to paralyse the enemy: when entire congregations are slaughtered on the spot, just for being congregations: when every house in thirty-one parishes is destroyed by official order, and massacres are a matter of routine?

The madness of deed was universal, but the Protestants also suffered from delirium of the mind. When their chapels were destroyed and their pastors scattered abroad or forcibly converted, the Protestants – like the Israelites

– went into the wilderness, *le Désert*. They worshipped in
secret but in great numbers among the wild and fantastic
rocks that characterize the limestone regions of the south
with their preacher enthroned in a portable pulpit made of
wood sections or black cloth and struts on the deck-chair
principle. From it, words of fire and symbol reverberated
over the surreal landscape in an atmosphere of fear and
tension lest the congregation be discovered. Every soul
was stuffed with hatreds, resentments, religious inhibi-
tions, horrors, griefs at oppressions: many were ill-fed to
the point of light-headedness, especially after following
their prophets in droves through the mountains with little
to feed them but what wild fruit they could find. The
Cévenols were a dour mountain-people starved of fantasy:
their folk-tales contain almost no magic or wonder, but
are full of homily and clever tricks. So when their
imagination finally took hold of them, they had no natural
resistance and it shook them as a terrier shakes a rat. The
reprisals that ended it all are known as *le brûlement des
Cévennes* after the burning of more than 400 villages and
hamlets: but before that the fire was in the head, dancing
to the tune of Psalm 68, the song of battles, which the
Protestants are even said to have taught to the blackbirds
of the Cévennes, so that it might never be out of the ears
of the oppressor.

It comes as no surprise to find, almost three centuries
later, that today's Cévenol is proud, private, intensely
distrustful of Paris and central authority – and still usually
Protestant. Pat Vallette and her husband Pierre, who were
waiting for me at a café table in Mende, gave me the
example of a murderer then at large. He was an outsider,
one of a group of drop-outs who squatted on an abandoned
farm. When they had made it productive, the owner
claimed it and turned them off. Left without a livelihood,
they robbed a bank and were recognized by a local butcher,
whom they killed.

'They still haven't caught the man,' Pat told me.
'Actually he's still in the Cévennes selling horses but the

locals won't give him up because they hate the police even more than they hate drop-outs.'

I went to bed that night thinking that I had had a surfeit of death, destruction and history. Even in my evening walk through the net of dark alleys that run through the old town, where the cream-coloured spires of the Catholic cathedral are always peering at you over the high-pitched roof-tops during the day, and a large illuminated cross on Mont Mimat forces its attentions on you after dark. I came upon a house where someone had recently died: outside the front door they had set a table against the wall, with a black-ruled book for people to write condolences in.

THE TWENTY-SECOND DAY

The sun had not yet got into the alleys when I left Mende, and was still going round the ring-road with the tourists. A quantity of over-enthusiastic flies had gone up high to meet the warmth, and were being snapped up for their pains by equally enthusiastic martins swooping round the cathedral towers. I snapped up a couple of fruit tarts from a laden *boulangerie* which smelled as if it had itself been baked that morning, filled my water bottle at a dribbly old fountain opposite, and took the avenued road south along the valley of the Lot, with pine-clad mountains crowding down to its orchards and water-meadows. The Lot is a little, clear river there; the valley was green as green, and the light twinkled in the leaves.

I was heading for a different, upland country. At Balsièges, the few early tourists took the main routes that lie along the rivers and I went straight on by the ancient church that is just big enough to support the single bell that lives in a stone hutch on the roof, but cannot quite manage a churchyard, so has a neat vegetable garden instead with a profusion of tall daisies under the wall for the

sake of appearances. The hill wound long and steep: half-way up, I was surprised to be passed at speed by a trainee racing cyclist standing on his pedals with his trainer on a phlegmatic moped at the back. I plodded after him in my leisurely bottom gear through a thinning landscape: almost at the top, I was gratified to come upon the cyclist and trainer again in agitated discussion over a map. Plainly, they had taken the wrong hill, and were facing up to the prospect of going down to the bottom again and trying another one. I bade them good day: they eyed my sagging personality critically, but I did not care. I had decided that hairpin bends offer an additional advantage to the travelling sun-worshipper of broiling you nicely on all sides – though my hands were now two-tone, with a white bar across the fingers where they went underneath the handlebars – and I was full of modest energy from my excellent dinner of the night before at le Lion d'Or in Mende.

Standing on one's pedals is no doubt a good thing, but

you have to see it in a gastronomic perspective. I had cast my eye over a panorama of terrine of smoked trout, pigs' trotters in a rich cheese sauce, and an even richer *confit d'oie*, with a modest bilberry sorbet in sponge and meringue flamed with brandy. The menu had called it a *flambé de Lozère*, for on that mountain the gathering of bilberries is a significant part of the local economy, along with the collection of medicinal herbs and wild mushrooms of various kinds (the *confit d'oie* had been distinguished by the presence of *cèpes*, that perfuming boletus we seem to have excluded from British cookery, among the potato, onion and potted goose).

The meal had also included a distinguished Roquefort, for not far to the south-west lies Roquefort-sur-Soulzon where the inhabitants made the most of their few natural advantages to produce what many people consider the emperor of cheeses, though my taste is for the gentler Bleu de Lozère which is to be found in local markets. The people of Roquefort were shepherds, and found that the mountain grasses and wild herbs on which sheep fed gave the milk an aromatic quality. But the particular asset was the cave system undermining the mountain of Combalou, which had caused it to collapse upon itself, leaving fissures to the air outside. Any cave provides evenness of temperature, but these fissures, called *fleurines*, add a constant gentle movement of air which makes the caves ideal for the curing of cheese and distributes the unique Roquefort mould to all the cheese there, which it enters through the holes pricked into them. It is a cheese of most respectable antiquity: Pliny approved of it, Charlemagne is said to have insisted on a personal supply and, today, cheeses come from as far afield as the Pyrenees and Corsica to ripen in the famous mouldy caves.

The land I came into on the top of the hills was obviously good for little else but sheep. I had noticed new plants as I came up: harebells growing giant, a yellow rock rose, white-and-yellow-flowered succulents. Cornflowers were the same as ever, but they gathered fresh petals in the

form of tiny butterflies, winged with red spots on metallic
blue, which clustered on them. There were the first wild
clematis of the Cévennes, with white star-bursts of heavily
scented flowers, bristly lavender and low-growing sloe
bushes, whose fruit are not only made into a liqueur but
also a children's pudding, when they have become sweeter
after the frost. On the *causses*, these highland plains, everything puts up a prickly resistance to the sun. Spines and
thorns are everywhere, in the few stunted conifers, the
innocent-looking junipers: even the grass grows spiky, and
the plants scrunch beneath your feet as if half-dried. There
are stocky, ferocious thistles and sometimes you come upon
la carline à feuilles d'açanthe, which is a flower as big as
the palm of a hand lying flat on a nest of prickles like
a yellow sun in the grass.

The *causses* were always a world apart: a tall, fair
caussenard would stand out from the crowd in a southern
market filled with short, dark plainsmen; the valleys were
full of small farmers with plots of land whereas the *causses*
had big self-contained ranches. The valleys grow splendid
fruit and vegetables: on the *causses* such wheat as there
may be is sparse and pale with stems hardly thicker than
the grasses. The top country was desolate even on that
burning day when the sky was deep blue in the middle,
whitish-blue at the edges, as if it were being heated in
a furnace. The only sounds were the distinct tinkle of
a flock of sheep on a distant slope and the thin whirr of
wind in grass. When I took the top off my water bottle,
the breeze hooted in it, as if a genie were coming out.

Where there were fields they were covered with grey
stones, studded with cairns of grey stones, rimmed with
banks of stones, walled with stones – all painstakingly
cleared to make a thin pasture. There are sometimes dry-
stone beehive huts, *cazelles*, just big enough to shelter two
people from the weather. But for the juniper and pine,
it is a yellow-grey country – even the box bushes tinge
to yellow except where they straggle out along the line
of underground water, and that is only on the slopes. Here

it is worthwhile to cultivate the tiniest patch of soil caught in a hollow in the rock: I saw a field of clover no more than 25 yards across. These islands of fertility are called *sotchs*, and mark a patch of earth in a depression where the limestone was dissolved by rain or a cave fell in geological times, which is why they are usually circles of green against the yellow. The Causse de Sauveterre, which I was travelling across and which is the northernmost of this succession of great *causses*, is well named.

When I had passed the solitary stones of the Tour du Choizal, the landscape was empty until I came to Sauveterre itself, a small cluster of messy farm-buildings on a rise with a great concrete pond doing its best to hold water for the animals. Then the road bent downhill, along the course of what it would be more correct to call a damp patch rather than a stream until I came out above a stupendous hairpin descent into the cleft of the river Tarn. It was a God's-eye-view of creation, seen at a rather early stage in geology when the form-work was still visible: a town of red-roofed houses like match-heads by the cyan thread of the river, hillsides of dark green brush beetling over the ripples of abandoned terraces and the edges of grey cliffs. The road crept back and forth over and under itself down the vertiginous sides of the valley: I crept with it to the sound of busy grasshoppers, an echoing bell from far below and the cautious rub of brakes.

Soon I was low enough to see the cars baking in the village of Ste-Enimie, for it is not to be expected that any place a fraction as impressive looking as the Gorges du Tarn will be destitute of tourists in high summer, though parking is scarce on the road that snakes along the river, so they tend to concentrate in spots. Apart from a lack of space which prevents the establishment of such essential amenities as fun-fairs, skyscrapers, cathedrals and chain-restaurants, the gorges have everything the holiday-maker could reasonably desire – sun, scenery, a beautiful river to share with the fish, pretty little towns to accommodate souvenir shops, and a good supply of legends, of

which that of the randy seigneur of Castelbouc who, for
his sins (or possibly his greater convenience), was trans-
formed into an enormous flying goat which disappeared
above his castle in a clap of thunder, is rather more interesting than that of Ste-Enimie herself, a princess whose
prayer to be saved from losing her virginity to a husband
was granted by a very prompt divine affliction – a horrible
skin disease which kept all her suitors at bay. Having got
rid of them, Ste-Enimie rather inconsistently asked for
her complexion back, and was duly directed to a miraculous spring by which she remained for the rest of her life,
enjoying her favourite occupation of washing the feet of
beggars – and, on one occasion, chasing the Devil down
the Tarn and throwing boulders at him, which can be
seen to this day downriver at Pas de Souci.

The town of the super-hygienic princess was undeniably
pretty, with her little chapel on the hill, a fine arched
bridge, tiny cobbled streets leading one out of the other,
one half-timbered house looking like an escapee from
Warwickshire, a great deal of trimness to the others, and
a stentorian clanger of a church bell. It looked as if it
had been much visited and holidayed in since they opened
up the gorges at the end of the last century, and would
be prepared to sell you anything. It was also full of people,
so I went off downriver past St-Chely-du-Tarn which is
set in a *cirque*, a vast meander of the river, and swam
in an amethyst pool beneath an overhanging rock where
there was only a scattering of people, most of whom were
fairly conventionally unclothed.

The southern rivers bring out a great deal of previously
undisplayed flesh: most women able to wear a bikini put
on only half of it, and in parts of the Ardèche – which
must be one of the most perfect swimming rivers there
is – are almost completely nude, much to the disgust of
the locals, who say: 'They don't do it in their cities –
why do they come and do it here?' The keenest nudists
appear to be the Germans, with the Dutch a close second:
since *camping sauvage* is not frowned upon in the Ardèche

as it is in the Gorges du Tarn, you come upon caves in the cliff-face lined with naked bodies, as if prehistory were still in progress. (In some parts of the country there can be so many tents pitched in the scrub along the river banks in an effort to escape the horrid togetherness of the organized camp-site that it is like walking through a housing estate with the dustmen on strike, since the simple life appears to produce little less rubbish than the sophisticated one.)

The self-consciousness of the nude tourist varies according to tan. In the early stages of the holiday there is a noticeable tendency to remain rigid, as if the tourist were working to the obscenity rules that operated under the old Lord Chamberlain, viz: that nudes were pure until they moved. At this stage, the bathing costume is often kept handy to allow for a quick cover-up in case anybody comes by. Since there is a constant procession of canoes down the river, somebody is always coming by, so this precaution proves to be unworkable, and the nude tourist gives up pretending to be not really there, and starts casting glances out of the corner of the eye at the people in the canoes, who are also often naked. Then follows the stage of the interested stare, succeeded by the indifferent stare, and the more hardened and presentable bodies eventually take to wandering up and down the bank to see if anything interesting will happen, which it hardly ever does. The most determined attempt to escape the boredom of sunbathing that I have seen was a gentleman I encountered about a mile from the nearest road – sitting on a rock playing a Bach solo suite on the cello. It must have given him a most peculiar-shaped tan. Generally there are a few yards of space between one group of sun-worshippers and the next, and this may be important in getting past the initial self-conscious stage of nudity: when the crowding at the riverside (which increases yearly) reaches a seaside intensity, it will be interesting to see whether people can keep it up.

None of this is to say that river-swimming is not among the greatest delights of this part of France. It is beyond me why anyone would prefer to lie cheek by jowl on a yelling beach where the sand gets into the butter and there is no shade and nothing to look at but sand, sea and other bodies if, instead, they could have shoals of little fish nibbling at their legs, a clear stream and a wooded valley loud with cicadas. However, it is very necessary to go about shod, since the pebbles are extremely knobbly – especially when the soles of the feet have some nineteen stone to support – and plastic water-sandals are sold everywhere.

Downstream of Ste-Enimie, the cliffs rise steeper and the valley narrows until the road is reduced to cutting through the outcrops in tunnels, and at this point is the Château de la Caze, where I stayed the night. The château stood by itself on the edge of the river with three round towers, two square ones and as many battlements as the most enthusiastic medievalist could possibly desire. It was once the home of the eight 'Nymphs of the Tarn', the daughters of Soubeyrane Alamand who built the castle in the fifteenth century: they were so beautiful, it is said, that no suitor could choose between them. I found the castle guarded by a fleet of fat trout in a moat through which the waters of a spring rushed to the river below, and two ancestral dogs – a boar-hound looking as if it had been kept liberally supplied with boars, and a three-legged Alsatian, that went everywhere at a hop.

In the gardens, I met a middle-aged Belgian and his wife emerging from lunch who asked me whether I had been up or just come down. Down, I told him, but I would be going up Mont Aigoual next day.

'It is not possible,' said the Belgian. He raised his voice to a medium shriek, and the three-legged Alsatian joined in. 'In one day?'

I assured him.

'I find it so fun,' said the Belgian, chuckling. He was not staying at the château he said, he had just come to lunch and had done very well on something for which he could not remember the English.

'Someone like you have in Scotland,' the Belgian explained.

'Haggis?'

'No, not haggis. Shalom?'

'Salmon?'

Salmon it turned out to be. He was from Antwerp, and had bought a house in the Ardèche six years before. 'It was for nutting,' said the Belgian, lowering his voice conspiratorially. 'I change everything: now we have two bathrooms. Forty people lives in now.'

'It sounds more like a hotel,' I said.

'Yes, hotel for the Belgian people. And English. We had a fellow from Manchester last week. We met him in a tank. In Antwerp in the war, and he is always a fellow.'

I asked him how he found the local people, and how they found him and his luxury home.

'We have money, you see, and if you have money it is always all right. But French are very funny, very bizarre people. You were ever in the south? How was the people there? Better than here?'

In fact, Pat Vallette had told me that the Cévenols had an ambivalent attitude to tourism and to the Belgians and the Dutch who were buying up the country. (There were hamlets that had no French in them at all, and no permanent residents.) Those who made money out of the holiday-makers naturally welcomed their cheque books, but the Cévenols were a proud people, and there were those who would rather see a house go to ruin than sell to a foreigner. But the most virulent opposition to tourists came from outsiders who had dropped out to the simple life. I saw a number of slogans resentful of the decline of everyday working life in the Cévennes: a scrawl of *Oc* (for Occitania) was common on road signs, though the general opinion was that that was the work of a very small group of people, and the uniform style of the slogans seemed to support that. In several years of holidaying in the Cévennes, I almost always found the people as friendly as anyone could wish, providing that you are not snooty with them. It was said to me that if you ask a Cévenol the way he will take great trouble to show you: but if you decide for yourself to take the wrong road, he will enjoy watching you learn the hard way.

The cocky sort of person does well to follow the advice the Belgian gave me, in hushed tones, as we parted: 'They are very bizarre people: be careful.'

I entered the château by means of a long-jump over the baronial boar-hound. A manageress with the statutory pallor of the hotel-keeper emerged from a small dungeon in the middle of the castle, where she lived like a diffident spider, to conduct me to my room with something of the air of Lady Macbeth ushering an important guest to the

principal bedchamber. We trod the polished cobbles and
stone flags of vaulted corridors past the chapel – which
contained a peculiarly revolting devotional picture of a
fat bare infant hugging a lamb, or possibly throttling a
sheep – and came to a tower room with furniture of
immense solidity. The bed was not actually a four-poster,
but did have four knobs: the wardrobe was big enough
to conceal at least two lovers and, locked with a key, big
enough to hold both of them in forever, should the injured
spouse remain permanently suspicious. Stunned by an
excess of medievalism, I restrained myself from searching
the hangings for the lever which plunged daggers into the
sleeper in the small hours, ignored the possibility of there
being an Iron Maiden in the bathroom, and went off for
dinner on the terrace – from which, in ancient times, cooks-
at-arms had doubtless poured down boiling *sauce béchamel*
on the heads of invaders. I was almost 750 miles from
London.

THE TWENTY-THIRD DAY

I left the château with the sun climbing down the cliffs,
bats and shadows vanishing together into the crevices:
below, the river was cool as cool, clear as clear and still
as still. As one side of the gorge paled to gold, what was
left of the darkness retreated across the water and hung
grey among the stone outcrops and the half-blind houses
of the village of Haute Rive, which were like outcrops
themselves. Haute Rive has no road: only a one-foot
footpath that runs along that side of the river, but they
had slung a hawser across the water, and a tin cradle went
over from road to village on rusty pulleys and chains like
a bosun's chair. In the cradle was a crate of empties waiting
for the morning delivery: they were not milk bottles, but
litres of *ordinaire*.

By contrast, the day felt special. Ahead was the peak
of my trip, Mont Aigoual – slightly shorter than Mont

Lozère but still almost 1600 metres high, and the last great barrier before the Mediterranean. My road would pass not far below the summit, and I was surprised to find myself relishing the prospect. The bicycle and I swept smoothly along in modest confidence to the village of La Malène, which during the Revolution hid its aristocrats, the Montesquieux, in caves for nine months – the baron, his three grandchildren and the baroness, who was blind and over seventy – and afterwards took up a collection to enable them to buy back part of their family estates, a devotion for which the baroness showed her gratitude by living to the age of ninety.

There was a surprise waiting at La Malène, a grey-roofed village even smaller than Ste-Enimie (which has no more than 600 people when you take away the tourists). The surprise zig-zagged up the side of the gorge like a snake with a bad case of indigestion: a prodigious hill, the old road to the village dating back to the days when the only way along a lot of the Tarn was by boat. '! 10 lacets dangereux' said the sign at the bottom, advertising hairpins whose horrors were only too visible. Also, '! falling boulders'. '! Indeed,' I thought to myself, engaging bottom gear in a determined manner. The next three miles took an hour of crawling past limestone screes and red rock where the stone was crumbling and had not yet turned grey (this was presumably the *calcaire doux* which is easy to work but hardens and changes colour on exposure to the air, and is distinguished from the brittle *calcaire vif*, also known as *calcaire de Ste-Enimie*). There were fissures and mysterious cave entrances: plants were rooting in the tiniest crevices, hanging and trailing over the rock (I even saw a trailing box).

Every time I looked back, La Malène was even more impossibly tiny in the rock-scape of even more impossible grandeur. I stood on the pedals, I persevered painfully, I stopped and puffed: but I did not regret the hill for it made me feel that I was making contact with the toughness of the land though I hoped that I would not come upon its like again. Nor was my pride lessened by an envious Fate which sent a racing cyclist to pass me at some speed on the very crest – though he had been nowhere in sight when I last looked back – for as he vanished there came the instant of the last push which sent me rolling over the top of the rise, and the magic clicking of the freewheel as I picked up speed on the down.

The down was brief, and when I started pedalling again I did not move quite as confidently as I had in the valley: there was a feeling that the brake was invisibly and slightly on, especially up the long slow climb to la Parade. I was on the Causse Méjean, the highest of the *causses*. It did not seem quite so poor as Sauveterre, but was still inhospitable country: when I stopped to make notes, a large black ant scuttled up and bit my toe in an exploratory manner.

'Dr Livingstone, I presume?' I said to the ant, sarcastically.

The ant called his friends. I left, and spoke to no one else apart from an old man tending his dahlias in the garden of an isolated house until I got to la Parade itself, which was a random scattering of stone houses at a cross-roads. There I was hailed by three boys on bicycles forlornly propping up a road sign. I could hardly understand their accent but gathered that some disaster had taken place: they were camping, they said, and one of their companions was '*crevé*': would I follow them? Looking up '*crevé*' in my dictionary, I was aghast to find that it meant split open. I sped after them along a track which went ever-deeper into wilderness, and was relieved to discover their companion in one piece nursing a punctured inner tube. I supplied a pristine puncture-repair kit, for I had had no trouble of that sort on my journey, and departed to a great many incomprehensible expressions of gratitude.

The population of Méjean seemed to consist of cyclists: I met four girls in bikinis who greeted me with '*Bon appetit*' in response to my '*Bonjour*', but fortunately they were going the other way so there was no temptation to keep up with them. Apart from cyclists, there were goats of a

peculiar voracity, gobbling at the scanty grass, which was
as much grey as green, and nudging each other on to the
next patch like a rugger scrum; and sheep, milling around
in packs in the midst of emptiness, tended by two black
spots – the larger, a shepherd taking it easy on a rock, and
the smaller, his dog, moving in an elaborate and tireless
patrol. It was the dead-centre of nowhere, and occasionally
a track would turn off the road in the direction of nowhere
itself. The only one with any traffic on it, however, was
the dead end to the Aven Armand, a pothole named after
Louis Armand who discovered it in 1897 which is not open
to the public. The limestone *causses* are honeycombed with
caves and passages through which the water makes its way
down to the gorges: their great speleologist was M. E. A.
Martel, who revealed the stone poetry of the underworld
in the 1880s with the flicker of candlelight and the brief
flash of magnesium flares. His statue stands at Le Rozier
on the Tarn, ornamented with pillaged stalactites which
look uncommonly dull in the light of day. Among his ex-
plorations was a five-day trip through the rose grotto of
Dargilan, which was discovered by a shepherd beneath a
fox's earth. It lies not far from the Aven Armand but very
separate on the far side of gorges which are a close second
in magnificence to the Gorges du Tarn, the Gorges de la
Jonte, which I soon saw on my right as the road began
a long descent into a country which was dry enough but
still seemed greener after the bareness of the *causse*; the
roofs of the town of Meyrueis reflected the sun in a silver
cluster far below.

There were trout nosing the current under the bridge
at Meyrueis, and a great many holiday-makers in shorts
nosing the hams, sausages and garlic-strings in the little
market which seems to be permanently busy in the summer
months. It was the prettiest of stone towns, with a succession of little bridges arching over the pebbly stream that
ran down behind the market to join the Jonte: an old
round tower guarding a bridge contained the tourist office
and supported an ancient clock and an alarm-bell in a

rusty cage; there was also a bright blue Virgin perched on a hill-top chapel. In the crowded souvenir shops, I found I could buy cow-horns with squeakers in them, twisty towers of brioche done up in cellophane called *châteaux*, Lozère cake with nuts and an extraordinary variety of polished rocks at prices ranging up to £550. But I could not find anywhere to sell me fresh milk – not even the plastic litre bottles of half-turned blobbiness which is what passes for it in the smaller shops of the south. The town *crémerie* offered milk which was *longue conservation* and milk powder which was even *longuer*, but told me that I must see a *paysan* for fresh milk. Since there was no indication of where one of these might be found in association with cows, I did not. Joy was in the market when I came out. She said she had bought Côtes de Roussillon instead.

'It will have to do,' I said. 'And by the way, if you see a flock of sheep, can you record them in stereo? They tinkle, you know.'

Meyrueis had a long wooded hill out of itself, and we lunched in a dell by a tiny ice-cold rivulet half-way up. Though the Causse Noir continues to the south-west with its black pines and fantastic rocks, my way went along its edge and the start of the granite which, unlike limestone, holds the water and nurtures forests. With the change in rock, I was no longer approximately but truly in the Cévennes, though it hardly seemed so at first, for the road ran through mountain farmland. Then I rounded a bend into a landscape of shaggy hill and crag; first there were chestnuts in flower as if hung with ropes of greeny-yellow fungus, then the road wound into tall pines that dropped cones round me as I travelled gently but continually upwards.

It was not a natural forest: Aigoual was created twice, first by God, second by Georges Fabre. He had a Cévenol father, but he was born at Orléans in 1844 and developed his love of nature in the Jardin du Luxembourg in Paris to which his mother used to take him as a child. He became a brilliant student of forestry, and could have had his pick of

the best jobs but he astonished his tutors by choosing to
come to Mende, which as far as everyone else was concerned was the backwoods in entirely the wrong sense, and
one of the least-regarded posts in France.

At that time Aigoual, whose name comes from the
Occitan word for water, was on its way to becoming a
desert, with its forests rapidly disappearing before the axe
to provide fuel for lime-burning and glass-making – and to
enlarge the pastures and winter fires of the local people.
Channels of erosion ran from top to bottom of the
mountainsides. Fabre looks from his photograph as if he
had entered a competition for the Best Impersonation of
Abraham Lincoln Prize (and so does his colleague Charles
Flahault, a professor at Montpellier University) but with
their successor Max Nègre, they master-minded the re-
afforestation of almost 40,000 acres in the course of a
century. Fabre himself designed the observatory which
was built in 1894, complete with battlemented tower, at the
summit of the mountain, L'Hort de Dieu, 'the Garden of
God': but, though Fabre established an arboretum lower
down, little grows at the peak except shiny, slippery
grasses. The weather is so Wagnerian that the little café
and refuge under the massive walls of the observatory has
to be fastened down to the rock with chains. It is quite
normal for gales to top 250 k.p.h. in the winter, and even on
a summer day the café's washing-line blows in the wind as
if the clothes still had people in them.

From Aigoual you look across mountain ranges and
plateaux to distant violet shadows and cloudy cliffs that
could be sky or land; they are Mont Ventoux across the
Rhône, the Alps, the Mediterranean, the Pyrenees. But the
best show is often close at hand, in the conflict of the winds
that have come over the Massif down from the north, and
the wetter clouds up from the Mediterranean, which are
pinned down, churning, in the valleys, until the cold makes
them give up their moisture. With snow on the ground
from November to May and the only way to the observatory by ski, the early foresters were tough men, and their

successors little less hardy. One man unable to get to a dentist is recorded as having pulled out thirteen of his own teeth with the pliers from the tool-kit of his useless car.

Relations with the local people were not always easy. At the start, they objected to the compulsory purchase of their farms and loss of timber rights. In 1970, they resented the creation of the National Park of the Cévennes, which was intended to promote tourism and conservation. *'Assez parc national pourri'* said one slogan I saw scrawled for the tourists to read. Rotten or not, the Parc National involves various compromises, especially for local people who remember the traditional way of life. Gathering of mushrooms and *cèpes* was an important perquisite of the peasant worth three times the wages of the wine-harvest, for a man and his brother might gather three or four hundred kilos in a day: now they have to get there before the outsiders arrive in their cars.

Though the gathering of bilberries is strictly limited to those who own the land, and the use of the *peigne* (a box with a comb of nails to drag through the plant) is banned, stacks of *peignes* still appear and disappear in the hardware stores. Another staple of the economy, particularly on the *causses*, was the use of *tendelles*, snares to trap thrushes, which is now frowned upon since there are hardly any thrushes left. The traditional thrush bait was the juniper berry, gathered in its second autumn when the fruit turns black; and the thrush was killed by a falling stone.

Even more dangerous to wild-life is the amateur hunter, manic and numerous.

'If you saw the last hare,' one was asked, 'would you kill it?'

'Yes,' said the hunter.

'But surely that is unreasonable?'

'But if I didn't, somebody else would,' was the reply.

There is an astonishing quantity of opinion scribbled over the Cévennes, considering the comparative shortage of walls. One slogan I passed said: *'Chasseur cévenol = grand guignol'*. On their side, the hunters objected to the release of pairs of vultures to replace those which were once seen in flights of thirty or forty in the days when farm animals were less carefully tended than they are now and the carcasses left to the birds on the *causse*; there was too much competition for game already, they thought. People living in the Cévennes have automatic hunting rights, along with those who own more than a certain amount of land, but there are some two million hunters in France who have to hunt somewhere, and the opening of the season is the cue for an invading army that strips the landscape of everything that moves.

'It is all killed in the first day,' a non-hunting local man told me: 'After September 15th, you can't find a partridge, a quail, a hare: they come out after wild boar, and when they can't get that, they shoot the nightingale.'

In fact the wild boar is the only species which ever manages to increase its numbers – perhaps partly because there are now farms of tame wild boar to provide for the ethnic chef, partly because *sanglier* has a different season, and mostly because it is difficult for the novice to shoot. If there is not enough game, there can be no question as to why: when hunting stopped during the war, the number of partridges on the *causses* tripled. The only reason that the French have been able to bang away indiscriminately so far is that they have a large country and a relatively small population: but in Aigoual, as elsewhere, they are coming up against the natural law that you simply cannot have your game and eat it. The only hunters I have any kind of sympathy for are local ones who do it for the pot. Country people have a right to things appropriate to their life, like the landscapes, hunting and manure: such are not the birth-right of the town-dweller, who has chosen a life with different trappings and should be allowed in the country only on sufferance and proof of considerable humility. But you cannot tell the French that: too many of them expect to be able to hunt, plunder and light fires as if they were trappers in seventeenth-century Canada.

But that long hot afternoon there were no shots, and the

only animal I met was the stone cat who dribbled spring water into my hands at a roadside fountain, cool and tasting of the woods. The forest made everything its own, concealing everything else but forest for a long time, until there was the yellow gleam of distant grasslands through the trunks, and I was suddenly aware that the road was running above a ravine of layered red cliffs with a silver waterfall fanning out from a great black cleft in the rock very far below. It was Bramabiau, 'the river that bellows like a bull', and the grasslands extending to the cliff edge were the plain of Camprieu, fertile by reason of once having been the bed of a mountain lake, until the water found out fissures in the limestone and began to enlarge the caverns through which the river runs today.

Martel was the first explorer of Bramabiau in June 1888, discounting the suicide who preceded him the previous January and whose remains he found wedged in the rocks on the way down (such suicides were not uncommon in this cave country). That unfortunate apart, Bramabiau was alive with the rush of the river and the thunder of water-falls, springs bursting from the rock, dark lakes, mysterious rifts down which the river would vanish, only to reappear further on. Martel was the bard of the underworld, and the primitiveness of his equipment only served to deepen his sense of wonder, which issued in a cataract of subclauses:

'I will say nothing more of the magic effect of the magnesium light under those vaults lofty as Gothic naves: I will only ask the reader to imagine our little party, deafened by the roar of the water, in profound night, with feebly twinkling tapers, scattered about the grotto seeking for fissures, communicating by whistles, cords stretched and ladders hanging over abrupt ledges, our shadows magnified on the walls or on the foaming river, under cupolas 150 feet high, or at the end of avenues 300 feet long.'

The advance of progress has brought a ticket-office to the Abîme du Bramabiau – I passed it a few yards further on – but until that day in June 1888 when Martel's party burst into the daylight above the ravine nobody believed that the Bramabiau issuing from the cliff had any connection with the modest stream that vanished beneath the rock less than a kilometre away, for things thrown in at the top were filtered out during their passage through the caves, and never came out again: in fact, the upper stream even has a different name. There it was, as I came out of the trees into a tremendous noise of grasshoppers: beneath the long bare curve of a grassy mountainside dotted with distant sheep was a tapestry of grasses and alpine flowers, richly lit by the evening sun, moving in the warm wind from the south. And through this golden plain of Camprieu ran a deeply set, pebbly brook with only a little water – quite unexceptional, except for its name (slightly askew on a sign-post by the bridge): Le Bonheur. I imagine that it was probably called after the Abbaye de Bonheur, whose ruins were still standing towards the end of the last century, but for me to come upon this sign was like getting a surprise present, as if the entire corpus of bureaucracy of the Republic had conspired with the French landscape to astonish me by stamping my ride with the seal of official approval.

A little further up the road I came to the brook again, now in a livelier mood, and wheeled my bicycle across the leaf-mould to record the sound of certified contentment – the ripple of Le Bonheur. There were pines on one side

and the sun misted through them: beeches on the other, and there the light was dappled; a meadow where the green and gold slept together in the grass; and in the water, which was clear but already growing dark, there were still gleams and flashes of the afternoon – and many afternoons. I sat on a rock watching the reels go round gathering the echo of a reality that would soon be gone, for the next day I would be within sight of the sea, and I meditated on long miles past, wondering whether I had really appreciated them as they deserved. As I was considering this, the tape ran out and flapped round until I got up and stopped it.

'That,' I thought, 'is the way things are.'

Later, when I read the map more carefully, I discovered that the stream I had recorded was not Le Bonheur at all, but something else: so happiness remained just as fugitive as usual. However, it was a softer option than recording sheep, as I heard from Joy when I got to the hotel at the chalet village of Espérou.

'They run away, and you have to run after them –' Joy informed me in tones of some disillusionment – '*all* over the hillside. Then they mob you and you have to run away from them or you get covered with flies. And your heels get caught in the turf.'

'I crossed a stream called Happiness,' I said.

CHAPTER 10

Pyramids of the Sun

THE TWENTY-FOURTH DAY

Espérou was well on its way to becoming the suburbia of the Elysian fields, being plentifully supplied with chalets home-made with TV aerials, chalets middle-income with TV aerials, chalets pretentious for the relieving of executive stress with TV aerials, and piles of breeze-blocks with which to build more chalets whose TV aerials had not yet arrived. Any one of the chalets would have been idyllic by itself and really they were not *that* close together – with certainly far more space than there was between the caravans and the tents of the cloth-dwellers, a nomadic people who infest this part of the country. There was also a ski-lift in Espérou, and a very wide road with a great deal of parking in the middle of nowhere to provide it with customers. The best thing about the hotel was its Italian waiter, who had taught himself English entirely from pop-songs and film sub-titles, which was not only creditable, but imparted an interestingly stylized quality to his conversation.

'Wanna *poulet*?' asked the waiter. 'Gotta great *sauce aux cèpes*.'

But though everyone else seemed to be working quite hard to make Espérou the sort of place discriminating people would never want to visit again, they had not yet finished the job. Though there were sufficient chalets to make the nearby woods look like a poverty-stricken Virginia Water, there were not enough to make it look like Sidcup. Though there were sufficient campers to crowd out the little shop-cum-café, there had not been enough to make it worthwhile to open a supermarket. There was still something of a rough and ready air of the isolated community: the hotel turned off the main stopcock at night to save water, so that in the morning even the most determined sleeper was jarred to wakefulness by horrid gurgles and nasty spasms in the pipes; I could not dial London; the shop-cum-café sold absolutely everything, though it seemed to have a tendency to fix its prices according to the altitude.

I went in to buy a film on the morning of my last day's cycling, with 780 miles on the clock and sixty-three to go to Montpellier: there were hoops of sausages hanging from the low beams; chocolate and cheese and the local paper *Midi Libre*; a big box of croissants just up from the valley and the morning delivery of bread still outside, piled to the roof of an estate car with the *baguettes* crushing their noses against the windows like commuters in a tram. The major difference was that most commuters come from breakfast: the loaves were going there, when the campers got round to waking up and pulling back the tent flaps.

I rode off looking for the edge of the mountains, which from the map could not be far off. The road plummeted at first, then rose through beech forest to a stretch of grass-land; but the south side of Aigoual was already appearing rougher than the north and this was a hill-country of scant pasture that smelt of heather and quickly became forest once more with the chill of the night still in the pines. I dipped down to cross the valley of the Dourbie, which at this point is no more than a tiny stream, only to be faced with a long climb. It seemed the sort of switchback that could go on forever, but suddenly – and I was almost past it before I noticed – there was a blue name-plate by the road-side announcing the Col du Minier – altitude 1285 m, and a stone something opposite. The stone something was intensely grey and appeared to have fascinated a pair of passing motor-cyclists who were standing before it in attitudes of great dejection. It was gone in a moment, but it came as a considerable shock to realize, a few yards down the road, that I had been face to face with a menhir. I

PYRAMIDS OF THE SUN

guiltily thought that I should have gone back and rescued the motor-cyclists, but knowing the power of the beast, I concluded that there was a fair chance that they were bored to death already.

The road began to look as if it might stay flat for a while, changed its mind, and led gently down. I became aware that beyond the beeches and pines on the valleyside, there was a great rift in the mountains; that the Massif was over. It was the last boundary. I stopped pedalling and it felt as if every mile of my journey had been climbing to that rolling moment: then, as I slipped downhill, I left it all behind. The trees thinned. I saw ranges of wooded mountains tumbling hazily over each other to either side of me, but in between them there was nothing but the sky, and somewhere beyond, very far below, the plains of Languedoc and, eventually, the sea. At that, I squandered all my sense of gravity, rushed down the hill far too fast, and only narrowly avoided squashing a mouse running across the road like a furry sausage on legs. My horn unscrewed itself with the jolting and fell squeaking into the road. Having stopped to screw it back again, I resolved that I ought to be more sober about the descent of such a once-in-a-lifetime thing as a 20-kilometre hill, and remained a while to pick raspberries – tiny fruit from tiny bushes growing out of the rock, but tart and deliciously wild. There was a pervasive buzz of flies in the forest, and a solitary bird; sometimes the rush of streams down the mountainside. As the road went lower, the beeches gave way to chestnuts and the chestnuts to scrub of evergreen oak in which shrilled the automatic song of cicadas, and a dull church bell mingled with a distant rasp of a tractor in the valley. I left the cool, leaf-mould scent of the woods in the shade, descending into smells of hot rock, dusty scrub, marvellously pungent mints and marjorams growing beneath the dwarf walls guarding the precipitous edges of the road.

I met a succession of sun-baked cyclists toiling up the hill towards me: it was a great pleasure to be able to bid them good-day in a cheerful manner, knowing that they were going up, and I was coming down. For an extraordinary time, the long zig-zags continued across the whole length of the mountain, and the valley remained blue with remoteness. Then I could pick out the huddled roofs of Aulas, from which the bell had sounded: then the white bell-tower; then it was gone, for both road and time have passed Aulas by, though it was once important, and a fortress. Its most interesting citizen was the mysterious duellist, Henri de Celadon, Chevalier de Lanuejols, who was born nearby at the Château de Clapisse in 1740. On the same day each year for twelve years, that nobleman left home and travelled to the Isle of Basthellasse in the Rhône, near Avignon. There he fought a duel, always with the same man, a gentleman from Lyons, who did not turn up in the thirteenth year, nor in the fourteenth. Only then did the Chevalier learn that his opponent had died of his wounds two years before. He never revealed the identity of the man who came from Lyons, nor why the duel was fought.

Shortly after Aulas, I came down to river-level in the valley of the Arre and through the orchards of Rochebelle to the town of le Vigan, where the road goes flat.

Le Vigan gets its share of tourists in the season, but it never stops being a useful sort of little town rather than a looked-at one. It has a general charm: many people must drive straight through the middle and never see the two best features, a delightful boulevard and a bridge which is charming, even by the standards of this country of beautiful medieval bridges, perpetual reminders of the Benedictine monks from the abbey of St-Guilhem-le-Désert who opened up the foothills of the Cévennes to prosperity.

Le Vigan, which was largely Calvinist during the centuries of religious war and persecution and saw some savage incidents, does not begin to know how to flaunt itself: what counts is the day-to-day of centuries. The museum here is the Musée Cévenol which is fascinatingly full of everyday life – once you get past the menhirs. The local author, André Chamson, is a kind of Hardy of the Cévennes, chronicling ordinary lives in books like *Les*

Hommes de la Route. The fountain flows in the place Bonald, the waters gush below the plane trees of the Place du Quai, but nobody makes a fuss about the sacred spring of Isis, whose temple was established in Roman times: history is certainly nice, but it is more important to the day-to-day to have a good hardware store.

In the past, ironmongers must have been the axle on which the simple technology of peasant life went round. (Food shops can never have been so important when the peasant families that came down from the mountains were largely self-sufficient: even today, le Vigan's tichy supermarkets are second-class citizens in comparison with the Saturday morning market in and around the square.) Hardware stores have an air of consequence still, and are great places of pilgrimage not only for real residents in need of a saucepan, and second-home converters in need of a little red notice to say 'Keep Out', but even for the most transient population of all, the campers, who are regular worshippers at the shrine of the Great God Camping-Gaz. In July 1979, le Vigan was living as normal and receiving tourists on its own terms.

EIGHTEEN ODDISH IRONMONGERISH FRENCH THINGS FOR THE BRITISH TO GO 'OOH' OVER

1. Gas lighters (funny)
2. Triple-barrelled mousetraps (peculiar)
3. Black iron cauldrons (good for gypsies)
4. Black iron firebacks (traditional, attractive)
5. Château-shaped clock-work spits (a more serious equivalent of our cottage teapot)
6. Waterless lavatories (suitable for deserts)
7. Traditional French hat-pegs (bulbously different)
8. Wooden-handled pocket knives with ferocious blades (actually useful)

9. An extraordinary variety of little gadgets for various inscrutable purposes connected with irrigation
10. Reversible grills for barbecues and medieval door furniture (to pretend you live in a hunting lodge)
11. Old fashioned bars of laundry soap (*savon de Marseilles*)
12. Old fashioned clothes-pegs (suitable for W.I. peg-dressing competitions)
13. Loads of *boules* (suitable for putting away in the cupboard after the holiday and forgetting about)
14. Funny brooms and besoms
15. Cévenol pitchforks (these are half-grown, half-made – particularly at Sauve – from the *micocoulier* or nettlewood tree. Two or three shoots are left to serve as prongs at the top of a stem which will make the handle: when the fork is grown it is heated in an oven and bent to its final shape)
16. All sorts of threatening notices

South of le Vigan, the road runs flat because it runs by the river: though the biggest mountains have gone, others still crowd the valley like giants' children, with tousled slopes of rock and scrub and grey stone houses staring out of un-kempt woods. The insidious charm of dereliction spreads over these hills and along the side-valleys: in the overgrown terraces, the tumbled stones, the holiday-maker admires the ruin of a society.

Often they were not just houses, but *mas*, hamlets of several families – self-contained sometimes even to the extent of having their own graveyard, burial in consecrated ground having been denied to Protestants during the persecution. The *mas* has the strength of the man in the Bible who founded his house upon a rock, if that man had not been a very experienced architect. It was not built so much as grown from a core, with cellars and animals close to the rock, which was often left with boulders pushing up through the floor and sometimes had a spring. To the family home above were added, as necessary, extra rooms, barns, workplaces, granaries, bread ovens, cisterns, entire new houses, so that an astonishing complexity and angularity of little roofs is one hallmark of the *mas* along with an extraordinary number of stone steps and split levels split over and over. A *mas* is probably one of the best places in the world for playing sardines, apart from a skyscraper constructed entirely out of broom cupboards. Large stones sometimes stick out of walls for no apparent reason, tie-stones left by the far-sighted builders to allow extensions to be properly joined to the original structure, though ever afterwards people would have to hop up and down stairs and in and out of the yard to get to them, since there would be no knocking a doorway easily through walls a yard thick. Everything was immensely solid, with nothing as fragile as a chimney pot but a sturdy stack with a stone on top to keep out the weather, so that the smoke curls from the sides like the horns on a Viking's helmet, and a roof of heavy stones (nowadays tiles firmly bedded in concrete) supported by chestnut trunks, with a stack of logs holding up the ridge only kept in place by weight. A Cévenol roof is a horrifying construction, especially if you have ever heard one fall in (which it does with a crash like a Hollywood earthquake).

Once I lived under such a roof for some weeks, and it was an alarming experience since there was a colony of wood-eating ants in the main beam, dropping a substantial pile of shavings on the floor below each morning. In that house, guests sleeping below were offered ear-plugs to keep out the noise of the field-mice scuttling around above; but in all other respects the *mas* was very good to live in, especially for those with the agility of a mountain goat. It was very cool in the heat with its thick walls and tiny windows, and for most of its history it must have been regarded as possessing the last word in mod. cons., with a cellar almost as good as a fridge, and a constant water supply to a hollow in the wall that served as a stone sink with a cork in the bottom to let the waste run away outside.

Wherever there is a *mas* there is a spring, though it may be far up on the hillside, and in summer is often no more than a patch of brilliant green among the brown grasses of the hillside surrounding a cleft in the rock. Nowadays, a plastic hosepipe snakes into the cleft and carries the water drop by drop to an enclosed cistern below and this must last until the rains come. Old systems of rock basins, one below the other, are also still in use and, for irrigation, tiny canals known as *béals* branch from pools high up the river and carry along the hillside above it to the tiny fields and the man-made terraces, each with its massive dry-stone wall retaining earth painfully carried up in baskets from below – and often carried back again in spring after the winter storms.

The terraces are called *bancèls* or *faïssas* locally: some terraces are still cultivated, growing magnificent garden-stuff, but most of the higher ones only sport worn-out trees and black vine-stumps, wasting grasses and weedy prickliness of one sort or another. The labour of fetching and carrying all day up and down the mountain on footpaths and steps built into the walls belongs to another age, though in one village where I stayed, goats were still driven up the *draille* daily to pasture on the mountain. Many of the *bancèl* walls stand remarkably firm without maintenance and if they crumble on the high terraces, the reversion to mountainside is undramatic. It is a different matter with the *béals*, which once provided not only irrigation but water power (most of the mills are ruins now, surrounded by inscrutable channels in the grass where the water once flowed, but I have seen them with full machinery remaining), for the water accelerates the destruction.

When the rain comes to the mountain valleys, it can be dramatic, even in summer. There was a storm while I was staying at the *mas*, which sent me indoors from picking plums in the garden because the sky was so black I could no longer see the fruit. Even the grey houses only just across the stream half-vanished in swirls of greyer cloud. Thunder drifted over the peaks: the electric lights flickered, flickered again with less determination and blacked out. The sound of the valley changed: the cicadas were quiet, the echo that was there in the dry disappeared; everything was absolutely still except for a dull rustling that grew to a tiny but ferocious pattering on the leaves. The rain fell in glinting needles that scored lines on the landscape until everything outside the windows vanished in sheets of water. It was so overdone, it felt as if some celestial stage-manager was putting on a show with a cosmic bucket. Water poured in torrents into the courtyard and instantly made a lake, rang down the drainpipes, gurgled into mysterious subterranean ways, made waterfalls down the steps, galloping and spurting down to the stream by every available channel. Then light came over the mountain and pushed the thunder gently but firmly down the valley: the electricity came back to life in a yellow glow (though it went off again after a particularly vicious thunderclap from the other side of the hill). The rain stopped spitting into the puddles and left its drops to go whoop! down the mulberry leaves like a watery helter-skelter, pushing each other off the end on to the next green slide. But the stream no longer trickled: it had become a torrent, and remained so for the rest of the day and all night. In the Cévennes, the water level can go up over four feet in an hour.

The next day I got into conversation with a local school-mistress, and remarked that I was impressed with the brand of weather they had in these parts.

'That's nothing,' said the schoolmistress. 'You should have seen 1968: it cost the commune thousands to fix the *béals*. All the cellars in the town were flooded: a friend of mine had rabbits in hers and she had to carry them out in sackfuls and let them go on the mountainside. But that was nothing to the frost of '66: I remember the passing bell going all day for the old people – we're not so well prepared for cold here. And I remember the frost that killed the mulberries before that.'

There were two trees at the heart of the Cévennes – *l'arbre de pain* and *l'arbre d'or*. The 'tree of bread' was the Spanish chestnut whose fruit was gathered from the mountainside in the last three months of the year and eaten fresh and boiled as well as grilled at the *veillée*, the after-supper chat that was the basis of social life; but most chestnuts were dried for almost a month in *clédas* – split-level drying-houses on the hillside with a slow fire below and the chestnuts above. The best of the dried chestnuts went to market and the remainder stayed at home to make *le bajanà*, a soup of very little else that was the staple of the mountain diet. As well as food, the chestnut trees provided wood for building, furniture, tool and basket making, vine-stakes, beehives (a section of hollow trunk with a stone on top); the leaves were gathered for litter and food for goats; the family pig got *les possas*, the debris from the skinning of the nuts which was accomplished by trampling them with hobnailed boots or using a machine called a *pizariri*, having first been put in sacks and thumped out of their spiny cases with wooden rakes.

For a thousand years, the chestnuts were grafted to ensure the best crop, with trees bearing for several hundred years after they came into full production at the age of sixty. But towards the end of the last century, cheaper nuts came from elsewhere to the makers of *confiserie*, and the quality declined. Many trees were cut down and the bark used for tannin: others, untended, were increasingly attacked through roots and leaves by two diseases, *l'encre* and *l'enothia*. On many hillsides today, *l'arbre de pain* is nothing but a spiky skeleton standing grey above the scrub.

The great frost of 1956 that killed off many of the white mulberries was no more than the full stop on a sentence already passed – for as 'the tree of gold', the mulberry was dead already. Silk-making spread through the Cévennes in the seventeenth and eighteenth centuries and reached a peak during the nineteenth with at least one mill in every town and valley, but by 1957 when the last *filature* closed, artificial fibres and foreign competition had ruined a market that had, literally, been golden, for Cévenol silk was a rich yellow and so fine that a Japanese machine imported to St-Jean-du-Gard continually broke the thread.

The process of *le magnan*, silk culture, was rather like nursing a sick baby in a betting shop and making a book on the result, for the profits were great, but uncertain. The worms were unbelievably delicate, subject to all manner of ailments and – for much of the life of the industry – disastrously misunderstood. Traditionally, it was appreciated that they needed warmth, so the *graines* would be incubated in little bags slung round the goodwife underneath her skirt and brought to the conjugal bed at night. The *magnanerie*, a long attic at the top of the house, would have seven or eight fires constantly burning to cherish the tables of greedy worms in their later stages, though the roof would remain uninsulated and hygiene be limited to a dousing with *eau de Javel*, the French equivalent of Jeyes' Fluid.

What went unrealized for many decades was the fact that the silkworms craved not only warmth but ventilation, and the intimate bag method of hatchery and the tightly-closed windows of the *magnanerie* (with the silkworms giving off gallons of extra water-vapour and the fires often without chimneys) hardly provided this. Every scientific method possible was used to make things more reliable. People burnt gunpowder to purify 'bad air', and there is one case recorded of a woman who brought the powder-box too close to the fire and blew a large hole in the floor, by some miracle remaining relatively uninjured herself. Understanding improved as the nineteenth century wore on, and Pasteur organized disease-free eggs from a central source, but the rearing remained chancy: half of the hopeful might have had reasonable success, one in ten the kind of harvest that would keep the family in comparative wealth for the next year.

Le magnan was mainly woman's work and – hard as it was – was at least kinder to the hands than gathering chestnuts. At the start of the incubation, worms needed watching round the clock, so that a woman would be up from four in the morning until eleven at night for a fortnight: there followed up to a month and a half of back-breaking labour as the worms went through their life-cycle, their appetites increasing almost exponentially at every stage. Man has seven ages, a silkworm five: in the first, worms from an ounce of *graines* would eat 6 kg of leaf (which had to be dry); 250 kg in the fourth; and in the last eight to ten days before the worms climbed up to the heather twigs placed for them and made their cocoons, the worms would eat a staggering 900 kg of mulberry leaves; these were collected in sacks with wooden hoops at the top to keep them open. Everything stopped in the rush to feed the worms: the silk-mill closed; the schoolmistress sat before empty benches; the parson took his holiday, for there would be no one in church. At the end of it all the cocoons would be taken off the heather and despatched to the *filature* in linen-lined baskets, each cocoon 8000 times the weight of the *graine* that produced it, and composed of up to a kilometre-and-a-half of silk. There would be a small celebration, because the silk merchant paid cash on the nail (though it was nothing to compare with the *carbonnade* when the pig was killed – perhaps because everybody was too weary).

I met a teacher who, with his artist wife, had produced 6 kg of cocoons one year: in the great days of the *magnan*, a really enthusiastic wife with a husband to help her gather leaves might have produced 150 kg.

'It took a whole large room,' said Liliane.

'They ate a tree a day,' said Jean.

'We never got any silk,' added Liliane.

'No,' said Jean. 'One night some people came to the door and said they'd heard we had silkworms and could they buy them for bait. Trout love them: there's a heavy fine if you're caught fishing with them. So we sold them for much more than we could ever have got for the silk.'

There is still a research station interested in re-establishing silk culture in the South of France using the Japanese Kokusco 21 variety of mulberry, which is frost-resistant, but I have not seen a recipe anywhere for persuading twentieth-century Europeans to undertake the amount of hard labour involved.

Nevertheless, Cévenol life keeps some of its variety and its make-do. The schoolmistress told me she still kept a family pig for *charcuterie*.

'It's all right if you don't count the work,' she said. 'But add up the price of the animal, food for it, buying it potatoes, and the sausages come pretty expensive. But buying a pig full-grown is out of our reach: this is a way of paying by instalments. It's a lot of work for something that for somebody else comes off a shelf in a shop. But it's a choice you make. It's the people who drop out from the towns who really have a hard time of it – they've no experience, they can't take the work. They don't often succeed.'

In spite of the fact that as I came out of le Vigan a large bumble-bee dive-bombed my forehead, fell inside my collar and stung my belly until it was removed by frantic shirt-flapping, I made good speed along the banks of the Arre, a tributary of the Hérault, though when the two join among the apple orchards of Pont d'Hérault, the Arre is, in summer at any rate, rather the larger of the two. The Hérault however is much the more lively, having jumped off Mont Aigoual in a waterfall and spent the following miles skipping over boulders in a great hurry. The name comes from *auraris*, the golden, and I met one holiday-maker with a small collection of glittering dust – probably mostly flakes of mica – which he had panned in several hours; but rivers to the east like the Gardons are where such serious gold-panning as continues is carried out.

The gold of the Hérault that I saw glowed from the branches of a peach orchard along the valley, just before I came to the ancient bridge of St-Julien-de-la-Nef, where

I stopped to swim. There is some coarse sand there, though the bed of the river is mostly boulders and worn pebbles, an alternation of rushing white shallows and blue-green pools. I floated on my back and watched the tree tops shining in the sun: alder, acacia and poplar grow along these banks, with dense bushes of willow overhanging the water and springing up in bonsai twiglets from cracks in the planes of rock which, mottled grey and brown, run geometrically down to the river, where they are sculpted into hummocks by the stream. Yellow-flowered fennel and *sariette*, a spiky pungent savory, are common along the roadside and among the rocks. *Saponaire*, the soap-plant, grows among the pebbles with dark, dull leaves and a pink flower: if you take rather a lot of it and scrub your hands with it for a very long time indeed, it will live up to its reputation and lather slightly. Out of the bushes an old man wheeled an even older bicycle laden with mallows, presumably for his rabbits. He shouted something at me that I did not catch. I made friendly noises from the middle of the stream: he shrugged his shoulders and went on his way.

I came out of the coolness and toasted myself on the rocks, keeping an eye out for the insect life, since there is a particularly large horse-fly by this river which likes to eat wet bodies, though it usually ignores dry ones. The Cévennes teems with flittery things of great energy: flies (common, horse, blue-bottle, and bright green-bottle colour); butterflies (black and white, black and red, orange and yellow, shiny blue); very-leggy black beetles as serious as undertakers; menacing droopy-tailed hornets; stag-beetles buzzing like Angels of Death with machine-guns; dowdy browny crickets that flash rich linings to their wings when they spring; sprightly green grasshoppers; the fastest possible ants, from large fierce black ones to red ants so tiny that their legs are invisible and they move about as if on casters; dragonflies like biplanes of painted silk; juicy green cicadas like twenty-first-century tanks; and a black scorpion that goes up walls like a pair of animated lazy tongs and loves to crawl into your bed – it is either innocuous and lucky, or capable of an extremely nasty bite, according to which local you ask about it.

When the horse-flies stopped coming, I judged I was dry, dressed and went back up to the bicycle, which I had chained to a post. As I unchained it, I noticed that the post had a purpose in life; it carried a notice, which had its back to me. Coming round to its front, I learned what the old man with the bicycle had been shouting about: '*Pollution – baignade interdite*'. I walked the bicycle across to the middle of the bridge and inspected the waters for any visible signs of corruption. There were shoals of fish swimming over the rocks as usual. They seemed to be all right.

'Oh well,' I said: but I was glad to discover later that the problem had only been temporary and had occurred some days before.

I rode on past the pool where the cold blue waters of the Vis tumble into the Hérault and came to Ganges, celebrated for particularly fine silk stockings (in 1938 – the last year of full production before the coming of the war and nylon – the town made 500,000 dozen pairs, a complicated statistic which works out at 12 million individual feet). Even more than le Vigan, Ganges is a town of undistinguished buildings and no detectable architecture at all apart from the church which has its front arches in pretty colours, almost as if it were Italian. A Renaissance château stood on the site of the present market-hall until the closing years of the last century, but was pulled down for the convenience of shoppers and stall-holders. It argues a fair degree of stupidity to pull down the only good building in your town, but perhaps the citizens were influenced by its reputation, for in 1667 it was the scene of spectacular brutality when the beautiful Marquise de Castellane was murdered for her money by her brothers-in-law who forced her to take poison and then when it had no immediate effect, pursued her through the streets with drawn swords and stabbed her before the eyes of a drawing-room full of ladies, where she had taken refuge.

Being Friday, it was market-day at Ganges and as I was

passing, a girl at a cake-stall who saw that I was English tossed back a rust-red head of hair and bawled at me provocatively in my own tongue to 'Come and 'ave some'. On investigation, it proved that her offer was limited to bags of croissants, but since I was off the bike, I stayed a while, for I rarely resist a market anywhere, and never in the South of France.

The Friday market at Ganges is made up of local stalls augmented by the Marché des Cévennes, which travels round the mountains in palatial caravans that instantly spring open into entire hardware stores, shoe shops and hat emporiums; it is also attended by a fleet of big and little vans stuffed with leather goods, jeans, dresses; table-ware of stripey olive-wood; thick plates ornamented with fruit, flowers and peasant pictures; cooking-pots, cheap cooks'-knives, balloon whisks, olive-stoners, garlic-presses; agricultural machinery, little pottery lavender holders, dried flowers, jewellery and richly coloured banks of thick home-dyed wool – all of which come out on trestles below bright umbrellas that pack the square by the market-hall, the road by the market-hall and the large car park. Somehow they all just fit in, and there is no space left over. There is life and warmth about the markets of the south: the sun goes straight to the heart by way of the vegetables. Other things are sold, but it is the food that counts, and the plenteousness is gladdening.

There is nothing special about Ganges market – for instance, it does not have the tankers full of Côtes du Rhône that fill your *bonbel* or demi-john with *appellation contrôlée* at Villeneuve-les-Avignon as if you were buying petrol, or the *tripéries* of Montpellier, replete with every possible size of brain, cooked *mamelle* (cow's udder, I hope), and scalded calves' heads wrinkling their nostrils against the counter-glass. If you go to the big supermarkets like Montlaur, you will find sixty different cheeses on a rack, a fish counter like a point-to-point in the Sargasso, fruit and veg. like an Amazonian market-garden, meat like the Roman circuses after the battle of the 10,000 accident-prone gladiators, 900 different kinds of table wine – I counted them – and thirty tills ticking euphoniously together. Ganges market is nothing compared to this: all you can say of it is that the entire West End of London, including Soho and Knightsbridge, can hardly rival it in quality, and that it sells some things that the West End has never heard of. Since Ganges has fewer than 5000 inhabitants, perhaps this modest praise will do to be going on with.

Walking through the Ganges market was like walking through a cornucopia of miraculous freshness. Housewives went by bearing trays of gold-red peaches of perfect ripeness from the man who had picked them that morning, their leaves still on them. There was earnest discussion taking place over the pears as to which were juicy today and which would be juicy tomorrow, and some extremely serious smelling of melons. At the entrance to the market-hall, where sharp-knived butchers were peeling off slices of steak as if they were taking off a wrapper, and where the butter came in primrose mountains, was a woman selling basil a good foot-and-a-half high planted in an old tin can, and scenting the doorway with its enormous leaves. There were red peppers bulging with sweetness, green peppers, yellow peppers, all like horticultural traffic lights; freckly potatoes, freshly dug, smooth-skinned; aubergines of lustrous purple; red rolls of obesity that were tomatoes; beans green, beans purple, with curly tails; thick ribs of chard; prickly ridge cucumbers; lettuce sold by the kilo very young, with the tightly-curled heads of *sucrées* ready to live up to their name; slim leeks, infant turnips and bunches of carrots tied up as an art-work in green and gold. Almost nothing except bananas came from outside the area; I could not buy an avocado pear. But there were fresh onions too big to get your fingers round tied up by green stems, dark red onions counted specially sweet for salads, long purple shallots, little white onions, little brown onions, garlic in strings – the violet is bigger and stronger, but rose garlic keeps best. There were cartwheels of rough country bread,

the homely partner in the French love-affair with crustiness; *saucissons de montagne*, hams coloured like a rosy
bruise; goat cheeses laid out sedately in wooden boxes,
some flavoured with mountain herbs.

The nasty end of a public execution was still going on
at the fish stall, where they give you a bunch of parsley
with your kilo of sardines or primeval-looking *bouillabaisse* mixture: a five-foot tunny had been laid out on a long
bench and methodically sliced with an enormous knife into
thick steaks a foot across – since it was late in the morning,
they were getting near the tail, and the best cuts had gone.
A housewife sold jars of her own rabbit pâté: the pickle man
had tubs of salted anchovies bristling with tiny bones, and
bright plastic buckets ranged in rows – olives black, green,
Greek, Nêmes, stuffed, crushed with garlic, *piquants*
(shrivelled up with angry red chillis), *à la grèque* (which
are nothing at all like the Greek): all his own recipe ('not
like the ones in the supermarkets') ladled by the kilo into

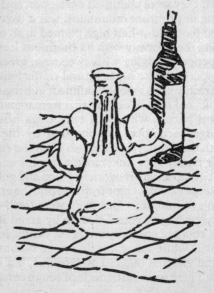

plastic bags, along with strong mixed pickles, twisted-up long chillis in brine and *cornichons*, sour little gherkins to eat with *charcuterie*. I concluded that perhaps the market at Ganges was, after all, a fair exchange for a measly old Renaissance château which was only good for murdering people in.

By the time I left, it was lunchtime and everything had gone quiet. There was not a car in sight at the T-junction by the paper shop where a blue-shirted gendarme had been waving and whistling at a traffic jam only an hour before. The midday sun fell like a hot blanket over the town, and even the shadows went to sleep under it. I pedalled south through the green shade of plane trees with trunks like an avenue of bones. The road came back to the river at Laroque, a tiny village scrambling up the said *roque* to an ancient tower. The road had most of its pavement on the river side, so that the waiter from the tiny café had to dash across the traffic to serve his customers at the line of tables under the trees. A club of the fattest possible black fish was holding a meeting in the deep water under the wall to discuss the remnants of the catering above.

After the weir at Laroque, the river disappeared in a detour of pebbly shallows: when it rejoined the road in the canyon half a mile along, its personality had changed with the geology. There was virtually no soil in the gorge: nothing but rock and such scrubs and trees as can scratch a roothold in a crevice. The river had smoothed its course as clean and white as a bath, jade water resting in a channel of bleached limestone. Above, rough cliffs laid geology bare with all its cracks and wrinkles, and streaks of ochre ran down the grey where the rock was newly exposed; and somewhere within the rock was the Grotte des Demoiselles. I turned back to the cave up a winding road from St-Bauzille-de-Putois (a saint whose career I have been unable to trace but whose name, St-Basil-the-Polecat, undoubtedly qualified him as *extremely* holy). As I rounded the corner, an old woman was just going into her house tightly shuttered against the sun: as the door closed I saw the flame of an oil lamp inside. In the Hérault, sun is for the tourists: local people, except those who have to work in the open, keep themselves as pallid as mushrooms and retreat into the dark whenever they can, emerging in the twilight for the late evening social life of the south – a little gentle sitting outside your house, a little gentle wandering to other people sitting outside their houses, some conversation, a glass or two.

The road pottered out of St-Bauzille through vineyards and new little villas before it set itself a hairpin climb up slopes dotted with cypress to what is now the main cave entrance in the side of the cliff, a concrete portico hung with vines swinging gently in the current of cold air from within. There was a small railway station in the portico with a bright red funicular which rumbled me up to the cave itself with a great number of the graveyard jokes which are a compulsory feature for any guided tour underground, along with the squawling baby at the back. The object of going up was to get to the pothole into which the original explorers descended in 1780 from the Plateau de Thaurac; it is still open to the sky, and anyone who fancies climbing down the solitary creeper that peters disconsolately into the cave could very likely save the entrance fee. La Grotte des Demoiselles (demoiselles are the nasty sort of fairy) is an awe-inspiring cave, particularly when you have no head for heights and come out on the site of the biggest chamber 'The Cathedral' and see the concrete staircase climbing down the side of the rock into almost invisible depths, inhabited by finger-nail-sized mannikins who, on inspection, turn out to be people trooping among the formations like mites in a stone broccoli forest.

Having spent an hour climbing up and down the cave's 647 steps, I blinked into the sunlight and got into conversation with the friendly lady in the ticket kiosk and her seamy-faced husband who was resting his leathery complexion in the shade with the other guides, torches dangling from their belts. It would be back to the fields for him after the holiday season, he said. Then he took me to the corner of the car park and told me to look at the rock above. Made of the same grey stone as the cliff and almost invisible against it was a wall with a doorway in it and a look-out point, fronting a cave not much more than fifty feet deep in which neolithic remains had been discovered.

'That is the Cave of the Camisards,' said the guide. 'The young people get the wars mixed up; they ask me if I mean the *maquisards*.' He pointed to the mountain above. 'But no: that is the boundary of religion. To the north, all the villages have two churches, *culte protestant* and *catholique*: to the south, they have one.' We said goodbye, and I went to the south into lower Languedoc, leaving the Cévennes behind.

After St-Bauzille, I was unpleasantly surprised to discover that I had not quite done with mountains. There was a long haul up to the 1000-foot Col de la Cardonille with the sun beating down, the water hot in the drinking bottle and the cry of cicadas all round. Blackberries that had been in flower on the mountains that morning were ripe here, but tiny fruit on stunted bushes. I was in a country more arid than any I had seen before, a land in which you cannot bear to place your hand on the stone at midday, and a patch of shade is a different world. The *garrigue* is a scrub desert where little grows above waist height, bleaker than the *maquis* of more friendly hill country, which has stunted trees to offer concealment to people such as the *maquisards*. To hide in the *garrigue* you would have to crouch behind a stone or in a dry gully – and there are plenty of both. The *garrigue* breaks into flower in the spring but if you want pleasure from it in summer, you must sniff for it – if the heat leaves you the energy – for the sun that flashes the dew off the rocks and draws the water from the earth thickens the sap in the twigs and distils aromatics in the tough leaves of the plants such as thyme, sage, hyssop, rosemary and lavender. The great product of the *garrigue*, until the advent of synthetic dyes, came from the shrub from which the *garrigue* gets its name: *garus* was Latin for the kermes oak, which grows where all else withers. On it lives a scale insect which, at one stage in its life-cycle, looks so much like a growth on the tree that until 1714 it was thought to be a vegetable, and that knobble was gathered in spring for the red dye, which was more permanent but not so bright as cochineal.

After the *col*, the road led down into what was hardly noticeable as a valley, any more than the stony bed of the Lamalou on its way to the curious rocks of the Ravin des Arcs was noticeable as a river, but by the standards of the chaos of nature around me, the village at the head of its unremarkable hollow deserved the title it had appointed itself on a tatty board by the roadside – 'Oasis of the *Garrigue*'.

The village of St-Martin-de-Londres is a true oasis, for water and rest are its being. It has two places of coolness – its fountain, and the beautiful Romanesque church cuddled in with random houses at the top of the town and approached by a massively vaulted cloister which does little to diminish the soft shock of darkness within the church after the whiteness of the sun. There was a priory here, for St-Martin and the surrounding country were developed, like most of the Cévennes, by the Benedictines of St-Guilhem-le-Désert, which is not far away across the hill in the spectacularly savage gorges of the Hérault, and from which came also a relic of the True Cross, which now spends most of its time in the Louvre. Mysterious carvings on the church's pulpit have been identified as Cathar symbols, though they were made centuries after the Albigensians had been officially wiped out.

St-Martin-de-Londres has nothing to do with some obscure Cockney holy man, though 'Londres' probably comes from *doundras*, from the Celtic for marsh, perhaps the same sort of derivation as the name of London itself. Incredible as it may seem in the grilling afternoon sun, the Val de Londres was a swamp until the monks drained it. Even today you pass flood warning notices on some of the roads to the twelfth-century Château de Londres, which is the only castle within many miles, a hotch-potch of battlements and Renaissance manor, and boasts several interesting medieval paintings.

But the life of St-Martin-de-Londres is at the fountain; its motto might be 'They also move who only sit and wait'. Under three gigantic plane trees and an infant one with a trunk a mere three feet across, I came upon an expectant world of old men sitting in the shade, a hippy junk jewellery stall, and a sub-culture of children and dogs chasing each other in and out of boredom. With the time-honoured detachment of the Midi, everyone was waiting – not for something interesting to happen, which would have been too much to hope for – but for something newish to pass by. The Café des Autobus wore its hopes on its sign: the other café, Chez Jules, enclosed them in a bracket after-wards – (Café des Touristes) – as if Jules were by no means convinced of the validity of being *chez*. St-Martin might be an oasis in watery terms, but without the passers-by off the *garrigue*, the town would shrivel away in the sun.

My arrival aroused a passionate interest in the observers, several of whom turned half an eye on my bicycle, before leaving one of their number to keep a permanent watch in case, after all, I should turn out to be unusual. He was a scrawny character with oversize feet, a nose hooked like a grappling iron and lips that hung off his mouth like ill-attached slices of melon; he eyed me as I cooled myself with the water that splashed confidently from the six half-human fish-heads of the mossy fountain where you drink, and flowed briskly round the circle of channels where you are allowed to wash, and then disappeared under the road as a stream. It was cold with a rasp of limestone in the taste. Whatever I looked at, whatever I did, the gaze followed me, except when a helicopter went over – probably from the air emergency service that operates over the sea and mountains – and everyone's eyes went upwards, even though there was nothing to see through the thick leaves.

'There go our taxes,' said someone.

I went to buy some beer at the little self-service. When I came back to sit by the fountain, my observer was still

at post. The bottle-top would not come off: his interest perked up. I wrestled with it: he nudged his neighbour. I went to my bicycle bag: other eyes turned to see what would come out. Pliers. Ah! With my pliers I banged on the bottle-cap: there was a hardly perceptible shaking of heads. Distracted, I missed my bang. The neck of the bottle broke. The man with the large lips pursed them as much as to say, 'Told you so.' There was general approval as I picked up the broken glass, threw it into a litter-bin and took to the road once more. I detected a general opinion that, though there had never been any prospect of my arrival being particularly interesting, I had done as much to help pass the afternoon as could reasonably be expected.

After St-Martin, the country was no longer quite so desolate as it had been before, and Pic St-Loup – whose grey crag curves dramatically out of the plain and flies gliders round itself all day – disappeared behind. I had been expecting the bas-Languedoc to be more *bas*, but the hills went on, ripples of mountain dying out before they met ripples of the sea, though even hills were something to cherish as I neared the end of my ride.

Vineyards became more and more frequent, for the Hérault is a prodigious producer of generally down-market

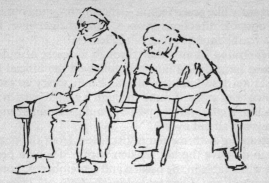

wine, like the rest of Languedoc, whose over-production has often brought economic crisis in the past, and in 1907 an actual revolt of *vignerons* with widespread demonstrations, deaths and mutinies in three regiments. Winegrowers' discontent has remained one of the important reasons for the leftish lean to politics in Languedoc (along with the resentment of the power of right-wing Paris). A frequent sight by the roadside is a rusting relic of an ancient propaganda campaign: a sign '*Le vin – le plus sain des boissons*', or an unscrupulous quote from Pasteur: '*Le plus hygiénique des boissons*'. I suspect that what he was actually saying was that clean wine is better than dirty water. The Hérault has been trying to improve the quality and the image of its wine: the frost of 1956 that killed the mulberries also put paid to many vines, and gave a first push to replanting with varieties better than the mediocre Aramon, notably Carignan and Grenache. But though Hérault has thirteen V.D.Q.S. wines and five *appellations contrôlées* (Clairette de Languedoc, and four Muscats, headed by Frontignan), four-fifths of the wine of Languedoc-Roussillon have no such distinction, as you can often see by looking at the vineyards. The vines I passed did not have the neatly-barbered look of Sancerre: rather, they grew exuberantly like green temple-dancers, throwing out limbs in all possible directions at once. After the *garrigue*, I was struck by the intense green of the leaves.

I penetrated Montpellier through a desert of building sites and tarmac, and unwisely followed the official signs to the Hôtel des Violettes which took me a weary way round the town. But at last I came through a walled garden with palms into a courtyard of wisteria and geraniums: and my journey was all but over.

A steaming bath melted my stiffness from the outside: then, to dissolve the last tension within, I took a beer to a trim white table in the garden and remembered, how less than a month ago, I had sat before the Café des Tribunaux in Dieppe with all the excitement of a new land ahead. Now, in the blankness of utter relaxation, I felt the calm of a familiar relationship. As I sat among the palms with the long road running through my head, I realized that – even though I might never be part of France – France had become a part of me.

FRANCOPHILIA – THE SYMPTOMS AND THE CURE
by Bulwer Wellington-Ffoulkes (M.D.)

There is no point in trying to pretend that the unpleasant disease of francophilia does not carry a social stigma. The old excuse of having picked it up by sitting at an unhygienic café table simply will not wash: inevitably, any sufferer has been guilty of engaging in intercourse with the french nation, and this is their God-given punishment.

The symptoms are well known and disgusting. The patient has a craving for *sauce béarnaise*, and a vacant expression overspreads the features at the slightest mention of Château Mouton-Rothschild;

in Tertiary Francophilia, the hands tremble uncontrollably in the presence of a Camembert and the tongue lolls hideously from the mouth, which slavers continually – this sometimes leads to the incorrect diagnosis of hydrophobia, when the patient is in fact more likely to suffer from hydrophilia.

In the treatment of this extremely contagious disease, it is vital to trace all contacts and isolate them in a francophilia clinic, where they can be bombarded with old frogs' legs and *tripes à la mode de Caen* until they return to health.

B.W.-Ff.

THE LAST DAY

At Montpellier I returned to the sprawling, disconnected twentieth century, for on a bicycle you do not carry your own cocoon as in a car, and I had been riding through a present which was simply the top layer of the past. But at Montpellier, there were parking meters (there cannot be anything more ridiculous in the whole of creation than a parking meter); crowds of people whose object in life was not to get mixed up with other crowds of people; old roads that strained with traffic and new roads that were emptier but worse; and new buildings that were cheap and tawdry and would never look right. The town has many delightful things about it, but I saw that its civilization had been put back on the drawing board. I had come back to the reality of too many people, our society of squirming maggots: and I was a maggot myself once more.

It was not that Montpellier was not trying to be pleasant. It had old streets built high and narrow to keep out the sun – for over the year, Montpellier has sun six days out of seven. Its medical school is the oldest in the world, and has brought a cosmopolitan collection of intellectuals into the town since the twelfth century – even today the university has more foreign students than any other in France. There is a botanical garden which is always shut when I want to go to it but is nevertheless the oldest in the country: there are substantial villas of discreet distinction within high-walled gardens, and terraces of two-storey houses in a yellowish stone which almost remind you of Bath, except that – though the doorways are imposingly framed – the windows have no mouldings, which give them that blank southern look as if they have stared at the sun too long and gone behind their shutters. The Place de la Comédie, whose smart cafés are better to look at than to pay in, is paved with marble and overlooked by a theatre of dumpy baroque, like a fat duchess in curlers.

But for the traveller who passes through and out again, this is all but drowned in a sea of suburbs and a desert of roads. In 1962 there was a cloud-burst of immigration over Montpellier which was suddenly swamped with former colonists from the newly independent Algeria. These *pieds noirs*, called 'black feet' because of the native Algerians' initial astonishment at their shiny shoes, were the main reason for the city's population rising from 123,000 to 200,000 in a few years, with a burst of commercial energy which cracked open the peaceful character of Montpellier as a university county town. At the glass town hall soaring above the over-shiny Polygone development and a truly hideous new hotel, I heard a familiar story of proliferating suburbs; and that some sixty acres were to be redeveloped in the largest project of its kind in Europe in an attempt to bring back people and vitality into the city centre.

I doubted that it would bring back Jean Joubert, a professor at the university, poet and novelist, with whom I had been to dine the night before in his old cottage near Castries – a house of unpretentious civilization and great solidity of stone and beam. He told me that Montpellier had been a small town when he had come to Languedoc from the north of France twenty-five years before: it had been like entering another world with its own art of living. There was a magic in the leisurely view of life that rejected rush and refused to put work on a puritanical pedestal, a warmth in the long conversations on the doorstep in the summer evenings, often going on until one or two in the morning. It was no longer the same, he said: in spite of its intellectual revival, Occitan was hardly ever heard in the village. On summer evenings, the doorways would contain nothing but the door – the people would be inside watching TV. The small farmers were disappearing so fast that the consensus in his village was that in twenty-five years there might be only three left – each with more land but a lot less independence.

'I came here because I was in love with an image of this country,' Jean Joubert told me. 'Progressively I discovered it was probably a myth, and that the myth is dying away. The man from the south was something very different from the man from the north: I can still see differences, but they are not so obvious. The landscape is still beautiful in spite of the fact that it has been distorted and disfigured occasionally. But the coast was so different to what you see now that it's extraordinary. It was a long sand beach, completely empty: there were dunes, a few fishermen.'

Even the blue sky had paled in the sun as I left the centre of Montpellier looking for the way to the coast so that I might dip a symbolic toe into the Mediterranean. You cannot expect any reasonable human being to love a road that goes round in circles, and the Montpellier ring road was no more cared about than most others of its kind. Subtopia followed as I turned due south along a cycle track shaded by bushy plane trees towards Palavas-les-Flots, the original seaside resort of Montpellier at the bottom of the Lez, which has traditionally combined the functions of river, canal and sewer. At the town hall, I had heard some emphasis placed on the fact that it was now safe to swim at Palavas, from which I deduced that it had not been so previously, and was told that a big purification scheme would shortly come into operation.

That day, however, I approached the coast across rather

ill-smelling marshland whose unfortunate nuances gave
place to a not altogether savoury sea breeze. Palavas announced its presence with rows of white houses, a funfair
taking a siesta and boats on the canal. The old part of the
town had an unexpected charm – there were back streets
of two-storey terraces of nineteenth-century vacation cottages, with grey rendering crumbling elegantly and bright
towels drying on filigree balconies. There, I felt human,
but as I went further I felt only the pressure of humanity.
Between Montpellier and the old walled town of Aigues-
Mortes (the Dead Waters) on the fringe of the Camargue,
the coast is unrelieved seaside unless you look inland to
the lakes and marshes, which only a fisherman does. The
country towards Sète to the west is a more honest and
varied one, with the vineyards of Listel '*Vin de sables*' and
the workaday world intruding itself occasionally in a way
that can only be gratifying to the tourist conscious of holiday freedom.

Beyond Frontignan, where every shop is full of Muscat
and *eau-de-vie*, the beaches are fresher, emptier and sometimes made of sea-smoothed fragments of shells: lorries
park along the beach road so that the drivers can watch the
girls and get in a quick swim.

But the beaches from Palavas to Carnon-Plage to La
Grande-Motte and le Grau-du-Roi are an enclave of pure
enjoyment with a furniture of gaudy umbrellas and brown
bodies. The sand is perfect, the sea would not drown a

poodle, the sun is continuous. A lorry-driver lorry-driving would be quite out of place, even supposing that there was anywhere for him to park. Some people can take the boredom of the beach; others fill in the time with failing to sail a *planche à voile*, Mediterranean nymph-spotting, fishing (with almost universal ill-success), and stumping over the sand in masks and flippers to seek out mussels and sea-urchins among the rocky breakwaters that have been piled up all along the coast. The mussel supply seems to be inexhaustible, no matter how many are dredged up and consumed on the spot. (There are also many small crabs, a bucketful of which makes a good soup.) The pressure of space on the beach is such that the French tend to behave with almost British reserve in order to maintain territorial rights. What is un-British is the effort the energetic put into making it clear to everybody around that they are really enjoying themselves in a special way that others cannot hope to emulate, and the relative lack of the D.I.Y. civil engineering projects you find in Britain: but that may be because the ultimate in sand-castles is ready-built just down the coast.

I rode the long shadeless road by the shore through the hotch-potch of seaside villas which may have been trying to be different but only succeeded in looking untidy, and shack shops that sold cool drinks and chips for the beach, ice creams and barbecued chickens. After a while, the tatty villas on either side were replaced by sand dunes, which I judged to be the ones Jean Joubert had described to me as having been preserved from development only after a struggle by environmentalists. But there was no preserving them from the lines of cars broiling by the roadside while the families broiled by the sea.

What Jean Joubert had told me of that country twenty-five years before was unimaginable, that white horses and black bulls had roamed a land of pool and marsh, as they still do in the nature reserves of the Camargue. For ahead were shapes that at first looked like white cliffs in a heat haze, and then resolved themselves into the futuristic structures of La Grande-Motte, with its pyramids of the sun. One curved like a ship in sail; another flashed its windows like a compound eye; all sloped tier upon tier of terrace and gay balcony down to the streets, the gardens and the perpetually golden sand. Somewhere in La Grande-Motte, greatest of the sun-cities of the coast, there were groves of trees and boulevards, but I ate my lunch of melon and peaches bought along the road in the shade of a willow patch I found by the main road on the edge of town, which had plainly been much used before, judging by the amount of litter. Then I searched out the hotel at which my rendezvous had been arranged and waited for Joy to bring the man who was one of the architects of the success of La Grande-Motte, sitting on the grass with my back against an undeveloped tree. A French dog came up.

'Gerroff,' I said to the French dog. It went and peed elsewhere, viz: against the next tree. I got up and waited in the sun.

Joy arrived with Georges Pagès, whose hair had slipped off the top of his head and collected in a fringe about his jawbone. He had been Tourist Manager of La Grande-Motte for its first fourteen years, and took me up into a high place to show me all the riches of his kingdom.

'It is my child,' said M. Pagès, with a crack in his voice as if it were indeed. 'In 1963 there was nothing in this country. All was desert: everything was nude. The only problem we have in the beginning was mosquitoes: but we have a struggle every year, and now we have no more mosquito in this country.'

He told me that La Grande-Motte, named after the farm that was the only previous habitation there, had grown to accommodate 1100 boats, 60,000 visitors at once, 18 km of walks and as many roads, a metre of green for every four of concrete, cinemas, a theatre and a resident population of 4000 numbering amongst them M. Pagès himself.

'Is it fun to live in?' I asked.

'It's quite different in different parts. We have funny

places along the seaside.' His delight in his town was unquestionable and irresistible.

'Architect is a Doctor in *psychologie*: he know people. Every time I leave this town in the morning, when I come back, I am proud of it. I look at it: it is my child.' M. Pagès cradled his voice, laughed and chuckled with pleasure. 'It's stupid perhaps – I'm sorry – it is wonderful.'

Given that the coast was going to be developed anyway, I was inclined to agree, having seen the slummy ribbon development at Carnon-Plage. La Grande-Motte has style, a grand design, the impress of an individual enthusiasm: it is at least a monument and perhaps you have to live there to find in it the humanity that bathed Georges Pagès, even if it eluded me.

We went to drink beer on the terrace of the Hôtel Frantel, with only two ceremonies left to perform. M. Pagès persuaded the hotel manager to find a pair of bathroom scales, and a weighing ritual was held on the front steps in the presence of a young lady photo-journalist from the local paper who said it was her first story, and it was a pity it was a rather inconclusive one, on account of the scales only reading up to 120 kg and the needle going over the top. But it was enough to show that I had lost little if any weight at all in the course of the 865·1 miles registered on the mileometer.

For the final moment of my journey, I carried the bicycle across the maze of golden bodies on the beach with not a mosquito between them and the sun, and placed my toe officially in the sea, which ruined the gesture by retreating from me at that instant. Joy opened a bottle of wine which may not have been the best champagne but was geyserish in the heat, and M. Pagès poured it over the handlebars with a short speech, at which the sun-worshippers around perked up and came to see what was happening.

'What?' said a mostly unclothed but well-provided lady, wobbling. 'Who?'

When told, she said, 'Oh!' and went away again.

'Faithful steed,' I said to the bicycle. 'I name thee

Velocimousse – "*mousse*" for lightness, "*velo*" for swiftness and bicycles.' There was a weak stammer of applause from those onlookers who thought that something else ought to happen and, if the eccentric who had brought his bicycle to the water could be sufficiently encouraged, perhaps it might. A nearby baby got sand in its mouth and started to scream.

I carried Velocimousse back across the bodies and fixed her to the rack on Joy's car. The frame still shone and the wheels were hardly dusty: the only mark of the ride was a yellow band all round the back wheel where the tyre was worn down to the canvas. We left M. Pagès waving in the sun beneath his pyramids, and drove off for a swim on a busy beach with the other tourists.

'Strange,' I thought, 'to think I've done it.'

I cannot suppose that I will ever make the journey again, but it made an impression on me that no other travelling has ever done. The green fragrances of the verges, the cool of the trees, the heat of the hills, the long, long landscapes, the turns of the road are still with me, and feel as if they will stay. France is more to me now as a country I passed through at its own pace on an honest, unhurtful means of transport: not a 2-litre intruder, but simply a fat man on a bicycle.

On Bicycles

How to buy one
You need a good touring bicycle along the lines of other
people's good touring bicycles. This means drop handlebars, paying out for a good frame with alloy fittings, and
even learning to use toe-clips. Sorry. Go to a good shop.
Read the standard reference paperback, *Richard's Bicycle
Book* (Pan).

Size and the frame
A cheap suit that fits is better than an expensive one that
doesn't: so with bicycles. The size is determined by the
frame, and varies in three ways:

Shape: Keep at the back of your mind that frames for
racing are made more sit-up-and-beg than the more comfortable touring frames you are likely to encounter, and
that compromise frames for general use also exist. A touring frame will be described as having an angle of 72° or
less. Women have to decide whether they are ever going
to want to ride in a skirt: if not, then a man's frame is
stronger.

Height: This is the most important factor, and there is more
than one formula for working it out. Most people need a
frame in the 20″-24″ range, and each ½″ is significant. If you
buy too small, then you feel like Quasimodo; if too large,
as if you were riding a camel (the lesser of the two evils).
You should be OK if – with your saddle set 2″ or 3″ above
the frame – your knee-joints are fractionally bent when
your foot is at the bottom of the pedal stroke. If the shop

won't allow you to sit on a bike in the shop and adjust the saddle to find the proper size, go to another shop.

Length: This is mainly determined by the height and the frame angle, and affects your comfort a lot, especially on a long journey. There is some adjustment under the saddle, but length is varied more by how far forward the handle-bars are set by the stem that holds them. To alter the length, change the stem.

Quality: A frame's quality is determined by what it is made of rather more than how it is put together. The best classic frames are made with Reynolds 531 tubing, which *always* bears one of four different patterns of label to tell you how many of the tubes in the frame are made of it and whether each main tube is thickened inside at the ends for extra strength (double-butted). It is important to find out from the bike shop *exactly* what the different patterns of Reynolds' label mean, or look them up in *Richard's Bicycle Book*, so that you know what you are paying for.

Wheels
If you have a choice, good wheels from a good wheel-builder are worth paying for, as you will find out if you ride heavy weights over rough roads. Twang the spokes: in a good wheel they are taut and can be moved only slightly against each other. In any case, you should have alloy wheels, which are not only lighter but better for braking in wet weather. Quick-release wheels are general and useful: less common is a device to allow each brake cable to be instantly slackened, so that the brake blocks do not get in the way of the wheel coming out. With slim tyres, its absence may not matter: with the rather more substantial tyres you may need for long touring, it does.

Fittings
In fact, all – or practically all – of the fittings on a good bicycle should be alloy – handlebars, seat pin, gear-

changing mechanism, chain wheels and cranks, brakes.
Alloy does not rust and is lighter: and apparently minor
reductions in weight (particularly of moving parts) can
make a considerable difference to the amount of effort
needed.

Gears

You need ten gears, provided by a combination of two large
chain wheels at the front, and five cogs at the back. You
can also get bicycles with 12, 15 and 18 gears, but the last
two especially lead you into an over-complicated life which
you would be better off to avoid. Three gears are quite
adequate for Holland, five if you cannot afford ten.

Ten gears are not as elaborate as they sound, especially
since, in practice, there are only eight. The derailleur
mechanism works by shifting the chain from side to side:
consequently, when it is at the extreme left at the back and
on the right at the front (or vice versa) there is too much
sideways strain on the chain for things to work well and
not wear badly. You get used to avoiding those two positions, as you get used to only changing gear while you are
pedalling.

You need wide-range gearing unless you are fit, light,
not carrying much, and living in fairly gentle country. Gear
ratios are complicated but to alter them is fairly easy and
cheap by changing the cog assembly on the back wheel
(though, if worn, you have to change the chain as well).
You can also alter the front gearing by changing the gear
rings on the chainset. In France, I often blessed Evans for
providing me with my fairly outrageous 33″ bottom gear.

Saddle

Leather saddles take about 500 miles to break you in, but
are then highly esteemed as the most comfortable, and
often transferred from bike to bike. Plastic ones need no
breaking in, no dressing with neatsfoot oil at the start, and
are less fussy about getting wet.

Brakes

Braking efficiency does not depend much on the pattern of brake: adjustment, rims and brake blocks are more important. Since I ride a lot with my hands on the top of the handlebars, I prefer the type of brake lever which has a side extension you can grasp from that position.

Tyres

The tubular tyre used by purists actually has to be unsewn every time you want to mend a puncture, and then glued back on to its special rim: they are excellent, therefore, for someone who likes glueing, sewing, and spending the extra that they cost. Other tyres are conventional 'wire-ons', and a heavier type is desirable for touring. Some inner tubes come with Schraeder valves, which can be blown up (perhaps literally) on a garage air-line: more common is the 'Presta' valve, which has a lock-nut which you have to unscrew before you can start pumping to any purpose.

Pump

A frame-fitting pump, being longer, is easier to use than the traditional type that clips between two prongs. It will have its own connector built in which you just push on to the valve. When doing this, I have found it possible to produce a most interesting effect whereby the pump handle and associated insides have been propelled instantly and violently over a distance of 20 or 30 yards. In spite of this interesting, embarrassing and potentially litigious tendency of mine, I greatly prefer them.

Handlebars

Drop handlebars are preferred for touring mainly because they give a choice of riding positions, which is useful on a long journey. The standard touring pattern, which has a slight lift on the top bends, is known as 'Randonneur'. Some form of padding – gloves or foam – between hands and bars helps to alleviate the thumping that they get from miles of rough road surface.

APPENDIX I: ON BICYCLES

Lights
The British fashion is for battery lamps which stay on when you stop: there is an easily detachable French variety which requires no mounting brackets on the bicycle and is reliable, which some other lamps are not.

Bags
You can buy very light panniers which will take a prodigious quantity of things: I used Karrimor Iberians in France, which come with a specially stout frame. I have found a handlebar bag much better than the traditional British saddlebag because it is much easier to get at things and you can carry it off on a shoulder strap when you leave the bike.

Locks
You must have a good lock for a good bicycle, and it will be expensive. Most formidable of all is the Citadel, a great hoop of solid metal: it is heavy, expensive and you have to write to America for new keys, but it is worth it if you have something it will go round, like a parking meter stem. In case I haven't, I also carry a long wire cable with lock attached, but in town I would not rely on this alone.

Tools
The vital things to carry on the road are a spare inner tube and tyre levers – and I add a puncture repair kit for the flat after that. A small number of spanners fit the more usual nuts, a couple of Allen keys adjust saddle and handlebars and a single screwdriver is usually enough. At home, the only special tools likely to be needed are one for tightening and undoing your cotterless cranks; a rivet extractor, so that you can take off the chain; and if you ever want to change the cogs on the back wheel yourself, you will need a freewheel remover *which fits your particular freewheel*.

Buying secondhand
It is not difficult or risky to buy a bicycle secondhand,

though in what is usually a seller's market, prices are sometimes inflated. If the paintwork is grotty (but original), count your blessings: it will be less attractive to the light-fingered. Buy a machine which was good in the first place: avoid those which look as if they have been pieced together from miscellaneous collections of old parts: be apprehensive of teenage mechanics.

The great evil of the secondhand bike is the twist. Never buy if the frame is bent out of true (which is unlikely, but possible): look down over the handlebars to check. Wheels only slightly out of shape can be pulled back cheaply. Bad buckling and rims which are no longer round (dented or flattened somewhere by a pothole perhaps) need replacement. Frame, front forks and wheels are expensive; double chain wheels can be dear; other parts are much of a muchness, but add up rapidly. Don't forget to include an allowance for irritation as you learn to adjust worn parts the hard way.

One great advantage of the secondhand machine, however, is that you may feel freer to decorate it according to your fancy, though you should bear in mind that, unlike canal-boat art – which is proletarian and cornucopic in character – Bicycle Art is armorial and aristocratic, since it derives fundamentally from the carriage trade.

As with the Greek vase and Campbell's soup-tin, Bicycle Art is carried out on a curved surface, but it has neither the battle, frolic or scene of daily life of the first, nor the recipe of the second. This may perhaps be attributed to the fact that, whereas a vase or soup-tin may easily be turned round so that you can continue drawing on the other side, to represent a continuous scene on a bicycle requires either special apparatus or special agility.

APPENDIX I: ON BICYCLES

HOW TO PAINT *THE RAPE OF THE SABINE WOMEN* ON A BICYCLE BY MEANS OF SPECIAL AGILITY

1. Bind a thick layer of cotton-wool or old rags to the back of the head.
2. Tie a stout rope to the ceiling of a large room uncluttered with chairs, lawn-mowers, long-haired dogs, Louis Quinze tables etc.
3. Attach the bicycle to the rope in an upright position, and gather your requisites.
4. Stand with your back to the bicycle. Bend over backwards, clasp your requisites firmly, and paint the side of the bottom tube that would be facing you if you were standing the right way round. WARNING – DO NOT PAINT THE SCENE UPSIDE DOWN: THE TOP PART OF A SABINE LADY SHOULD BE IN THE DIRECTION OF YOUR CHIN.
5. When you have painted the first side of the tube, kick out your legs in a forward direction. This will have the effect of bringing you rapidly into a supine position.
7. Paint the continuation of the scene on the underside of the tube, edging your way backwards as necessary. Rise gradually to a sitting position as you approach the far side of the bicycle, and to your knees in order to conclude the scene on the top side of the tube.
8. Congratulations! You have now painted *The Rape of the Sabine Women* on a bicycle. You may now proceed, if you wish, to a representation on the top tube (*The Last Supper* is recommended as a subject owing to its excellent breadth).

NOTE It is beyond the scope of this Appendix to advise upon individual aspects of the design: it is assumed that you have already studied those aspects of *The Rape of the Sabine Women* that you find interesting.

APPENDIX II

On Journeys

Joy's route described in this book was extremely successful, though anyone duplicating it might like to detour to some nearby towns which I missed. Were I riding it again, however, I would be inclined to stay further away from Paris after Les Andelys, and come down to the Loire to the east of Orléans. On the final stage of the trip, I would recommend crossing the river at Ganges and coming down to the sea by way of St-Guilhem-le-Désert which, though itself rather full of gawpers, is exceptionally picturesque and set in the most striking country.

Any professional writers contemplating the trip may be interested to know of a closed shop operating in this area under the aegis of ASBPPPAT, the Amalgamated Society of Bicycling Persons in Pursuit of Poesie and Allied Trades. This trade union – which in 1979 was able to achieve a 100 per cent membership of all workers then pedalling in France in pursuit of gainful literary employment – has negotiated with Michael Joseph Ltd the following conditions of work which shall be deemed henceforth to govern all activities among the comrade workers carrying out this trade:

1. The Bicycling Operative (BO) shall be provided with protective clothing, viz., an eccentrically-stitched chamois leather seat, which may be applied either to shorts, knickerbockers, plus-fours, doublet and hose etc. but not simultaneously. Nor shall the stitching be so eccentric as to invite comment from such as hold the Working Arses in derision.
2. The BO shall be provided at all times with a Bicycle

Operative's Mate (BOM), to provide assistance and comfort and to officiate at tea breaks (*qv*). The BOM shall be certified by the National Union of Female Surveyors to be in full accordance with the BS/15/A/3/, viz., British Standard Pulchritude and Development, though in no case should this development be such as to interfere with the handlebars (or, without prior agreement, rub on the back of the BO, if a tandem), otherwise the mounting of the BOM shall be at her own discretion.

3. Demarcation agreements shall be observed in respect of altitude and gradient. On an upward slope of more than 1 in 8, the Incorporated Guild of Mountaineers and Piton-Drivers shall be called to belay safety lines, and members of the Submariners' Friendly Society shall be in attendance at sea level, to observe the Plimsoll line and in case of sharks.

4. Any stretch of road not complying with the Factory Acts or Chadwick's Public Health Act shall rate time and a half. Dirty money shall be payable in wet weather; and an incompatibility allowance in the event of encountering any Frenchman speaking his lingo at over 300 w.p.m. In view of the possibility of thunderstorms and the inevitability of encountering what the French themselves admit to be *oiseaux sauvages*, danger money will be payable at all times.

5. Tea-breaks. Tea shall be *appellation contrôlée* in the interests of promoting international harmony and maintaining the dignity of the BO. The BOM shall be mother.

Fraternally,
Tom Vernon
(President, Secretary, Praesidium and Membership,
AMALGAMATED SOCIETY OF BICYCLING
PERSONS IN PURSUIT OF POESIE AND
ALLIED TRADES)

Index

Index

343

Fontana Paperbacks: Non-fiction

Fontana is a leading paperback publisher of non-fiction, both popular and academic. Below are some recent titles.

- [ ] THE POLITICS OF INDUSTRIAL RELATIONS (second edition) Colin Crouch £2·95
- [ ] NATTER NATTER   Richard Briers £1·50
- [ ] KITCHEN HINTS   Hilary Davies £1·25
- [ ] MRS WEBER'S DIARY   Posy Simmonds £2·50
- [ ] A TREASURY OF CHRISTMAS   Frank & Jamie Muir £2·95
- [ ] THE VIDEO HANDBOOK   John Baxter & Brian Norris £1·95
- [ ] A BOOK OF SEA JOURNEYS   Ludovic Kennedy (ed.) £3·50
- [ ] BEDSIDE GOLF   Peter Alliss £1·95
- [ ] DAY CARE   Alison Clarke-Stewart £1·95
- [ ] THE WOMAN QUESTION: READINGS ON THE SUBORDINATION OF WOMEN   Mary Evans (ed.) £3·95
- [ ] WAR FACTS NOW   Christy Campbell £2·50
- [ ] CHRONICLE OF YOUTH   Vera Brittain £2·75
- [ ] FRIGHTENED FOR MY LIFE   Geoff Coggan & Martin Walker £1·95
- [ ] HIGH PRESSURE: WORKING LIVES OF WOMEN MANAGERS   Cary Cooper & Marilyn Davidson £1·95
- [ ] TRADE UNIONS: THE LOGIC OF COLLECTIVE ACTION   Colin Crouch £2·50
- [x] THE KINGDOM   Robert Lacey £2·95
- [ ] A FOREIGN FLAVOUR   Rose Elliot £2·95
- [ ] SEVEN DAYS TO DISASTER   Des Hickey & Gus Smith £2·50
- [ ] P.S. I LOVE YOU   Michael Sellers £1·75

You can buy Fontana paperbacks at your local bookshop or newsagent. Or you can order them from Fontana Paperbacks, Cash Sales Department, Box 29, Douglas, Isle of Man. Please send a cheque, postal or money order (not currency) worth the purchase price plus 10p per book (or plus 12p per book if outside the UK).

NAME (Block letters) _____

ADDRESS _____

_____

_____